The Craft of Argument, Concise Edition

Joseph M. Williams

University of Chicago

Gregory G. Colomb

University of Virginia

Longman

New York • San Francisco • Boston
London • Toronto • Sydney • Tokyo • Singapore • Madrid
Mexico City • Munich • Paris • Cape Town • Hong Kong • Montreal

Senior Vice President and Publisher: Joseph Opiela
Acquisitions Editor: Susan Kunchandy
Executive Marketing Manager: Ann Stypuloski
Senior Supplements Editor: Donna Campion
Media Supplements Editor: Nancy Garcia
Production Manager: Joseph Vella
Project Coordination, Text Design, and Electronic Page Makeup: Thompson Steele, Inc.
Cover Design Manager: Nancy Danahy
Cover Designer: Wendy Stolberg
Manufacturing Buyer: Al Dorsey
Printer and Binder: Courier Corp.
Cover Printer: Phoenix Color Corp.

Library of Congress Cataloging-in-Publication Data

Williams, Joseph M.
    The craft of argument, concise / Joseph M. Williams, Gregory C. Colomb.--1st ed.
        p. cm.
    Includes index.
    ISBN 0-321-09186-8 (alk. paper)
        1. English language--Rhetoric. 2. Persuasion (Rhetoric) 3. Report
    writing. I. Colomb, Gregory G. II. Title.

PE1431 .W65 2002
808'.042–dc21

2002025476
CIP

Please visit our website at http://www.ablongman.com

ISBN 0-321-09186-8

1 2 3 4 5 6 7 8 9 10—CRW—05 04 03 02

Brief Contents

Detailed Contents

Topical Contents
of the
Writing Process Sections

Teaching the Craft of Argument

Our aim in *The Craft of Argument* is to help students integrate the skills of writing, thinking, and arguing so that they can write arguments that are clear, sound, and persuasive. To that end, we discuss argument in ways that are rooted in the rhetorical tradition that began even before Aristotle's *Rhetoric*, but are different enough from most current texts on argument to deserve some explanation.

What Distinguishes Craft from Other Books on Argument

- **We emphasize that writers make arguments not just to gain their readers' agreement but to enlist them in solving a problem.** Therefore, we put problem finding, framing, and solving at the heart of planning, drafting, and revising written arguments. Only when we understand the problem we address *from our readers' points of view* can we make an argument that they will take seriously

- **We show students the differences between the kind of problem most familiar to them, pragmatic problems, and the kind of problem that may be less familiar to them, conceptual problems.** Most teachers expect students not only to address conceptual problems, but also find and formulate their own. Throughout this book, we help students meet the demands of finding academic, conceptual problems that they care about, but that they can also imagine their readers caring about.

- **We steadily emphasize ethos.** We show students how they project an ethos through every element of their argument: by how clearly they write, how baldly they state their claim, how thoroughly they support it with evidence, how candidly they acknowledge and respond to objections. Even when their argument fails to achieve agreement, they can still call it a success if readers think that they made it in ways that seem reasonable, thoughtful, and fair.

- **We devote considerable attention to informal reasoning and integrate sound critical thinking into our discussion of argument and writing in every chapter.** To that end, we have not segregated advice about reasoning and arguing from advice about writing, because we believe that the skills of writing support and illuminate the skills of reasoning, and vice versa.

- **We have included a "writing process" section in every chapter.** These sections show students how the processes of planning, drafting, and revising can help them not only generate the substance of an argument, but reflect critically on the thinking it represents.

- **We have tried to synthesize two aspects of argument that most books on argument keep distinct: dialectic and rhetoric.** Dialectic is commonly defined as a process of two people questioning each other in search of as-yet undiscovered truth (a claim that they can support), a topic now pursued by those calling their work "pragma-dialectical." In contrast, rhetoric focuses on one person's finding and arranging support for a known claim in order to persuade another to accept it. In our view, dialectic and rhetoric are two perspectives on the same process. Questioning and being questioned helps students both to discover a claim worth making and to find the support that gives them and others good reasons to accept it. It is a process students engage in every time they have a conversation with friends about an issue they care about. We show students how to create sound written arguments from those familiar speech genres by imagining themselves exchanging questions and answers with their readers or their surrogates (a thread that may remind some of Bakhtin).

How *Craft* Participates in the Rhetorical Tradition

Despite those differences from current books on argument, *Craft* is rooted in the 2,500-year-old tradition of rhetoric and argumentation. We aim at helping students develop a public voice appropriate to written arguments in a variety of civic, professional, and academic forums. We believe that thoughtful readers are likely to assent to a claim only when they see good reasons, and evidence, when they understand the logical connections among claims, reasons and evidence, and when they see their own doubts and questions acknowledged and answered. We believe that at base argument is not a coercive device (though it can be), nor even a product of human rationality (though it is), but the fundamental competence by which rationality is created and shared.

Craft's Roots in Aristotle

We have been struck by how closely (though unintentionally) we tracked Aristotle's *Rhetoric*. We begin, as did Aristotle, by identifying the problems that occasion different kinds of arguments. He focused on the oral arguments occasioned by civic events—trials, funerals, and political decision-making—the triad that has led to the familiar categories of forensic, epideictic, and deliberative arguments (or fact, value, and policy). We believe, however, that that division obscures a more basic distinction between arguments that want us to *do* something and arguments that want us to *understand* or *believe* something.

Although we do not treat arguments about values as a distinct category, we do not ignore them. In fact, we emphasize how the values of both readers and writers shape all arguments, whether the aim is action or belief.

As did Aristotle, we address not just invention and arrangement, but style and ways that the psychology of readers and writers interact. (Those last two topics claim little or no space in most current books on argument.) As did he, we put aside syllogisms, focusing instead on warranted claims. And like his aim, ours is relentlessly focused on "how to," on answering two pragmatic questions:

- What does an audience expect in a sound argument?
- How do we express that argument to meet their expectations?

As did Aristotle, we also focus on the role of feelings, of emotions in making a sound argument. Far from rejecting emotion as an element of an argument, we emphasize its importance in framing the problem the argument addresses and in choosing the language to express it.

Craft's Revision of Toulmin

Like many recent books on argument, we have profited from one of the most influential works on argument since Aristotle, that of Stephen Toulmin. We are especially indebted to these three insights:

- Arguments differ in different fields but share a family structure.
- That common structure is based on a logic of question and answer.
- We understand that structure best not in terms of formal deductive logic, but rather of the informal logic of everyday conversation.

As important as those three insights are, we believe that teachers of argument who embrace Toulmin's formal layout make a pedagogical mistake. Recall that he represents an argument in a figure of six elements:

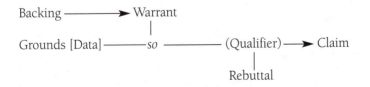

Students and teachers alike have found it difficult to apply some aspects of Toulmin's account of argument to the task of producing their own arguments and analyzing the arguments of others. To make Toulmin's insights more useful to students at all levels, we have modified his layout in five ways.

1. We removed the arrows. Toulmin wanted to represent the movement of an argument, but most arguments start not with a statement of grounds but with a problem, followed by a claimed solution, followed by intertwined grounds, warrants, and rebuttals. And as a model of reasoning, his layout is psychologically unrealistic. When we *reason* about a problem, we do not start with grounds, then think our way to a claim (its solution). We begin with the problem that motivates us to search for a solution in the first place, and find a tentative hypothesis based on the facts then available to us. We then use that hypothesis (C. S. Peirce called it a "hypothesis on probation") to find more data that we hope will confirm or disconfirm it. This kind of thinking is called abductive, a kind of reasoning that Toulmin's layout cannot represent.

We do not intend our layout to represent any "real time" process either, not of reasoning, drafting, reading, or analyzing an argument. It represents only five elements required in every argument and some formal relationships among them. We intend it as a tool for understanding and discovering arguments, for planning and drafting them, and for thinking about the arguments of others.

2. We dropped "backing." Toulmin needed backing to explain how arguments differ among different fields, but that is not our concern. Moreover, *backing* refers to the grounds that support a warrant viewed as a claim in its own argument. We can more usefully analyze that arrangement as two distinct arguments, one embedded in the other. So backing is redundant.

3. We dropped "qualifier" as a distinct element. Qualifications such as *probably, most,* and *may* are crucial not just to the accuracy of an argument, but to the construction of its writer's ethos. But qualifiers are not a singular element of an argument like a claim or a reason; qualifiers color every element—claims, reasons, evidence, warrants, and rebuttals. Far from ignoring qualification, we show its crucial role in projecting a thoughtful ethos in every element of an argument.

4. We divided the single element "grounds" into two, reasons and evidence. Careful readers accept a claim about a contested issue only when they see two distinct kinds of support: reasons and the evidence on which those reasons rest. This distinction reflects a psychological and social imperative: We consider a contestable claim only when it rests on something more "solid" than the arguer's mere confidence in it; we ask for support, for reasons. But reasons provide only the logical structure of that support; evidence is the basis on which that structure of reasons rests, something brought in from "outside" the argument. An argument consisting only of a claim and reasons can seem unsubstantial, but it would seem opaque if it consisted of only a claim and raw evidence such as numbers or quotations. Readers need reasons to help them understand the logic and organization of an argument; they need evidence to understand the basis of those reasons in something they can think of as "external" reality.

5. We replaced "rebuttal" with "acknowledgment and response." Many have noted that Toulmin's notion of rebuttals is a problem. He defines rebuttals as limits on the scope of a claim:

Since Harry was born in Bermuda, he is a British subject, _{claim} **unless he renounced his citizenship, or unless one of his parents was a diplomat, or unless . . .** _{rebuttal}

But in ordinary language, what we call a *rebuttal* responds to objections *of any kind*—not just to the scope of a claim, but to the source or sufficiency of its support, to the soundness of logic, to the definition of a problem, to alternative solutions. Rebuttals are essential to every thoughtful argument because they acknowledge and respond to a reader's predictably different beliefs and interests. So as have a few others, we expand Toulmin's *rebuttal* to refer to responses to any anticipated alternative, objection, or criticism.

We believe, however, that the term *rebuttal* can encourage responses that are too aggressive, so we substitute something more amiable and accurate: *acknowledgment and response.* That term encompasses two actions: first we acknowledge readers' views by presenting them fairly; only then do we respond to them, and not always to refute them, since mature arguers concede the force of plausible alternatives.

In addition to those five modifications, we fill two gaps in Toulmin's account. First, we explain the ambiguous nature of evidence, which literally exists outside an argument and so can only be represented inside it. Readers are led by our prototypical image of evidence to want "external" evidence that is concrete, palpable—a smoking gun and fingerprints. But we must recognize how that differs from the representations writers offer in its stead—a *description* of a smoking gun, an *image* of fingerprints.

If students learn to distinguish between the evidence "itself" and the reports of it used in arguments, they will be better prepared to read others' reports of evidence critically and, when they write, to report their own so that their readers can know where and how they obtained it. No one asks where anyone found a reason; we must all ask where someone found evidence.

The second gap is in Toulmin's account of warrants. So far as we know, no book on argument has explained how a warrant that is true can nevertheless fail. For example,

You should eat fish _{claim} because it does not raise your cholesterol. _{reason} As we all know, everyone should eat foods that provide roughage. _{warrant}

Each of those three propositions is arguably true, but the warrant fails as a guarantee of the *relevance* of the reason to the claim. We offer what we think is the first intuitively satisfying explanation of how a warrant soundly establishes the relevance of reasons and evidence to a claim, and of how it can fail.

Using This Book

This book has four parts:

- Part 1 surveys argument and its relationship to problem solving.
- Part 2 looks at the five elements of an argument in detail.

- Part 3 discusses reasoning, particularly about meaning and causation.
- Part 4 treats the role of language in arguments.

After Part 1, you can teach the other parts in any order. You can also teach the chapters in any part in any order, even assign different chapters to different students who need work on particular issues.

Features

To help students learn *and use* these principles, we have incorporated several kinds of learning experiences.

- Most chapters include brief examples that illustrate various points of arguments.

- Writing Process sections appear in each chapter, explaining how students can apply the principles of argument to their process of preparing, planning, drafting and revising a written argument.

- Most chapters also include several activities, called "Inquiries," that spur further thinking about argument and its uses.

- Each chapter concludes with a concise summary of its main points.

  Finally, there is a Teacher's Guide that provides more than a hundred activities including classroom activities for discussing issues, identifying questions and problems, generating and testing answers, and then developing the elements of argument needed to support them.

  We hope that this book can help you do more than show students how to write respectable academic papers. We hope that it encourages students to think about argumentation as a subject in its own right, as something at the heart of their public experience in their neighborhoods and workplaces, as well as larger civic arenas. Since argument is central to what it means to be not just a rational human being but a socially rational citizen, and since irrational persuasion has never been more widely—and cynically—attempted, we believe that there are few matters students need to know about more than how to make—and judge—sound, rational arguments.

Acknowledgments

As we say repeatedly, every writer needs a reader's help because readers know one thing that writers never can: they know what it's like to be our readers. We two have been immeasurably helped by those readers who reviewed this book during its development. They told us things that we could never have known on our own (and sometimes didn't want to hear). But they read our work better than we ever could, and we have been grateful for their always helpful comments, even when they stung.

Students who profit from this book can thank the following reviewers, as do we: Jonathan Ayres, University of Texas; R. Michael Barrett, University of Wisconsin, River Falls; David Blakesley, Southern Illinois University, Carbondale; Stuart C. Brown, New Mexico State University; Jami L. Carlacio, University of Wisconsin, Milwaukee; William J. Carpenter, University of Kansas; Peter Dorman, Central Virginia Community College; Ellen Burton Harrington, Tulane University; Eleanor Latham, Central Oregon Community College; Carol A. Lowe, McLennan Community College; Margaret P. Morgan, University of North Carolina, Charlotte; B. Keith Murphy, Fort Valley State University; Twila Yates Papay, Rollins College; CarolAnn H. Posey, Virginia Wesleyan College; Deborah F. Rossen-Knoll, Philadelphia College of Textiles and Science; Mary Sauer, Indiana University Purdue University Indianapolis; Laura Wendorff, University of Wisconsin, Platteville

We are especially grateful to those who taught versions of this book in its formative stages and to their students, who provided invaluable feedback: Thomas Fischer, Paula McQuade, Dev Parikh, Peter Sattler, Bryan Wagner, and Carol Williams.

We would also like to thank Susan Kunchandy for seeing this manuscript through to production, and Alec MacDonald for his reliable work tracking down sources and helping assemble the index.

And finally, those closest to us.

There is no way to say how much the growing family has meant to me. The best days are when we're together—Christopher, Oliver, Megan and Phil, Patty and Dave, Christine and Joe, and now the twins, Nick and Kate. And of course Joan, she who for so many years has put up with my "Just one more minute." Her deep well of patience and good humor still flows more generously than I deserve.
—JMW

I was born to a clan of arguers, and my daughters have inherited the tradition. But what they learned along with their love of argument was that good argument never threatens love. Robin, Karen, and Lauren have kept me on my toes, my arguments well-tested, and my heart full. This last they got from their mother, my companion for more than thirty years. Sandra has always been the heart of it all.
—GG

Part 1

The Nature of Argument

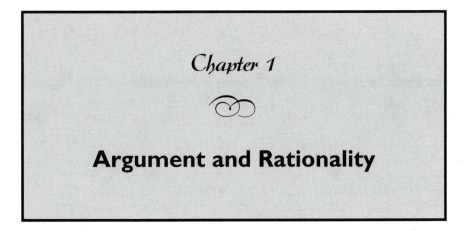

Argument and Rationality

Argument is not verbal combat, but a means to cooperate with others in finding and testing good solutions to tough problems. Bad arguments can divide us, but good ones strengthen the fabric of our communities—civic, academic, professional—by helping us justify not only what we think and do, but why others might have good reason to do the same. But even when our arguments fail to achieve that agreement, they succeed if they help us explain why we and others differ, in a way that creates mutual understanding and respect.

What Is Argument?

How many arguments have you heard or read today? Probably more than you can remember. Television and talk radio are so full of them that arguing now seems to be a national sport—and the nastier the better. Some talk shows are less interested in offering a thoughtful exchange between reasonable adults than in staging a battle between combatants eager to shout each other into silence. And when public figures tire of attacking each other, plenty of columnists and talk show hosts carry on the battle with venomous pleasure.

That image of argument as close combat is encouraged by our language: Opposing sides *attack* each other, *advancing* claims, *marshaling* reasons and evidence, and *defending* them from *counterattack.* So it's not just the likes of Jerry Springer who encourage verbal violence; the English language itself inclines us to think of argument as warfare.

But forget the battles. How often can you recall people calmly trading claims over issues as trivial as the future of the Rolling Stones or as important as the morality of suicide, then quietly supporting their views with reasons and evidence? As calm as they are, those exchanges are also arguments, because an argument is not defined by its hostility, but by the exchange and testing of claims and reasons in order to solve a shared problem:

- Your friend says she doesn't want to eat Japanese because she had Korean last night, but you want vegetarian. So you talk it over and compromise on Indian.
- Your teacher rejects a claim that apes can count because it is based on flawed data. You mention an article claiming that they communicate by sign language, but your teacher criticizes those studies too.

Even if you spent the day reading, you probably had silent arguments with writers. You read, *Cloning has no moral implications,* and think, *Wait a minute. Every action has a moral dimension. I wonder how he would explain . . .* You may even have argued with yourself, if in your own mind you had to wrestle with a vexing personal problem: *So what do I do about my chem class? I have no shot at med school if I don't get at least a B. But can I? It would mean no social life for the rest of the term. But do I really want to be a doctor? . . .* Argument is a staple of our interaction not only with others, but with ourselves, in the privacy of our own minds.

We are making an argument with you right now, offering what we hope you will take as good reasons to accept our claim—that an argument need not be antagonistic, that it is not something we *have* but something we can collaboratively *make* to solve a problem in a way that meets all of our best interests. And we hope you are thinking, *Wait a minute, what about . . . ?*

What Good Is Argument?

Argument Makes Us Rational

We humans pride ourselves on being rational creatures, but it is easier to say what rationality is not than to say what it is. It is not a set of facts or rules of logic. Nor does it have much to do with education or intelligence. It doesn't even mean being right, because we can rationally believe what is wrong. For thousands of years it was "rational" to think the world is flat, because that's what the evidence of our senses tells us.

We start to become rational when as children we ask for reasons why we should think or do as others tell us to. And as we mature, we learn, when asked, to give reasons for what we think and do. But to do that well, we have to develop other aspects of rationality. We have to acquire the self-control to size up a problem before jumping to a solution, a pause that gives us:

- the patience to gather information from experience, observation, or research, and the judgment to know when to stop;
- the ability to use that information to reason our way to a sound conclusion.

But even that is a limited kind of rationality, something, it is claimed, chimps can do. We become most humanly rational when we can reflect on and test our own reasoning. To do that, we must learn to exercise

- the resolve to look for evidence that might contradict our solution (but also the good sense to know when to stop);

- the courage to change our mind when the weight of evidence contradicts our beliefs (but also the confidence not to change beliefs lightly);
- the imagination to evaluate the long-term consequences of believing in or acting on our conclusions (but not at the expense of not believing or acting when belief or action is necessary);
- most important, the ability to reason about our reasoning, to recognize and question assumptions, inconsistencies, and contradictions (but not to try to resolve every conceivable one).

At least that's how we're supposed to think rationally. The fact is, few of us do so consistently, no matter how intelligent, well educated, or experienced we are. Just about all of us reason in ways that are quick and simple, bounded by short-term self-interest. What's remarkable is that even when we rely on quick and simple thinking, we still make so many good decisions. But when we make bad ones, we can almost always point to the same cause: We didn't step back to assess whether we drew a sound conclusion based on good evidence and sound reasoning, or whether we reached the conclusion because we wanted it to be true. If so, we didn't exercise our deepest rationality.

So rationality is not just thinking soundly. It's sound thinking about the soundness of your thinking, a competence that depends on your ability to listen to a questioning voice. It's best when you find others to ask questions for you. But when you can't, you have to imagine a voice murmuring insistently, *But wait. What about . . . ? What would you say to someone who said . . . ?* In short, rationality is itself the ability to conduct arguments—with others when you can, but always with yourself.

How Common Are Critical Thinkers?

When one researcher investigated how well people critically reflect on their beliefs, she found that few were able to. She questioned 160 people about problems such as unemployment and school dropouts. Those interviewed ranged from ninth graders to college graduates to experts in the problems she posed. When someone offered a cause of the problem, she asked questions like these:

- How do you know that is the cause? What evidence would you offer?
- How would someone disagree with you? What evidence might he offer?
- What would you say to that person to show she was wrong?
- Can you imagine evidence that would show your view to be wrong?
- Could more than one point of view be right?

Fewer than half could think of any evidence to support their views. Though two out of three could think of an alternative view, fewer than half could think of an argument that might support it, and even when offered a counterargument, fewer than half could think of an answer to it. In other words, most of those questioned could not imagine another point of view based on sound reasoning, or think of any good evidence to support their own!

Source: From Deanna Kuhn, *The Skills of Argument* (New York: Cambridge University Press, 1991).

Arguments Sustain Communities

Personal rationality defines our innate humanity, but we are also social creatures who live and work with others whose views differ from our own. So if
you hope to be a rational *citizen* in a rational *community*, you must be able not
only to *form* rational beliefs, but to *give* others good reason to believe that your
views deserve if not their agreement, then at least their respect. Even when no
one agrees with your claim, you can still find a measure of success if others
think you argued for it thoughtfully, with reasons that would seem reasonable,
were they in your shoes.

When your individual arguments seem consistently sound, you earn the
lasting reputation of someone who thinks well. In every argument you make,
you project an image of your character or personality, a quality that some call
your *ethos*. Some of us project an ethos that others dislike: quick to judge,
closed-minded, aggressive, even abusive. Others project an ethos that seems
thoughtful, open-minded, confident, but not arrogantly so, the kind of character that thoughtful people tend to trust.

Once you earn a reputation for judicious thinking, you have the confidence of those whose agreement you seek. A reputation for sound thinking is
particularly important when you argue about complex problems with uncertain solutions. It's especially then that readers depend not just on the soundness
of your argument, but on your reputation for making good ones.

Arguments Define Academic and Professional Communities

Arguments, especially written ones, are also the lifeblood of academic and
professional communities. Scientists, engineers, college professors, and countless others—they all make arguments to support solutions to problems in their
fields. They make those arguments first in their own minds, then in conversation with colleagues, then in writing for their wider community.

Most professional communities make arguments to address problems that
can be solved only if someone *does* something:

Problem: The Malaysian economy has collapsed.

Solution: What we should *do* is lend them money.

We call these *pragmatic* problems—problems that have tangible costs that we
can't tolerate. To eliminate them, we propose *doing* something.

In academic communities, on the other hand, researchers often dig into a
problem not to fix anything, but to help others *understand* something better:

Problem: We do not understand how European trade influenced the
Malaysian economy in the seventeenth century.

Solution: What you should *know* is that it created a new commercial class of merchants and traders.

Academic researchers call questions like these *problems,* but they are problems of a special kind: They are *conceptual* problems that we can always phrase as questions: *How big is the universe? Do birds really descend from dinosaurs?* Such problems are "about" the world, but their solutions tell us not how we can improve it, but how we can understand it better. Researchers may believe that the more we know about the world, the better we can deal with its problems. But in the short run, they aim not directly at proposing an action, but at better understanding. Those who work on questions like these sometimes call what they do "pure" research. (We'll discuss problems in more detail in Chapter 3.)

Whatever kind of problem a writer poses, though, pragmatic or conceptual, she has to support her solution with an argument so that others in her community can reflect on it, test it, maybe improve it, or if necessary, reject it. As we start the third millennium, we depend on knowledge at least as much as we depended a century ago on steel, coal, and electricity. And just as our forebears in an Age of Industry had to learn to judge the quality of vehicles, tools, and other products, so must we in an Age of Information learn to judge the quality of the arguments on which we base our beliefs and actions.

Arguments Enable Democracy

Arguments are also at the heart of this messy way of governing ourselves that we call *democracy.* A dictator doesn't have to make arguments, because no one dares question his claims, much less his reasons. But in a democracy, those who govern us are, at least in principle, obliged to answer our questions. We elect people to ask questions and make arguments on our behalf, and we pay journalists and political analysts to write books, articles, and editorials that contribute to those debates. But whenever a government official is questioned on our behalf, that official is reminded that she is in principle answerable to us. We put our democracy at risk when we let our leaders think they can have their way without first giving us good reasons.

Of course, even the best arguments won't always succeed, especially when they threaten the self-interest of the powerful. Some critics claim that what finally counts in the political world is not logic and evidence but power and influence, so rational arguments are exercises in futility. But that view both ignores occasions when good arguments have prevailed and excuses those who exercise power from having to justify their arbitrary use of it. In the short run, those with power may still get their way, but their weak arguments at least reveal that they did not get it because they were right.

Developing Democracy Means More Arguments

Here's a news report about democracy in Thailand. Note the metaphors of warfare.

> Sumalee Limpaovart thought she was simply a mother protecting her child. But she found herself a warrior in the front lines of a struggle for democratic openness that is being fought today in Thailand and across East Asia. When her six-year-old daughter was rejected by an exclusive government school earlier this year, Mrs. Sumalee did something that would have been unthinkable here only a few years ago: She challenged the decision, using a new freedom of information law to demand the test scores of the other children. In the end, Mrs. Sumalee found what she had suspected: One-third of the students admitted had failed the entrance exam but had been accepted because of their families' status or gifts to the school.
>
> It was just one of the many small, sharp battles that have multiplied in recent years as a bolder, better-educated middle class begins to rise up against the paternalistic order of the past. As they do so, a society built on harmony and civility is becoming increasingly argumentative, confrontational, and noisy.[a]

The historian Robert Conquest makes the same point on a larger scale. He describes the suppression of independent thought by all three twentieth-century totalitarian regimes—communism, fascism, and nazism:

> "Scientific" totalitarianism, which appears to be the rational, ordered form [of society], contains greater elements of irrationality than does the civic culture . . . [because civic culture] contains the element of debate and argument. . . . The totalitarian state contains within itself all of the elements of a more extreme irrationality: the elimination of real debate and criticism.[b]

[a] *New York Times*, August 10, 1999.
[b] Robert Conquest, *Reflections on a Ravaged Century (New York: Norton, 2001), pp. 83–84.*

What's Not an Argument?

Explanations

Some claims and reasons look like arguments, but are not. Consider these two statements:

> Tanya: I have to go home. claim I'm so tired I'm making mistakes. reason

Tanya makes a claim and offers a reason, but we cannot know whether they constitute an argument until we know her intention:

> Ron: Leaving? About time. You've been working for hours.
>
> Tanya: I have to go home. claim I'm so tired I'm making mistakes. reason

Tanya offers Ron a reason not to *convince* him that she should go home (he seems to think she should), but to *explain* why she must. Contrast this:

Ron: You're not leaving, are you? Don't leave! We need you!

Tanya: I have to go home. _{claim} I'm so tired I'm making mistakes. _{reason}

Tanya offers the same claim and reason, but now to *convince* Ron to accept a claim that she thinks he will not accept just because she makes it. That's not just an explanation; now it's an argument supporting the solution to a problem.

So for an exchange to be an argument, it has to meet two criteria:

- The first is its form. When you make an argument, you offer someone a claim (a statement saying what you want that person to believe or do), and support it with at least one reason (a statement that gives that person a basis for agreeing).

- The second criterion is the intention of the participants. To make an argument you must also believe the other person will accept your claim *only if* you give her good reason to do so.

For an exchange to be a *thoughtful* argument, however, it has to be more than a one-sided offer of reasons:

- You make an argument that is both sound and fair when you also acknowledge and respond to views that might qualify or contradict your own. Tanya would be obliged to respond if Ron said, *But you promised to stay until we finished!*

We use explanations and arguments for different ends, but we usually have to weave them together when we argue about complex issues. You might argue, for example, that the campus bookstore should not sell sweatshirts made in a third world country, but in doing that, you would have to explain something about that country's economic conditions and the cost of living there.

Three Forms of Persuasion That Are Not Arguments

There are other forms of persuasion that superficially look like arguments, but lack a key quality of sound and fair ones. Here are three common ones:

Negotiation feels like argument when you and another person trade claims and reasons about, say, the right price of a car. But when you negotiate, you can offer any reason you want, so long as you reach an outcome that both of you can live with. While you ought not lie (on general principles), you are not obliged to be candid. So you are not unethical when you do not reveal the highest price you are willing to pay.

Propaganda resembles argument when it offers claims and reasons, but propagandists don't care whether their reasons are any good, only whether they work, usually by exploiting the emotions of their audience. Nor do they care what others think, except to know what beliefs they have to defeat. Least of all do they care whether another point of view should change their own. In honest argument, you must be open to the possibility that opposing claims and reasons might change your mind.

Coercion solves problems by threat, by making the cost of rejecting a claim intolerable: *Agree or suffer!* Though we think of coercion as a paddle, a carrot can also coerce when it is a bribe: *Agree and I will reward you.* Those who present themselves as authorities also seek to coerce if they argue *Agree because I know better than you do.* So do those who try to shame us into agreement: When Princess Leia of *Star Wars* pleads, *Help me Obiwan Kenobe, you're my only hope,* he must either help her or betray his deepest values.

Negotiation, propaganda, and coercion are not always irrational, or even unethical. We coerce, propagandize, and negotiate with children, but we call it parenting. Nor would anyone be irrational to threaten or negotiate with terrorists holding hostage a school bus full of students. Our challenge is always to know what form of discourse best serves the cause of a civil and just community.

Stories

Stories are as old as arguments, maybe older, but they appeal to a different kind of reasoning. In some ways, stories are more persuasive than arguments:

- When you tell a story well, you can make your listeners feel awe, fear, pleasure, or disgust. When you make a good argument, they may feel an ineffable sense of intellectual pleasure, but it is less viscerally compelling than anger or delight.

- When you tell a vivid story, you seem to describe what "really" happened "out there" so that its truth appears self-evident to the mind's eye of your listener. When you make an argument, you have to offer patterns of abstract reasons and claims that must not only reflect your reasoning, but accommodate that of your readers.

- When you tell a good story, you hope listeners will, at least for a time, suspend their critical judgment, so that they will not think, *Wait a minute, that can't be!* but instead wonder only *What happened next?* In fact, if we question a story told as a real personal experience, we risk serious conflict, because we seem to question the storyteller's truthfulness. When we write a thoughtful argument, we *expect* readers to question our reasons, our evidence, our logic, even the need for an argument at all, and we do not take offense at their doubts.

Very inexperienced writers sometimes think that a good story makes a good argument. And some great stories do imply their own point so clearly that we understand their intention. But a story alone can never itself be a claim, or even a reason. That's why so many moral tales end with an explicit message like, *Be careful what you wish for.* Lacking such a moral flourish, a story forces us to infer the claim it is supposed to illustrate. Used as evidence, however, a good story can support a reason or claim with great power.

When Arguments Go Bad

Though argument is central in our civic, social, professional, and mental lives, it can create discord when we manage it badly. Combative argument disrupts rational thinking, but so do claims and reasons that seem reasonable to us but wholly irrational to others, particularly in multicultural settings. For example, conflicts in southeastern Europe have created an immense human tragedy. The facts are clear: More than 600 years ago, Turkish forces inflicted on Serbians in what became the Yugoslavian province of Kosovo a defeat so great that it is part of Serbian cultural memory. Later, after Kosovo was inhabited mostly by ethnic Albanians, many Serbs believed that to recover their national honor, they had to drive out the Albanians and reclaim Kosovo as their own, which their government tried to do. Many in the rest of the world condemned the Serbs, believing it was irrational to think that a defeat six centuries before justified retaliation today. *They're mad!,* people claimed.

The problem is that some aspects of every culture can seem mad to others. The United States, for example, seemed irrational to many in the rest of the world in the way we dealt with President Clinton's sexual conduct, because they don't share values so deeply entrenched in our thinking that we can't imagine questioning them. When different communities disagree over fundamental values, they often can't get beyond simply trading claims.

Does that mean that different cultures can never agree? On some issues, perhaps not, especially when assumptions are so deeply buried that they have to be excavated before they can even be seen, much less understood. But if arguments can't settle some issues, they can help us understand why they do not. In a society of diverse values like ours, we need more than goodwill and tolerance. If we are to respect the views of others, we need an amiable, civil way to understand why we hold the values we do and why, on some issues, we should not expect to agree. Argument is an essential tool for maintaining the fabric of a culturally diverse society.

Logic, Character, Emotion/Logos, Ethos, Pathos

We hope you've noticed that we have not defined rational arguments as exercises in cold logic. Some philosophers exclude feelings from sound reasoning, but feelings are part of our human rationality: No rational person could write an argument about the Holocaust or slavery and be unmoved. We have all acted on conclusions that seemed logical but felt wrong, then regretted ignoring our feelings.

But how do we support a claim whose reasons are based on feelings alone? How do we demonstrate that our feelings are right and those of others are wrong? We can't justify a claim simply by saying how strongly we feel about it. We have to explain our

(continued on next page)

(continued from previous page)

claims—and our feelings—in ways that seem rational. And that means with good reasons and evidence.

Those who write about arguments distinguish three kinds of force in them:

- When we appeal to our readers' logic, we base our position on a force we call *logos*—the topic of most of this book.

But two other kinds of force depend on our ability to elicit feelings in our readers:

- When we appeal directly to their feelings of pity, anger, fear, and so on, we appeal to their *pathos*. (We raise this issue mainly in Part 4.)

- When we project a trustful, open-minded character, we hope readers will be moved by our *ethos*. (We discuss that force throughout this book.)

We can separate these appeals for analysis, but in practice they are so intertwined that to distinguish them may be mere hairsplitting.

WRITING PROCESS
Argument and Rationality

We aim to help you write sound arguments, but the habits of many first-year writers hinder them from doing that. They read with no sense of purpose, take copious notes, then plunge into drafting and go where chance takes them. Or they plan in detail, then write up their argument exactly according to plan, ignoring opportunities to discover something new. Experienced writers know they have to think, prepare, and plan before they draft, but they also expect to change their minds as they draft and revise, particularly when they imagine how their readers will respond to their reasons and evidence.

That's a lesson some writers take a long time learning. When they read an argument in a newspaper or magazine, they see the neatly printed product, but not the hours of drafting, revising, editing, and reediting that went into it. And so they think professionals dash off a draft, maybe spell-check it, and print it out. To be sure, some writers do that; the other 99 percent of us wish we could. We have to plan, draft, re-plan, re-draft, revise, re-draft, revise again, . . . until we run out of energy, interest, or time. But as vexing as that process can be, experienced writers know how necessary it is. So they not only expect it, they plan for it.

To start you on that learning curve, in each chapter we discuss strategies that experienced writers use to produce effective arguments in a reasonable time. We organize this advice into four categories (1) Thinking-Reading-Talking, (2)

Preparing and Planning, (3) Drafting, and (4) Revising. Those steps look sequential, but don't try to follow them step-by-step. Be ready to loop back and forth.

THINKING-READING-TALKING

You begin work on an argument long before you sketch your first outline of it, even before you take your first notes. In this section, we show you how to use your time from the moment you get an assignment. Since most of what you read will also be arguments, you can use what you learn about writing them to help you read them more effectively. The best way to understand what you read is to write about it as you go. Mark it up: underline, highlight, comment in the margins, talk back to the writer by writing out questions or reservations.

Get an Overview

Start by skimming to create a framework for more careful reading. Ask these questions of your authors:

- What problem do you solve? What question do you answer?
- What is the solution to your problem, the answer to your question?
- Do you want me just to think something or to do something?
- What reasons support your claim?
- What evidence supports your reasons?

Why not just read straight through? Because once you have a framework, you can read faster, understand better, and remember longer. Here is a procedure for skimming to create that informed framework:

Articles

1. Locate where the introduction stops and the body begins. That may be marked with a heading, extra space, or another typographical signal.
2. Skim the introduction, focusing on its end. You are most likely to find there a statement of the problem or question that the author addresses. Highlight it. You may also find the main point, the answer to the question, the solution to the problem. If so, highlight it too.
3. Skim the conclusion. If the main point was not at the end of the introduction, you should find it here. Highlight it.
4. Look through the body for headings that reveal its organization and sequence of topics.
5. Skim just the first paragraph or two of each main section.

Books

1. Read the table of contents and the opening section that contains an overview. It might be called "Introduction," "Preface," or "Chapter 1."

2. Focus on the beginning and conclusion of the overview, looking for a statement of the issue, problem, or question the book addresses.

3. Read the conclusion, noticing how it relates to the overview. Look for the main point. Highlight or summarize it.

4. Skim the first and last few paragraphs of each chapter.

Web Sites

Many of the texts posted on Web sites have the same structure as published articles, and you can use the approach above. Otherwise, do this:

1. Look for an overview or introduction. It might be a home page or page of its own.

2. Look for a site map to see how it is organized into topics and sections. If you find no map, read through the major links on the home page.

Once you have a general sense of a text, question it as you read it. Jot down disagreements, questions, alternative points of view. This is a useful habit, because it helps you imagine your readers doing the same with you.

When you've finished reading a section, write—or at least mentally rehearse—a brief summary. Think of it as your "elevator story"—what you would tell someone between the first and the tenth floor.

PREPARING AND PLANNING

Expert writers know that the more they plan an argument, the faster they write it and the better it will be. Nothing replaces experience, but what you learn to do now mechanically, you will do automatically later. In time, you'll discover the rituals of preparing and planning that work best for you.

Focus on Your Problem

Start planning your argument by knowing what you want it to achieve. What do you gain if readers agree? What do you lose if they don't? Do you propose ways to improve the world or just ways to understand it better?

- Your problem is *conceptual* if you solve it by getting readers simply to *understand* something better. What do you want readers to *understand* about Super-K and Wal-Mart?

  Megastores force small family stores out of business, replacing the intimate spaces of small stores where neighbors could meet with huge impersonal barns where everyone is a stranger, thereby eroding community values.

- Your problem is *pragmatic* if you solve it by getting readers to *do* something or to support such an *action* by others. What do you want readers to *do* about megastores?

> Because large megastores erode the quality of community life, this county should pass zoning laws to keep Wal-Marts out of rural areas.

You explicitly signal a pragmatic problem with words like *should, must, have to,* and *ought to.* But you can signal readers that you want them to act, or at least support an action with other words:

> By creating new zoning laws, we could . . .
>
> The creation of new zoning laws would . . .

Inexperienced writers commonly—and mistakenly—assume that when they don't explicitly say what they want their readers to do, their readers will "get it," but too often they don't. So be more explicit than you think you have to be.

Think About Your Readers

Keep in mind that what you count as a problem your readers might not, and what you think are good reasons and evidence, your readers might reject. You might think there's a problem with rising college tuition, but a recent graduate might not care one bit. So once you understand what problem you want your argument to solve, imagine how your readers will react to it. (We'll discuss these issues in Chapters 3 and 4.)

Don't imagine yourself behind a podium reading your argument to a faceless crowd in a dark auditorium; imagine them as amiable but feisty friends sitting across the kitchen table, interrupting you with hard questions, objections, and their own views. In that situation, you have to respond to their questions and objections, especially questions like *So what? Why should I care?*

Real Versus Stipulated Readers

You may, however, face a challenge if your teacher tells you that your real reader—teacher, grader, or classmate—is not the one you must address: *You are a researcher at Ace Advertising, working on the new V-Sport Vehicle account, and your manager wants an analysis of how Ford and Chrysler ads appeal to consumers under twenty-five.* So you have an actual reader (your teacher) and a stipulated reader (the imagined manager). If you know about ad managers, you may be able to anticipate their questions. If not, you can only imagine yourself in their shoes, then decide whether your real reader will imagine the same thing.

If your assignment stipulates your reader is "the general public," you have a bigger problem because there is no such reader. But if that's your assignment, assume (though it is not true) that this "general public" reads publications such as the *New York Times,* the *National Review, Scientific American,* and so on. Alternatively, assume that the "general public" is like yourself. They have read what you have, but have not discussed it and want to hear more.

Use Sources to Learn About Readers Indirectly

If your sources address readers like yours, study how they imagine them.

- Note what they assume you know; unfortunately, it will be in what they *don't* say. Is there background information that you wish the writer had explained? If writers don't explain it, they assume you know it.
- Note what they assume you do *not* know. You will find that in background information, terms or concepts that they define, and principles of reasoning they explain or defend.
- Note what evidence they explain and what they just mention. When writers explain evidence, they may believe it is new or controversial. When they mention it, they may assume it is familiar to their readers.

Talk to Readers If You Can

The best way to learn about readers is to talk to them. It's what experts do.

- Before an architect draws up a proposal, she finds out everything she can about her clients, from their finances to their family habits.
- Before a lawyer drafts a pleading, he checks out the judge who will hear the case by reading her decisions and asking other lawyers about her.

You might not be able to do that kind of detailed research, but it is a good idea to find out what your readers know and believe.

> Suppose Elena is preparing a proposal for a Center for English Language Studies to help students whose first language is not English. She could visit administrators to find out what they know about ESL students, whether they have dealt with the issue before, who will have a say in approving her proposal, and so on.

It's also wise to find out how they react to your argument before you write it:

> Once Elena has a proposal, she could visit readers to gauge their reactions to it. Do they think there is a problem? Do they think resources should be invested in other services? Do they have a cheaper alternative? Readers often judge an argument more generously when they are familiar with it before they read it.

Of course, for most students, talking to readers means talking to their teacher. But that's not a bad thing. Not only will it help you anticipate your teacher's responses, but it will prepare her to read your argument more generously by giving her a stake in seeing it succeed. When you can't talk to readers directly, imagine someone who is smart, amiable, and open-minded, but inclined to disagree with you; write to that person.

To Outline or Not to Outline

Experienced writers have mixed feelings about outlines. When the two of us left high school, we were glad to be shut of formal outlines with their roman numerals and letters, an "ii" for every "i." We no longer make elaborate outlines, but we do depend on sketchy ones for the general shape of our arguments. If you like formal outlines, use them, but don't reject a scratch outline because you reject a formal one. Find the kind of outline that works best for you, even if it is only a list of topics. Whatever it is, don't start a serious first draft without one. (We'll discuss plans in more detail in Chapters 5 through 8.)

DRAFTING

You may not yet be drafting an argument, but when you start, think of doing it in two overlapping stages: drafting and revising. We all revise as we draft, but it's useful to reserve time after you've finished a first draft to look at it fresh. We are all amazed at how much less convincing an argument seems the day after we wrote it. You'll write better and faster if you draft first and revise later.

When to Begin Drafting

It might seem logical to begin drafting only after you're dead certain of the solution to your problem, but that can be a mistake, because one way of discovering a solution is to do some writing to help you explore your problem. Start by formulating a few tentative solutions—call them *hypotheses*. You don't have to be 100 percent sure you are on the right track; think of this early writing as an opportunity to "audition" claims. Once you can articulate even a tentative claim, list reasons that would encourage a critical reader to take it seriously. That list can become your scratch outline *after* you arrange those reasons into an order that readers can recognize.

Styles of Drafting

Some writers draft slowly and carefully, others as quickly as they can. Most experienced writers are closer to quick than to careful, but draft in whatever way works for you. There is no best way, and both involve trade-offs:

- *Careful drafters* have to finish one sentence before they begin the next, get each paragraph right before they move on to another. Slow and careful drafters need meticulous plans, but even small changes can cascade, each requiring another, finally forcing changes bigger than the original plan allows. If you draft slowly, plan carefully.

- *Quick drafters* expect to revise, so they don't stop to find exactly the right phrase. When they get on a roll, they leave out quotations, data, even whole paragraphs that they know they can fill in later. When they bog down, they jump ahead or go back to parts they skipped, edit for grammar and spelling, or look for that right word. Quick drafters know they risk rambling, so they leave lots of time to reorganize and rethink their argument. If you draft fast, start early.

REVISING

Experienced writers know that once they figure out what they can say, they still have to say it in ways that meet their readers' needs and expectations. In fact, many experienced writers spend more time revising than drafting.

Your biggest obstacle in revising will not be too little time, but too much memory. None of us can read our own writing as our readers will, because we remember too well what we wanted to mean when we wrote it. So we read into our writing what we want readers to get out of it. Our readers, however, have to depend on what they see on the page.

Given that problem, you have to get distance on your draft. Set it aside until it is no longer fresh in your memory, or ask someone to read it back to you, out loud. But the best strategy is to revise your draft in a way that deliberately sidesteps your too-good understanding of it, a process we'll explain in every chapter that follows.

INQUIRIES

These inquiries offer a wide range of questions, puzzles, things to do, suggestions for class discussions, short papers, and even research papers, all intended to help you understand the nature and uses of argument. We offer them not as tests or review questions but as spurs to further thought.

1. Imagine that someone discovers a group of people isolated in some part of the world and claims that they are "completely irrational." Can you explain what would count as evidence that a whole society is completely irrational? Could an irrational society survive?

2. We can only speculate how rationality evolved, much less why. Here is a fable about its origins:

   At first, our forebears solved problems like the disputed ownership of a rock by hooting at or beating on each other until one retreated. The first advance in the technology of dispute resolution occurred when one of them found he could effectively claim ownership of the rock by clubbing the other with it. It was a pivotal moment: No longer was size or strength the only means of persuasion; humankind had developed the intelligence to make tools, especially those we call weapons. But the greatest change in our means of persuasion occurred when our ancestors replaced stones with words. Imagine that it might have happened like this: Once, when one of our forebears wanted to settle the question of who owned a useful rock, he uttered the equivalent of "Mine!" The other one in the confrontation might have just lunged at the one claiming the rock, but instead did something that must have amazed the other. She (or he) asked something like "Why?"—an act that transformed a physical confrontation into a verbal one. Then the first one did something more amazing yet. Instead of ignoring the question and just whacking the other with the rock, he (or she) offered the other a reason: "I found it." But the most amazing moment of all came when the other agreed: "OK, your rock." When they settled the issue not with blows but with good reasons, they together created the kind of talk we call argument and marked the beginnings of shared rationality, the ability to share our beliefs and the reasons that make us hold them, in the hope that others will agree.

In that story, humans began to offer claims and reasons to avoid violence. Can you imagine other ways that argument could have originated? (One of us [JMW] thinks this story must have a nub of truth; the other [GGC] thinks it unlikely.) Since we can never know for sure, you can be as fanciful as you like. Is the idea of "origin" even possible to speculate about? Does the fact that our metaphors for argument are so predictably drawn from images of combat offer any assistance here?

3. What metaphors do we use when we talk about reasoning? Are they as misleading as those we use for argument? Here is an example:

   I tried to resist the force of her logic, but it was so overwhelming that I could not stand up to it. I was simply compelled to accept her reasoning.

   . What metaphors do we use when we talk about expressing an opinion? (You might look up the original meaning of *express*.) Are they misleading? Here is a pair of passages that depend on different metaphors:

   It is important for me to *express* my ideas *honestly*, so I *lay out* my thoughts on the page as directly as I can. When I just *let it flow*, when I can *pour* my ideas out without any interference, I write most sincerely.

   It is important for me to *share* my ideas in a way that makes them *attractive* to readers. I try to *dress them up* with good reasons, to *show* them to *best advantage* and *hide* any weaknesses or rough spots.

   If those two speakers argued in the way their metaphors suggest, how would their arguments differ?

4. We've suggested that people make arguments to solve problems. Are there arguments that we have just for the sake of having them, regardless of whether the outcome resolves an issue? List some occasions when you have participated in or witnessed such an argument. Was it appropriate in the circumstances?

5. In your experience, are children more likely to argue just for fun than adults? Boys more than girls? Men more than women? People at home more than people at work? Why?

IN A NUTSHELL

About Your Argument . . .

We do not define an argument by its abrasive tone, the belligerent attitudes of arguers, or by the desire to coerce an audience into accepting a claim. Instead, we define an argument by two criteria:

- Two (or more) people want to solve a problem but don't agree on a solution.
- They exchange reasons and evidence that they think support their respective solutions and respond to one another's questions, objections, and alternatives.

You make an argument not just to settle a disagreement. Good arguments help you explore questions and explain your beliefs, so that even when you and your readers can't agree, you can at least understand why.

. . . and About Writing It

Your first task in writing an argument is to understand the problem that occasions it. Why (other than the fact that your teacher assigned it) are you writing it? What do you want it to achieve?

- Do you want your readers just to understand something, with no expectation that they will act? If so, why is that understanding important?
- Do you want your readers to act? If so, what do you expect to accomplish? What problem will that action solve?

Once you understand your problem, try out a few solutions, pick one that seems promising, then list reasons that would encourage readers to agree. You can use that list as a scratch outline or, if you wish, expand it into a formal one.

Draft in whatever way feels comfortable: quick and messy, or slow and careful. If you are quick, start early and leave time to revise. If you are slow, plan carefully and get it right the first time, because you may not have time to fix it.

Chapter 2

Argument as Civil Conversation

In this chapter, we show you how to build an argument out of the answers to just five kinds of questions that we ask one another every day. Then we show you how to use those questions to have a conversation with yourself to develop a written argument that your readers will judge to be thoughtful and persuasive.

The Questions of Argument

You make arguments so often that you probably never reflect on how you do it. You know that you have to support your claims, but do you know what to support them *with*? What do you say to someone who cannot follow your logic? to someone who says your support is irrelevant? How do you keep the tone friendly, even when there is a lot at stake and others are asking challenging questions?

Some writers consistently make arguments that support their claims in ways that we find convincing, or at least reasonable, while projecting an ethos that strikes us not as aggressive or coercive, but cooperative and considerate. How do they do it? More important, how can *you* do it?

To write arguments that readers judge to be thoughtful, you have to do two things:

- You must build arguments that include all the elements of support that readers look for in a sound argument.
- You must anticipate and respond to questions or objections that readers would raise, were they there to talk with you.

When we read such arguments, we feel we are working with a writer who has earned our trust by meeting our expectations and respecting our views.

It's easier to earn that trust in conversation than in writing, because you don't have to guess what questions to answer; others are there to ask them. If you answer willingly and candidly, you not only create the building blocks of an argument but project the ethos of someone who makes reasonable arguments that respect the views of others.

It is harder to earn that trust when you are "conversing" with a pad of paper or computer screen, because then you have to ask those questions of yourself. But that is a skill you must learn, because even a written argument is a collaborative dialogue with other voices, real ones when possible, but more often a voice that you must imagine on your reader's behalf.

Fortunately, there are only five kinds of questions, and you have asked and answered them countless times. The first two are obvious:

1. What's your point? What are you saying, in a nutshell? In short, what are you **claiming** that I should do or believe?

2. Why should I agree? What **reasons** can you offer to support your claim?

When you answer those two questions, you create the core of your argument.

The next two questions are more challenging. They ask you to demonstrate the *soundness* of your argument:

3. On what facts do you base those reasons? How do we know they are good reasons? What **evidence** do you have to back them up?

4. What's your logic? What principle makes your reasons count as relevant to your claim? (We'll call that principle a **warrant**, something we'll explain in a moment.)

To ask yourself the final question, you must imagine your argument from your reader's point of view:

5. But have you considered . . . ? But what would you say to someone who said/objected/argued/claimed . . . ? Do you **acknowledge** this alternative to your position, and how would you **respond**?

When you ask and answer those five kinds of questions, you create the substance of a sound written argument. In this chapter, we look at those questions as we ask and answer them in conversation, then discuss how to assemble their answers into a written argument that will encourage your reader to see you as thoughtful, judicious, and fair.

Argument's Roots in Civil Conversation

Here is a conversation among Sue and Raj, two friends home on spring break from different colleges, and one of their high school teachers, Ann. After chatting about Raj's school, Ann asks Sue about hers:

Ann: So what's new at your school?

Sue: I've been tied up with a student government committee working on something we're calling a "Student Bill of Rights."

Ann: What's that?

Sue: Well, it's an idea about how to improve life on campus and in class.

Ann: What's the problem?

Sue: We think the school is just taking us for granted, not giving us the services we need to get a good education.

Raj: What's your idea?

Sue: We think the university should stop thinking of us only as students and start treating us like customers.

Ann: Why customers? What's behind that?

Sue: Well, we pay a lot of money for our education, but we don't get near the attention customers do.

Raj: Like how?

Sue: For one thing, we can hardly see teachers outside of class. Last week I counted office hours posted on office doors on the first floor of the Arts and Sciences building. [She pulls a piece of paper out of her backpack.] They average less than an hour a week, most of them in the afternoon when a lot of us work. I have the numbers right here.

Ann: Can I see?

Sue: Sure. [She hands the paper over.]

Ann: [reading] Well, you're right about that one floor in that one building, but I wonder what a bigger sample would show.

Raj: I agree about office hours. We've got the same problem at my college. But I want to go back to something you said before. I don't see how paying tuition makes us customers. What's the connection?

Sue: Well, when you pay for a service, you buy it, right? And when you buy something you're a customer. We pay tuition for our education, so that means we're customers and should be treated like one.

Ann: But an education isn't a service. At least it's not like hiring a plumber. Doctors get paid for services, but patients aren't customers.

Raj: Does your idea mean that we just buy a degree? And what about the saying, *The customer is always right?* My test answers aren't always right. I don't want teachers pandering to me like advertisers do.

Sue: Nobody wants anyone to pander to us. We just want to be treated reasonably, like better bus service from off-campus dorms or the library to be open if we need to study late. And most of all, we want teachers to be more available. A lot of us work when we're not in class. Why should we have to take off work?

Raj: You're right about teachers. I've had trouble seeing my psych prof.

Ann: How about the idea of students as clients? When you go to a lawyer, he doesn't tell you what makes you happy just because you pay him. And good lawyers worry how you feel, so maybe it should be the same with a university. Maybe a school should treat students like clients.

Sue: "Students as clients." Doesn't sound as catchy as students as customers, but it's worth talking about. Thanks for the idea. I'll bring it up.

Sue, Ann, and Raj didn't settle their questions once and for all. But they understand one another's views better, and they can think about those issues more clearly because Sue offered a claim and Raj and Ann helped her test and develop it by asking her just five kinds of questions. Let's look at that conversation from that point of view, as a developing argument.

Two Friendly Questions About What Sue Thinks

When Ann asks Sue about what's new at her school, Sue raises the problem that motivates the rest of the discussion:

Ann: So what's new at your school?

Sue: I've been tied up with a student government committee working on something we're calling a "Student Bill of Rights."

Ann: What's that?

Sue: Well, it's an idea about how to improve life on campus and in class.

Ann: What's the problem?

Sue: We think the school is just taking us for granted, not giving us the services we need to get a good education.

Ann and Raj then ask the two questions that elicit the gist of Sue's argument.

What are you claiming?

Raj: What's your idea?

Sue: We think the university should stop thinking of us only as students and start treating us like customers. _{claim/solution}

What are your reasons?

Ann: Why customers? What's behind that?

Sue: Well, we pay a lot of money for our education but don't get near the attention customers do. _{reason}

Most of us welcome those two questions, because they invite us to share what we think and why we think it.

Two Challenging Questions About the Basis of Sue's Argument

If at this point, Ann and Raj agreed with Sue's position, they could let the matter drop. Or if Ann felt defensive about criticism of other teachers, she could counterattack: *That's silly!* If, however, they weren't convinced but still thought that Sue's problem was worth considering, they could ask two more questions about the deeper basis of her argument, not to prove her wrong, but to understand why she thinks she's right.

On what evidence do you base that reason?

Raj's first question is about facts, and Sue offers some:

Sue: Well, we pay a lot of money for our education, but we don't get near the attention customers do. _{reason}

Raj: Like how? [*What evidence do you base that reason on?*]

Sue: For one thing, we can hardly see teachers outside of class. Last week I counted office hours posted on office doors on the first floor of the Arts and Sciences building. [She pulls a piece of paper out of her backpack.] They average less than an hour a week, most of them in the afternoon when a lot of us work. I have the numbers right here. _{summary of evidence}

Ann: Can I see? [*What hard evidence do you base your summary on?*]

With that last question, Ann verges on seeming uncivil, because she implies that she does not trust the factual accuracy of Sue's report. But she is not overtly *disagreeing* with Sue's claim, only assuring herself that Sue has a good basis for it. Sue agreeably offers Ann her data:

Sue: Sure. [She hands the paper over.]

With a little help from her friends, Sue has assembled the core of her argument and tethered it to the first of two anchors that every argument needs: the evidence on which she bases her reason.

| **Claim** | *because of* | **Reason** | *based on* | **Evidence** |

How does your reason support your claim?

Every argument needs one anchor in sound evidence and another in sound reasoning. When, however, Ann and Raj ask for that second anchor, *how* her reason supports her claim, they seem to challenge Sue even more sharply than when they asked for evidence, because they ask for something more fundamental; now they want to understand the logic *behind* her reasoning.

> Raj: I agree about faculty hours. We've got the same problem at my college. But I want to go back to something you said before. I don't see how paying tuition makes us customers. What's the connection?

Sue may be factually correct: Students do pay good money for their education, but Raj doesn't see how that fact is *relevant* to her claim that they are *therefore* customers. Raj questions why Sue thinks her claim *follows* from her reason.

To answer, Sue has to analyze her own thinking, to find a general principle that explains why she thinks her reason is relevant to her claim.

> Sue: Well, when you pay for a service, you buy it, right? And when you buy something you're a customer. general principle We pay tuition for our education, reason so that means we're customers and should be treated like one. claim

There are technical terms for the principle that connects a reason to a claim. Logicians call it a *premise,* others an *assumption.* When that premise is explicitly stated, we call it a *warrant.* Like all warrants, Sue's has two parts:

(1) a general circumstance, which lets us draw

(2) a general inference.

Graphically, a warrant looks like this:

(1) General circumstance   — lets us draw→   (2) General inference

Sue offers this general warrant:

(1) person pays for service reason   so   (2) person is a customer. claim

If Raj and Ann believe Sue's warrant, Sue can apply it to her specific circumstance and draw her specific claim:

When a person pays for a service,   that person is a customer. warrant

Because we pay for our education, reason   we are customers. claim

Warrants do more than state static facts. They state the principles of reasoning that justify (warrant) our conclusions. Warrants usually justify us in connecting a reason to a claim, but as we'll see they can also justify the connection between evidence and a reason. We should alert you that warrants are hard to understand. Everyone struggles with them—including the two of us. (We explain them in more detail in Chapter 7.)

The Most Challenging Question: *But What About . . . ?*

The answers to the first four questions create the framework for an almost complete argument: A **claim** is supported by a **reason**; the **evidence** backs up the reason; and the **warrant** links the reason to the claim (another links the evidence to the reason). But those four elements alone cannot guarantee that your argument will succeed, because readers bring to arguments their own views. So they are likely to see things differently—draw different conclusions, think of evidence you didn't, and so on. And their different views motivate the fifth—and toughest—question: *But what about . . . ?*

In face-to-face arguments, we have the advantage of hearing another person's point of view directly, and we can answer then and there. But when we write, we must *imagine* our readers' questions, objections, and alternative views by creating a voice in the back of our mind insistently asking, *But what about . . . ? But what would you say to someone who argued . . . ?* If you cannot imagine your readers' questions and then acknowledge and respond to them, you will seem unwilling or unable to examine your own ideas critically and readers will judge your ethos and the quality of your mind accordingly. It may seem paradoxical, but readers have more confidence in your argument when you show them that you recognize its limitations.

Here are some of the questions and objections that Ann and Raj offered, not all of which Sue answered:

- Ann questioned the quality of Sue's evidence about office hours:

  Well, you're right about that one floor in that one building, but I wonder what a bigger sample would show.

- Raj points out a cost of accepting Sue's claim, one perhaps greater than the cost of the existing problem:

  Does your idea mean that we just buy a degree? And what about the saying, *The customer is always right?* My test answers aren't always right. I don't want teachers pandering to me like advertisers do.

- Ann offers an alternative solution and a bit of an argument of her own:

  How about the idea of students as clients? When you go to a lawyer, he doesn't tell you what makes you happy just because you pay him.

Raj and Ann could have asked Sue more questions:

Exactly what do you mean by "enough" office hours?

Do you have other reasons to think you aren't being treated well?

What do you think teachers would say about that? Or parents?

Do you think you could actually get the school to adopt that policy?

But each of those questions is just a variation on one of the others: *What do you mean by* asks you to state a claim or reason more clearly; *Do you have any other reasons* asks for more reasons; *What do you think teachers would say . . .* raises another objection.

Some students question why they should risk exposing themselves to contrary views: *Why should I imagine other views and maybe let them change my own? Isn't my job to stand up for my own beliefs?* True enough, but when you address a serious problem, it is in your own best interests to find its best solution, regardless of the one you prefer. Furthermore, in conversation, you would seem not just arrogant to ignore objections but foolish. You carry the same ethical burden when you write. What makes it so heavy in a written argument is that you must not only write in your own voice, but listen to those of others.

Review: Modeling an Argument

You might better grasp how those five questions work when you see how their answers combine into the structure of a complete argument, the way that atoms combine into molecules. Since some of us understand a structure better when we can picture it, we'll offer diagrams showing how the elements of argument work together.

The Core of an Argument: Claim + Support

In its simplest form, an argument is just a claim and its support:

> Because major college sports have degenerated into a corrupt, money-making sideshow that erodes the real mission of higher education, _{reason} they must be reformed. _{claim}

We can represent the relationship between a claim and its support like this:

Reason	*therefore*	**Claim**

That diagram does not represent the only order of those elements. We could reverse them:

Claim	*because of*	**Reason**

> Major college sports must be reformed, _{claim} because they have degenerated into a corrupt, money-making sideshow that erodes the real mission of higher education. _{reason}

To keep things simple, we'll regularly put the reason on the left and claim on the right. In real arguments, they can occur in either order.

Distinguishing Claims and Reasons

Some students puzzle over the difference between claims and reasons, pointing out that reasons also seem to make claims. They're right; those terms can be confusing. In fact, every sentence you write makes a claim in some sense of the word. But in order to keep the parts of argument distinct, we'll use *claim* and *reason* not in their loose, ordinary sense but as specific, technical terms:

- We'll use the term *main claim* to refer to the one claim that states the solution to the problem that the *whole* argument addresses. It is also the *main point* of the whole argument, the statement the rest of the argument supports (in high school, you may have called it a *thesis*).
- We'll use the term *claim* to refer to *any* statement supported by a reason.
- We'll use the term *reason* to refer to a statement that supports any claim, whether it is the main claim of an argument or a subordinate claim.

What all that means is that before you can decide whether a particular statement is a claim or a reason, you have to know how it is used. Here is a statement used as a claim:

> **Children who watch lots of violent entertainment tend to become violent adults,** claim because they slowly lose their ability to distinguish between reality and fiction. reason

And here is that same statement used as a reason:

> Violence on television and in video games should be moderated claim because **children who watch lots of violent entertainment tend to become violent adults.** reason

But there is one more complication: A statement can be *both* a reason and a claim *at the same time* if it supports some larger claim but is also supported by its own reason. Here is that statement used as both at the same time:

> Violence on television and in video games should be reduced claim 1 because **children who watch lots of violent entertainment tend to become violent adults.** reason 1 supporting claim 1/claim 2 supported by reason 2 They become so used to constant images of casual violence that they assume it is just part of daily life. reason 2

This can get confusing when you try to analyze a complex argument down to its smallest parts. But when you are dealing with your own arguments, you have only to remember that reasons support claims.

Anchoring the Core: Evidence and Warrants

In casual conversation, we might support a claim with just a reason:

> Larry: We'd better stop for gas here. claim
> Curly: What reason do you have for saying that?
> Moe: Because we're almost empty. reason

This is so trivial a matter that Curly is unlikely to respond, *What evidence do you base that reason on?* or *Why should the fact that we're almost empty mean that we should stop for gas?* But when an issue is contested, readers usually want to know both that you've based your reason on sound evidence and that your reason is relevant to your claim: you satisfy that need to know by offering evidence and a warrant.

Evidence

In that argument about college athletics, the issue is serious enough that readers would expect some evidence:

> Major college sports must be reformed, _{claim} because they have degenerated into a corrupt, money-making sideshow that erodes the real mission of higher education. _{reason} **In the last three years, we have had forty-six reports of athletes receiving money and 121 of athletes being exempted from academic requirements that other students must meet.** _{evidence}

Reasons and evidence might seem to be just different words for the same thing, but they are not:

- We think up reasons.
- We don't "think up" evidence; it must seem to come from "out there" in the world, something we can point out to our readers.

For example, we couldn't point to athletics degenerating into a sideshow, but we could point to someone handing athletes money or exempting them from academic requirements. (We discuss the difference between reasons and evidence in more detail in Chapters 5 and 6.)

To emphasize the difference between reasons and evidence, we represent the core of an argument like this:

| **Claim** | *because of* | **Reason** | *based on* | **Evidence** |

Think of evidence as anchoring your argument in facts.

Warrants

Readers may agree that you based a reason on good evidence, but still deny that it supports your claim because they do not understand how it is *relevant* to that claim and so doesn't "count" as a reason. In that case, they want you to state a principle that connects your reason to your claim, what we've called a *warrant*. Here's an example,

> **When an institution has its most eminent faculty teach first-year classes, it can justly claim that it puts its educational mission first.** _{warrant} We have tried to make our undergraduate education second to none _{claim} by asking our best researchers to teach first-year students. _{reason} For example, Professor Kinahan, a recent Nobel Prize winner in physics, is now teaching Physics 101. _{evidence}

We can graphically show how the warrant connects the claim to the reason:

| When an institution has its most eminent faculty teach first-year courses | it can justly claim to put its educational mission first. _{warrant} |
| Because we ask our best researchers to teach undergraduates, _{reason} | we have tried to make our undergraduate education second to none. _{claim} |

We can add warrants to our diagram in a way that shows it connecting a claim and its supporting reason:

Think of warrants as anchoring your argument in logic. If you are feeling a bit uncertain about warrants, you are right to. They are very difficult to grasp. We devote all of Chapter 8 to them.

The Fifth Question: Acknowledgments and Responses

Readers are likely to have alternative views, and thoughtful writers imagine, then acknowledge and respond to them. Someone familiar with college teaching might argue, for example, that famous researchers don't always make good teachers, a view that a skilled writer ought to anticipate:

> When an institution has its most eminent faculty teach first-year classes, it can justly claim that it puts its educational mission first. _{warrant} We have tried to make our undergraduate education second to none _{claim} by asking our best researchers to teach first-year students. _{reason} For example, Professor Kinahan, a recent Nobel Prize winner in physics, is now teaching Physics 101. _{evidence} **To be sure, not every researcher teaches well, but recent teaching evaluations show that teachers such as Kinahan are highly respected by our students.** _{acknowledgment and response}

We can add acknowledgments and responses to our diagram to show that they address all the other parts of an argument:

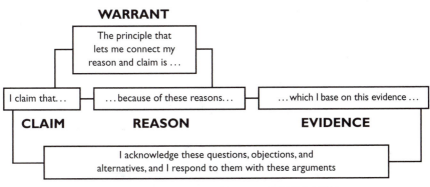

Crafting Written Arguments

When we are asked and answer the five questions of argument in conversation, we don't organize them in advance; we and our partner just go where the conversation takes us, rarely in a straight line to a conclusion. We manage well enough, though, because the back-and-forth helps us clarify points, elaborate on difficult concepts, even figure out what claim we can plausibly support. But when we write, we have to decide on our own what to say and in what order, with no second chances.

Although you can vary the order of elements in a written argument, you can rely on some standard orders: The default order for the first three elements is CLAIM + REASON + EVIDENCE. Since you will rarely support any serious claim with only one reason, you simply add REASON + EVIDENCE pairs. You sandwich them between an introduction that states the problem and its solution (your main claim), and a conclusion that restates that claim.

We can't tell you exactly where to put warrants and responses, except to put them near what they apply to:

- Locate warrants just before or after the claim they apply to, so that readers understand how your reason connects to your claim. (We know warrants are still murky; we promise they will become clearer.)

- Locate acknowledgments and responses where you suspect readers will think of objections and questions. Alternatively, put them all after the core of your argument.

Here is a simple plan for an argument:

Introduction: Problem + Solution/claim

Body:

    Warrant

    Reason 1 + Evidence 1

    Reason 2 + Evidence 2

    Etc.

    Acknowledgment and Response

Conclusion: Restatement of Problem + Solution/claim

Sue could organize a written argument following that plan. In a one-paragraph introduction, she states her problem and solution:

Recently, student government has been studying complaints about life at Midwest U. Some are minor, such as the bursar's office closing at 2 P.M. But others are major, such as teachers not keeping enough office hours. This problem suggests that the university cares little about our needs, apparently thinking of us only as transients, paying to be here but deserving little consideration. If this issue is ignored, we risk gaining the reputation of a "student-unfriendly" place that will gradually erode our reputation and ultimately threaten the quality of our education. _{problem} We believe the university should think of us not just as students, but also as customers vital to its success. _{solution/claim}

Then she lays out the body of her argument, starting with a warrant:

> When someone pays for a service, she deserves to be treated as a business treats its customers. _{warrant} Students pay for the services of teachers. _{reason 1} According to the Academic Senate, student tuition represents more than 60 percent of the funds used for faculty salaries. _{report of evidence} But we don't get the consideration that customers do. _{reason 2} For one thing, many faculty do not keep enough office hours. _{reason 2.1 supporting reason 2} In a survey of the first floor of Arts & Sciences Hall, office hours averaged less than an hour a week. _{report of evidence} No business would survive if it treated customers like that. _{reason 3, not supported by evidence} Of course, this is only a small sample, _{acknowledgment of anticipated objection} but it indicates a wider problem. _{response}
>
> Admittedly, we cannot push the analogy too far—the university can't educate us if it treats us like customers in all respects, especially in class. _{acknowledgment of alternative} Still, if thinking of us as customers leads the university to make our experience more productive, then we think the principle of "student as customer" is worth considering. _{response/restatement of claim}

In that example, Sue made every sentence answer one of the five questions, but not every sentence in every argument has to, because in an argument about a complex issue, you may have to explain some matters. For example, if you argue that gasoline additives cost more than their environmental benefits, you might have to explain the chemistry of carbon-based combustion. But don't explain concepts until you need to use them in your argument. Some writers explain everything first as background, but that's risky. Not only do you make readers remember the explanations until they become relevant, but you may make them impatient for the meat of your argument.

Thickening Your Argument

If you support your claim with as little as Sue does, you are unlikely to earn assent to the solution of a problem as complex as whether a college takes its students seriously. Experienced writers know that readers reject arguments that seem "thin," "undeveloped," or worst of all, "simplistic." When they make such judgments, they implicitly think something like this:

- You offer only one reason for treating you like a customer. I need more.
- You offer some evidence, but I need more and assurance that it is sound. You say teachers keep too few office hours, but you surveyed only one floor in one building.
- You offer a warrant but not an argument that it is true. Why do you think that just because someone pays for something, that person is a customer? I can't agree.

- You acknowledge that you have little evidence about office hours, but you claim that it still shows there's a problem. I need an argument before I accept that.

- You write about complex issues, but you don't explain them so that we can understand them.

You build a nuclear argument out of the answers to the five core questions, but you typically have to treat each statement of a reason, warrant, and response *as a subclaim inside its own argument* with its *own* reasons, evidence, warrants, and responses. In so doing, you "thicken," "broaden," and "deepen" your main argument. Readers judge an argument to be more complete—and the mind of its maker to be thoughtful and thorough—when they see simple nuclear arguments assembled into complex ones.

WRITING PROCESS
Argument as Civil Conversation

PREPARING AND PLANNING

Three Strategies for Designing an Argument

There are three strategies for developing a plan or blueprint for your argument:

1. Do not plan at all: Just let the argument fall out of your head onto the page as it will. Some writers do that successfully; most of us cannot.
2. Follow a stock plan you get from teachers or textbook writers like us. The problem is that while some stock plans are reliable, many are not—and you have to know which one is right for your situation.
3. Create a new plan for every argument. To make this strategy work, you first have to know a lot about your particular readers; second, you never benefit from experience. The set of common plans is a fairly small one that experienced writers improvise on, the way a pianist vamps on a tune or a basketball player varies the moves of a set play.

We suggest combining the second and third strategies. Think of a stock plan as scaffolding that supports a structure as you construct it but that does not look like the finished work. Base your argument roughly on one of our stock plans, but don't let it tyrannize your thinking or writing.

Stock Plans to Avoid

Before we offer some reliable plans, we should mention four stock ones that you should avoid:

The Five Paragraph Essay

¶ 1. *Introduction:* There are three reasons why you should floss your teeth.

¶ 2. The first reason is . . .

¶ 3. The second reason is . . .

¶ 4. The third reason is . . .

¶ 5. *Conclusion:* So we see there are three reasons to floss.

That may have worked in high school, but it reminds college teachers of high school thinking and is too simpleminded to accommodate complex problems.

A Narrative of Your Thinking

A blow-by-blow account of how you thought your way from a problem to its solution will engage those interested in the workings of your mind, but most readers care more about its product. An unrevised first draft usually records only the history of your struggle to write it.

A Summary of Your Sources

When you make an argument based on what you read, avoid a summary that tracks the order of its ideas. You will seem only to rehash them.

Thing One and Thing Two

If you write about two (or more) objects, such as people, books, or places, avoid dividing your argument into two parts, the first based on Thing One, the second on Thing Two. In comparing *Romeo and Juliet* to *West Side Story,* for example, don't devote part one to *Romeo and Juliet* and part two to *West Side Story.* Instead, organize your argument around aspects of the two works, such as their themes, actions, emotional impact, and so on. If you cannot avoid the obvious two-part organization, at least use phrases in the second part that recall and connect it to the first: *In comparison to Romeo and Juliet . . . , In contrast to Romeo and Juliet . . . , West Side Story shares with Romeo and Juliet . . . .* Otherwise, your argument will read like two unconnected summaries.

Sketch a Plan for Your Argument

Before you draft, make an outline, no matter how sketchy. As you gain experience, you may get by with just a scratch outline—even one you don't have to write down. But in your early papers, you're likely to need all the help you can get. Here's a low-cost way to plan a paper systematically.

Stage 1: Prepare Your Materials

1. On one page, sketch the problem or question and a plausible solution or answer.

Binge drinking is out of control. _{problem} Rather than ban drinking, we have to do a better job of identifying students likely to binge dangerously so that they can be counseled. _{solution}

2. At the top of separate pages, write the main reasons that would encourage readers to agree.

Assume that you need more than two or three. If you think of more than five, pick only the most persuasive ones.

> R1: Only a few students are the real problem drinkers.
>
> R2: When rules can be ignored without penalty, all students disrespect the administration.
>
> R3: Blanket prohibition deprives responsible students of a right.
>
> R4: Regardless of prohibitions, students will drink.
>
> R5: When the reckless drinkers are identified, they can be counseled.

3. After each reason, sketch the evidence (data, facts) or the additional reasons that support that main reason.

This is hard. You can think up reasons, but you have to hunt down evidence. If you can't think of any, you at least know what to look for.

> Only a few students are real problem drinkers. _{reason} A study in the *Journal of the American Medical Association* suggests that fewer than one in five student drinkers cause most of the problems. . . . _{evidence}

4. At the bottom third of each page, sketch relevant objections and alternatives that your readers might raise; then respond to them.

> It has been claimed that bingers cannot be controlled through education. _{acknowledgement} But researchers at the University of Washington have found otherwise. _{response} In their study, . . .
>
> It is true the administration has a legal responsibility to set rules to protect students. _{acknowledgement} However, a rule that cannot be enforced protects no one. _{response} We have seen this happen before. . . .

5. On another page, sketch a conclusion.

Do not just repeat the main claim from your introduction. You can restate it in more detail, but add something to indicate the value of your solution.

> Banning drinking will only encourage contempt for rules. It did not work during Prohibition, and it won't work now. Instead we have to help students make better decisions for themselves. If we can identify students most at risk for bingeing dangerously, the university can counsel them before they develop a pattern of bingeing. In that way, the university can do what it does best, educate, and avoid the kind of intrusion into students' lives that poisons students' attitudes and doesn't work anyway.

Stage 2: Organize and Arrange Your Materials

1. Decide where to locate your main claim (the solution to your problem).

The plan just sketched has you state your main claim twice, once at the end of your introduction and again at the beginning of your conclusion. But you have another choice. Each implies a different "social contract" with your reader:

> Choice 1: State your main claim twice, once at the end of the introduction and again in the conclusion.

When you do that, you in effect say to readers at the end of your introduction: *You know my problem and its solution, so you are in control of your reading. You know the most important things I have to say, so you can stop, read on, or skip around.*

> Choice 2: Save your main claim for the conclusion.

When you make readers wait until your conclusion to read your main claim, you in effect say to them: *I am in control, so follow me as I reveal my reasoning, and in the end I will reveal the solution you have waited for.*

Readers occasionally agree to that second contract with pleasurable anticipation, but only if they enjoy following the twists and turns of an intellectual journey. In fact, some teachers, especially in the humanities, prefer an argument that unfolds like a mystery story. Most of us, though, want to control our own time, so we prefer to see a statement of your main claim early, at the end of your introduction.

Some students hold back their main claim, fearing that if they "give it away" too soon, readers will lose interest and stop reading. That's a mistake. If you pose a problem important to readers, they will read on, even if they see its solution in the introduction. Conversely, no one is motivated to read about a trivial question just because you play hide-and-seek with its answer.

Other students think that if a reader might resist their main claim, they should sneak up on it. Only a skilled writer can lure readers toward an unwelcome conclusion that they don't see coming a long way off. And even if you do pull it off, readers may feel you have tricked them. Your best chance to win over hostile readers is not by manipulating them, but by acknowledging differences from the start. If they are so set against your claim that they refuse even to consider your argument, you won't persuade them in any event. But if you approach them as readers who give a fair hearing even to positions they do not like, they may not accept your claim, but they will at least grant that you have good reason for believing it, not a small success.

If you do hold off your main claim until the conclusion, give readers some guidance about what to expect: End your introduction with a sentence that introduces the key concepts that you develop in the body of your argument, and if you can, make that sentence more rather than less complex. Compare the following two ways of ending an introduction to an argument about binge drinking:

> In fact, **times** have **changed**, and universities have to **understand** those **changes** if they are to address **drinking** effectively.

> In fact, the **traditional role** of a university, **in loco parentis**, is more **complex** now than a generation ago, because it involves issues of **civil**

> **rights, privacy,** and **student autonomy.** Not until it **understands** where it
> **stands, legally, pragmatically,** and **morally,** can this university formulate
> workable **policies** to address the problem of **binge drinking.**

The boldfaced words in the second state more of the key themes in the argument. Of course, once you announce those themes, you must develop them.

Neither social contract, point-first or point-last, is intrinsically better.
They're just different, each implying a different relationship among the author,
reader, text, and circumstances. Most of us, though, most of the time prefer to
see a point early because that puts us in control of our own reading.

2. Decide where to put each reason in its section.

Just as you have to decide where to state the main claim of your whole argument, early or late, so you have to decide where to put each reason in its own
section. Since each reason is the point of its section, you can put it at the end of
the introduction to that section or in its conclusion. Here too, the default
choice is to state the reason early, at the end of the introduction to that section.

3. Decide how to order the sequence of sections.

The challenge now is to shuffle the separate pages with reasons into a sequence
that will make sense to readers. First, group reasons on the same topic. For
example, how would you group the five reasons to counsel students rather
than to ban drinking?

> R1: Only a few students are the real problem drinkers.
>
> R2: When rules can be ignored without penalty, all students disrespect the
> administration.
>
> R3: Blanket prohibition deprives responsible students of a right.
>
> R4: Regardless of prohibitions, students will drink.
>
> R5: When the reckless drinkers are identified, they can be counseled.

We can group those reasons into those involving all students and those
involving just irresponsible ones:

> R1.1: Blanket prohibition deprives responsible students of a right.
>
> R1.2: When rules can be ignored without penalty, all students disrespect
> the administration.
>
> R1.3: Regardless of prohibitions, students will drink.
>
> R2.1: Only a few students are the real problem drinkers.
>
> R2.2: When the reckless drinkers are identified, they can be counseled.

Now choose one of the standard orders for those reasons: more important
to less important (or vice versa), more familiar to less familiar, less complex to
more complex. If readers cannot see how you have ordered your reasons, they

are likely to think your argument incoherent. So state up front the principle you are following, or introduce each section (*not* each sentence) with transitional words such as *more important, therefore,* and *on the other hand.* (To learn more about ordering reasons, turn to p. 107.)

4. Decide where to put evidence.

If you put the reason in the introduction of its section, evidence must follow. You can, however, open with evidence and move toward the reason it supports:

> College athletics is becoming a scandal. _{problem} In the last three years, we have had forty-six reports of athletes receiving money and 121 cases of athletes being exempted from academic requirements that other students must meet. _{evidence} Clearly, athletics is degenerating into a corrupt, money-making side-show that erodes the real mission of higher education. _{reason} Major college sports must be reformed. _{claim}

We can easily manage short sequences of EVIDENCE + REASON + CLAIM, but when an argument opens with lots of evidence, we might not have any idea what that evidence is relevant to. So if you present evidence before its reason, introduce it with a sentence or two suggesting at least what topic the evidence relates to.

5. Decide where to put warrants.

This is the hardest choice, because you have to decide whether to state warrants at all. You almost always omit them when your readers share your values, assumptions, definitions, and so on. If they don't, you may have to state them as warrants, typically before the reasons they apply to, and maybe even support them with their own reasons and evidence. For example, after reading the following little argument, we could reject the claim at the end by objecting that what children watch is irrelevant to their psychological development:

> Every day, children are bombarded by TV violence. _{reason} The average child sees almost twelve acts of violence a day, most more graphic than necessary, few causing permanent damage, and even fewer condemned or punished (Smith 1992). _{report of evidence} When that kind of violence becomes a pervasive part of their experience, _{restatement of reason} it is likely to damage their psychological development. _{claim}

On the other hand, if the writer can first get us to agree to a general principle about the influence of example on child development, then she is more likely to get agreement later that her reason (violent TV) in fact supports her claim about damaged development:

> **Most of us believe that when children enjoy stories about admirable actions, they are more likely to become healthy adults.** _{warrant 1} **Isn't it likely, then, that when they see degrading behavior, they will be hurt by it?** _{warrant 2} Every day, children are bombarded by TV violence. _{reason} The average child sees . . . _{evidence} . . . [Watching TV violence] is likely to damage their psychological development. _{claim}

The argument now opens with two warrants, followed by a reason, evidence, and claim. We may be more inclined to think that the reason supports the claim if we first accept the general principle (*when children see degrading behavior, they are hurt by it*). Of course, if we might reject those warrants, the writer has to back them with their own supporting arguments.

6. Decide where to put acknowledgments and responses.

Ideally, you should acknowledge and respond to questions or objections the moment readers will think of them. Unfortunately, few of us are smart enough to do that. But just by acknowledging *some* objections and responding to them *anywhere,* you show readers you are aware of some alternative views, if not theirs in particular.

7. Decide what you have to explain.

Are there concepts, definitions, processes, background, history that readers need to understand your reasons and evidence? Explain where necessary.

All of this suggests the stock plan we sketched earlier:

> Introduction: Problem + Solution/claim
>
> Body:
>
>> Warrant
>>
>> Reason 1 + Evidence 1
>>
>> Reason 2 + Evidence 2
>>
>> Etc.
>>
>> Acknowledgment & Response
>
> Conclusion: Restatement of Problem + Solution/claim

We know that plans like these seem formulaic, but think of them not as blueprints but as rough sketches that you modify and develop. As you gain experience making arguments, you'll know when to forget these plans and go with your intuition. But even then, it's a good idea to have *some* plan before you start.

DRAFTING

When to Stop Planning and Start Drafting

It is so much easier to keep reading than to start writing that many of us just go on researching in order to put off the tougher job of drafting. Resist that trap:

Set a deadline to start drafting by back-planning from your due date. Decide how much time you need to draft, add 20 percent, then add another 20 percent for revision, if you are a quick drafter; if you are slow and careful, add more. Then leave time to proofread.

Draft a Working Introduction

You may have been told to write introductions last, after you have drafted something to introduce. That's a good idea, but you should also sketch a working introduction to focus your thinking as you draft. Try this plan:

1. **Start with a sentence or two of shared context for your problem:**

   > For centuries, drinking has been a part of college life. For some students, it is almost a rite of passage. But as we all know, it has become deadly.

2. **Add a sentence or two that articulate the problem:**

   > To control the risk, the university wants to pass regulations banning alcohol at all student events, even fraternity and sorority parties.

3. **In a sentence or two, state what the problem does or will cost readers:**

   > Students ignore these rules, which encourages contempt for university authority. And if the rules are enforced, responsible students will be deprived of a legal right.

4. **End your introduction with the gist of your solution to the problem:**

   > Student Government must join the Greek Council in opposing these rules and support instead educational programs.

REVISING

Match Your Introduction to Your Conclusion

Leave time to revise, but when time runs out, here is a quick fix to ensure that your introduction and conclusion at least do not contradict each other.

1. **Draw a line after the introduction and before the conclusion.**
   Readers are confused when they can't see those boundaries. If you can't find them easily, your readers may not find them at all. Always start a new paragraph after your introduction and at your conclusion.

2. **Highlight the main claim.**
   - If you stated the main claim at the end of the introduction, highlight it there and again in the conclusion.

- If you stated the main claim for the first time in the conclusion, highlight it there but also highlight the last sentence or two of the introduction.
- If you put your main claim anywhere else, revise to put it first or last.

3. **Compare the highlighted sentences in your introduction and conclusion.**
    - If they do not agree, revise the one in the introduction to match the one in the conclusion, because what you wrote last probably reflects your best thinking. If you repeat the main claim in both places, do not make them identical, but they should seem closely related.

4. **If you have time, repeat this process for each section longer than a page.**
    - In its introduction and conclusion, highlight the reason/claim that is the point of that section.
    - Put it at the end of its introduction, or at least in its conclusion.
    - If it is in the introduction, be sure it harmonizes with the conclusion.

INQUIRIES

1. Some say that ethos and reputation work best in the dark: they have the most effect on those who know least about the issue being debated. They believe that the more you know about the person (as opposed to just an image) and the more you know about the facts of the case, the less you should be influenced by ethos or reputation. Do you agree that if an argument is strong enough, the character of the person making it should not matter? What if a less trustworthy person makes a stronger argument than a more trustworthy person? Why do ethos and reputation matter to you, if they do?

2. How much are you influenced by reputation? Identify people whose judgment you trust, including public figures and people you know personally. List the features in their *manner* of arguing. Are they passionate or reserved? Do they qualify their statements or speak with unqualified certainty? Do they acknowledge the contributions of others? Do they use statistics? Anecdotes? What is their tone? Is there a pattern in the attributes of arguers you trust? If so, what does that say about you?

3. The five questions underlying argument can be asked in relatively explicit ways or with just "Umm" or "Oh?" Observe two or three conversations in which people make arguments. Notice how many different ways they ask others to expand and explain their arguments. Are their questions explicit or implicit? How often do people push enough to get the hard evidence on which someone bases a claim?

4. Are arguments at work different from arguments in school? If you have a job, notice how people make arguments with those above them, below them, and on the same level. Do they offer as much evidence as academic writers do? Do they acknowledge alternatives? What would explain the differences?

5. Are advertisements arguments? Few say explicitly, *Buy this car!* or *See this movie!*, but they still try to get you to do something specific. Most of them give reasons, and the photograph or drawing of the product seems to count as something like evidence, something you can see with your own eyes. Try analyzing them as arguments. What difference does it make whether we call them arguments or not? Look for advertisements that seek to persuade by means other than reasons and evidence. Can you find an ad that acknowledges another point of view?

IN A NUTSHELL

About Your Argument . . .

We build arguments out of answers to just five kinds of questions we ask one another every day:

- What are you claiming?
- What reasons do you have for believing that claim?
- What evidence do you base those reasons on?
- What principle makes your reasons relevant to you claims?
- But what about . . . ?

In conversation, someone asks us those questions, but when we write, we have to imagine those questions on our readers' behalf.

You anchor your argument on two of those answers: evidence and, if necessary, warrants. If your readers do not accept those elements, you can't make an argument at all. You must report evidence explicitly. You leave most warrants implicit, if you and your readers share assumptions, but you usually have to state them when you address contested issues. Most of us assume, however, that we and our readers share more than we actually do, so it is wise to be more explicit than you think you have to be.

Those five elements constitute the core of a simple argument, but you may have to treat each reason, warrant, and response to a different point of view as the claim of another, subordinate argument. That's "thickening" your argument.

. . . and About Writing It

You have four initial tasks:

- Understand the problem that occasions your argument.
- Formulate hypotheses that are plausible candidates for a solution.
- Pick the best candidate.
- List the reasons that encourage your reader to agree with your solution.

Once you have reasons to support your claim, think about evidence to back up those reasons. Then imagine someone asking *But what about . . . ?*
Avoid these stock plans:

- The five paragraph essay
- A narrative of your research and thinking
- A summary of your sources
- Organizing parts around things rather than ideas and concepts.

Here is a plan for drafting your argument:

- Sketch the problem and its solution.
- List reasons that you think your readers would accept as sound.
- Articulate the evidence on which you think those reasons rest.
- Order those reasons in a way that will make sense to your reader.
- Imagine objections and respond to them.

Next, draft a working introduction:

- Start with a sentence or two of shared context for your problem.
- Add a sentence or two that articulates the problem.
- State what the problem does or will cost readers.
- Finish with a sentence that sketches the gist of your solution to the problem.

Set off your introduction and conclusion from the body of your paper, and then compare the last sentence or two in your introduction to the most important claim in your conclusion. If they do not complement each other, change them so they do. (You will more likely have to change the one in the introduction.)

If you can, do the same in each major section: Set off its introduction and (if it has one) conclusion and compare them. The main point in each section should probably appear at the end of the introduction to its section.

In this chapter we discuss how to motivate readers to take your argument seriously by posing a problem they care about. We distinguish two kinds of problems—pragmatic and conceptual. We then discuss how to write introductions and conclusions that "frame" your argument in ways that help readers understand it.

You can occasionally choose whether to make an argument face-to-face or in writing, but often you have no choice. You have to argue in person when you have no time to write or need a personal touch. You have to write when you can't meet readers in person, you need time to plan and test your argument before giving it to them, or they want time to study it.

But writing has drawbacks. If you don't know what your readers are like—cooperative or prickly, generous or difficult—you might not know the right tone to take. Nor can you correct their misunderstandings or respond to surprising questions. You can only try to anticipate them and hope for the best.

But a written argument must overcome an even bigger disadvantage. When you make an argument face-to-face, you draw others into it with your look, your voice, your body language. If, for example, you ran into the dean of students after a bad day at the health service, you could visibly communicate your feelings with your frustrated look and passionate voice. And the dean would probably respond more intently than if he were alone in his office reading your angry letter. Human presence engages us as words on a page rarely can.

So when you make an argument in writing, you have to overcome the handicap of your absence by offering readers good reason not only to accept your claim, but to engage your argument at all. The most devastating response you can get from a reader is not *I don't agree* but *I don't care*. In this chapter, we discuss how you motivate readers to care about your argument by showing them that they have a problem that you can solve.

Two Kinds of Problems

We write arguments to solve problems, but problems are of two kinds:

- One kind requires us to ask *What must we do to change this situation?* We'll call that kind of problem *pragmatic*.
- The other kind leads us to ask, *What must I find out to understand this issue better?* We'll call that kind of problem *conceptual*.

The two kinds of problems require different kinds of solutions that need different kinds of support.

Pragmatic Problems

You face and solve pragmatic problems every day. A pragmatic problem is a situation that you want to eliminate, like AIDS, genocide, sagging profits, rising tuition—whatever makes you angry, sad, disgusted, frightened, pained, guilty, ashamed, discouraged, or even just annoyed, for yourself or empathetically for others. You solve a pragmatic problem only when someone *does* something that breaks the chain of causes and effects that makes you or, more important, your reader unhappy. (Of course, we also solve problems by getting someone *not* to do something, like not wasting energy.)

Pragmatic problems motivate written arguments everywhere in the professional world and in academic areas such as business, engineering, and architecture, where researchers solve problems ranging from ineffective advertising to crumbling bridges. A pragmatic problem can be as small as a loud radio or as big as global warming.

Conceptual Problems

A conceptual problem, on the other hand, is like a riddle, a puzzle, a mystery—something we can state as a question and solve with just an answer: *How old is the universe? Why don't apes cry?* Left unsolved, a conceptual problem does not cause sadness, anger, or pain, but not knowing the answer frustrates our human need to know more about the world, even about something as trivial as why the biggest nuts in a can end up on top. Such questions don't interest everyone, but they do motivate researchers to devote their careers to finding their answers.

Some people, especially politicians, think we waste money trying to solve such problems: *Who cares,* they ask, *why the biggest nuts end up on top? How will that improve the world? Why should our taxes support the search for an answer?* Scholars defend "pure" research of this kind by arguing that all knowledge is valuable, because it helps us understand the world better. That was the defense of a University of Chicago professor who, puzzled by the mixed nuts phenomenon, spent a lot of time figuring it out. (As it happens, his answer helps shipping companies pack granular materials more efficiently, construction companies build tougher roads, and drug companies make better pills.)

But even when an answer has no practical application at all, researchers still pursue such questions, simply because they believe that we must understand every aspect of our world better. It's an impulse that all of us have felt, even children: *Why is the sky blue? Why can't kitty talk? Where did I come from?*

Sometimes, we have to solve a conceptual problem before we can solve a pragmatic one, because before we can know what to *do* about a pragmatic problem, we have to understand better. For example, politicians will know what to *do* to fix our Social Security system only after researchers solve the conceptual problem of *understanding* how society will change if people have to retire later. When researchers work on conceptual problems to solve a pragmatic one, they call their research *applied*.

Pure Research and Larger Questions

A "pure" historical question has recently come closer to an answer that will not change our world, but might help us understand some of its history better:

Did Thomas Jefferson have children with his slave Sally Hemings?

DNA evidence suggests that he could have, but so what if we never find out? *Well,* the historians answer, *until we know, we can't answer bigger questions.*

Until we know for sure, we can't know whether his actions contradicted his claims about equality and morality.

But so what if you don't know?

Until we know that, we can't evaluate his moral values.

But so what if you can't?

Until we can, we won't understand the author of some of our key political principles.

Some might still ask, *So what? Who cares?* Well, many historians care. And now so do a few others who will use the answer to solve a pragmatic problem: Only blood relatives are entitled to lie in the family cemetery at Monticello, a right now claimed by Sally Hemings' African-American descendants. (When Jefferson's white descendants met to decide whether to let them in, they voted to create a separate cemetery for them.)

The Structure of Problems

In your career, you will be asked to write arguments addressing both problems, pragmatic and conceptual. To do that successfully, you must understand how they differ, because you have to write different arguments about them.

Pragmatic Problems

We'll start explaining pragmatic problems with an example that you would never write about but makes our point: Imagine you are driving to a final exam that you must pass to graduate. You partied last night, then slept through the alarm. You'll probably be late, but even if you make it, you'll probably fail, because you didn't study. You hit a traffic jam; now you *know* you won't make it. Do you have a problem?

Your situation seems to have the makings of a problem, because it is going to end up making you very unhappy indeed:

CONDITION ————— leads to ————→ **COST**

Didn't study + Traffic → Missed exam → F → Don't graduate → BAD feelings
Running late   jam

Then in the next car you see your instructor. As you slump down out of sight, you realize you no longer have a problem. In fact, that traffic jam is your solution! The exam will be put off, and you'll even have more time to study:

CONDITION ————— leads to ————→ **BENEFIT**

Traffic → Delayed exam → More time to study → Chance to graduate
jam

No cost, all benefit, no problem.

Here's the point: Every pragmatic problem has two parts:

- **Part 1:** An event, condition, or circumstance unsettles your world. We'll call this part of a problem its ***destabilizing condition.***

We usually name a problem by naming just its condition: *racism, cancer, AIDS.* But every problem has a second part:

- **Part 2:** That destabilizing condition must have an effect that you believe will make you—or someone you care about—feel bad. We call this part of a problem its ***cost.***

By this definition, a situation that at first seems very bad may not be a problem if it exacts no cost: a painless disease that will kill you tomorrow is no problem for you today if an asteroid is going to kill everyone on earth tonight.

When you write an argument addressing a pragmatic problem, you must make readers see this two-part structure, especially the costs of leaving the problem unsolved, because it is the costs that your *readers* want to avoid that motivate them to read your argument. Sometimes, you don't have to state the cost of a problem because it seems obvious—we all know the cost of AIDS, homelessness, or genocide, for example. But more often you do have to state the costs because they may not be obvious. For example, you might write to the administration arguing that your student health service should have separate waiting areas for men and women. But until you can point out the *costs* that *the adminis-trators* pay for a single waiting room, they are unlikely to see the problem.

Identifying Costs by Asking So What?

Since readers are motivated to read by the significance of a problem's costs to them, you must begin by imagining your problem from their point of view. To do that, imagine your reader repeatedly asking *So what?* until one of your answers makes her say, *Oh no! What do we do?* Here's an example:

> Industries are releasing chemicals that are creating a hole in the ozone layer.
>
> *So what?*
>
> Less ozone means more ultraviolet light.
>
> *So what?*
>
> Too much ultraviolet light causes skin cancer.

If she again asks *So what?,* you might question her moral rationality. But if you still needed to motivate her to care, you'd have to try again:

> More skin cancer means higher health care costs and many deaths.

If, however improbably, she asks *So what?* again, you have failed to state your problem in a way that helps her see it as hers. You can only shrug, baffled at her values. Only when she says *What do we do?* will you know that you have identified costs that motivate her to read about the solution to her problem.

When you state your problem in your introduction, imagine a reader asking *So what?* until you are certain that your answer spells out why that reader should care about the problem you have solved. Then state that answer as the costs that make your condition a problem for readers.

Conceptual Problems

A conceptual problem also has a destabilizing condition and a resulting cost, but they differ from those in pragmatic problems. In a pragmatic problem, the destabilizing condition is *any* situation that a reader finds intolerable: If winning the lottery made you unhappy, it would be a pragmatic problem for you. But in a conceptual problem, the destabilizing condition always is the same:

- In a conceptual problem, the **destabilizing condition** is always something you don't know or understand but want to: a puzzle, a gap in understanding, a discrepancy or contradiction between a new fact and old ones—anything that leaves you so uncertain, confused, or even just so curious that you want to resolve it.

We can always express the destabilizing condition of a conceptual problem as a question:

> How many stars are in the sky?
>
> How do children respond to the fragmented structure of network TV programs?

Conceptual problems also differ from pragmatic ones in their costs. In a pragmatic problem, the cost is some kind of tangible unhappiness. In a conceptual problem, on the other hand, the cost of the condition is another gap in knowledge or understanding. It is also intangible, however, so instead of calling it a *cost* we'll call it a *consequence*.

- In a conceptual problem, the **consequence** of its destabilizing condition is something *else* that you don't know, another question whose answer is *more* significant than the answer to the first.

Therefore, a conceptual problem consists of not *one* question, one thing you don't know, but *two*.

That is less confusing than it first seems. It works like this: You have the first part of a conceptual problem, its condition, when there is something you don't know but need to. You can always phrase the condition as a question:

How many stars are in the sky?

How do children respond to the fragmented structure of network TV programs?

You have the second part of a conceptual problem, its consequences, when you can say why you want to find out the answer to the first part. You can also phrase that second part as a question. Imagine someone asking *So what if you don't know that? So what if you can't answer that question?* For a pure conceptual problem, your response is something else you don't know that is more important. For example:

If we can't answer the question of how many stars are in the sky, _{condition/first question} then we can't answer a more important question: Does the universe have enough mass for gravity to hold it together? _{consequence/larger question}

If we can't answer the question of how children respond to the fragmented structure of network TV programs, _{condition/first question} then we can't answer a more important one: Does TV affect their ability to concentrate? _{consequence/larger question}

If the second question is one your readers want you to answer, then you've stated a consequence that makes them think that your first question is worth asking and that an argument supporting its answer is worth reading.

But what if you think that your reader might again ask *So what?*

So what if you don't know whether the universe has enough mass to hold it together?

At that point, you'd have to pose a yet larger question whose answer is *even more* significant to his understanding:

If we can't answer the question whether the universe has enough mass for gravity to hold it together, _{second question} then we can't answer a more important one yet: Will the universe one day cease to exist? _{consequence/larger question}

If that person asked *So what?* yet again, you could only think, *Wrong audience.*

Finding consequences is often the hardest step for students new to the academic world. Experienced researchers like your teachers know what large questions interest others in their field. So they can usually tell whether a specific question they want to answer connects to one of those larger questions. But you won't if you are just starting out in a field or haven't even chosen one. You will have to rely on teachers, colleagues, and lots of reading to help you discover which questions are *worth* asking.

But the first and most important step in this process is just finding a question that *you* want to pursue, simply because it interests *you*. Once you find that first question, keep asking *So what if I answer it?* If you are engaged in a long research project, you may not find the best—or even a good—answer until you are near its end. Don't be discouraged: that happens to everyone. But don't wait till the end to start asking *So what?* The sooner you can state the larger question that your specific question helps you answer, the better you will understand your problem and the more easily you will answer it.

The Wider Coherence of Conceptual Problems

Those new to academic research face another challenge with conceptual problems: not only must they answer their question, but they must make that answer fit with everything else known and believed by others in the field, from basic facts to political and ideological values. We will accept a solution to a conceptual problem only if it fits our entire mental landscape.

For example, *Why did the mammoth, camel, and other large mammals disappear from North America about 12,000 years ago?* Not much seems to ride on the answer, beyond understanding ancient natural history. But one answer has generated heat because it conflicts with larger ideological positions. Most researchers once thought those creatures died out because of disease or climatic change, but some now think that they were hunted to extinction by the earliest Native Americans. That claim is heatedly opposed by other researchers who believe that those first peoples lived in harmony with nature, and so *in principle* they could not have wiped out whole species. So despite the evidence, what killed those creatures *must have been* climate or disease. They find any other answer ideologically unacceptable because it contradicts too much of what they already accept as true. That's why some historians can't accept the idea that Jefferson had sex with a slave: it contradicts too much of what they believe about his character.

It is this need to make new ideas cohere with old that most challenges those just entering a field. When they make a claim about a complex issue, they can't know all the facts, principles, theories, and political views that their claims must harmonize with.

Framing Problems in Introductions

Readers understand your argument better and remember it longer when you motivate them to read it closely. You do that best when you state your problem in your introduction in a way that helps readers see their stake in your solution. Most introductions have three parts: (1) an opening segment we will call *common ground*, (2) the statement of your problem, and (3) its solution. We'll start in the middle, with the core of every introduction, its problem.

The Core of Your Introduction: Destabilizing Conditions and Costs

To state a problem explicitly, you must state its destabilizing condition and its pragmatic cost or conceptual consequences.

Some costs may seem too obvious to state, but it's risky to assume that your readers understand them as you do. For example, binge drinking among college students has obvious costs, but different readers may see different ones:

1. It threatens the lives of drinkers and those around them.

2. It encourages moral weakness.

3. It tarnishes the image of the university.

4. It exposes the university to legal action for its damages.

When you state each cost as something worth caring about, you imply that you and your readers share certain values: cost (1) implies that you both feel anguish over injury and death; (2) implies that you condemn moral weakness; (3) that you fear loss of prestige; and (4) that you fear loss of money. Each cost also implies that the problem can be solved in a different way:

1. Since bingeing threatens lives; prohibit students from drinking.

2. Since it erodes morality, teach moral virtue.

3. Since it makes the university look bad, launch a public relations campaign.

4. Since it exposes the university to lawsuits, limit the university's liability.

Those different costs would encourage us to write different introductions. Contrast how these next three introductions describe the problem:

1. When students drink, many "binge," consuming large amounts of alcohol at one sitting until they pass out. _{destabilizing condition} We cannot end bingeing, but we must control it. _{promise of solution}

That introduction implies that binge drinking is a problem, but names no costs; it fails to answer the question *So what?* By answering that question, these next two introductions state costs, but they imply different readers with different values and call for different solutions.

2. When students drink, many "binge," consuming large amounts of alcohol at one sitting until they pass out. _{destabilizing condition} Bingeing is, tragically, far from harmless. In the last six months, it has been cited in three deaths from alcohol poisoning, two from falls, and one in a car crash. It crosses the line from fun to reckless behavior that, if uncontrolled, kills and injures not just drinkers but those around them. _{costs} We cannot end bingeing, but we can control its worst costs by educating first-year students how to manage its risks. _{promise of solution}

3. When students drink, many "binge," consuming large amounts of alcohol at one sitting until they pass out. _{destabilizing condition} This behavior not only tarnishes our image, but exposes us to liability if a student injures himself or others. Until this problem is solved, we risk criticism from the state legislature, with possible cuts in our budget, and increased insurance costs, either of which will delay faculty salary increases. _{costs} We cannot end bingeing, but we can control its damage by educating the public and the legislature that the problem is caused by lax parenting. _{promise of solution}

An Alternative Way to State Pragmatic Costs

You can state a problem positively by rephrasing its costs as the potential benefits of its solution. This introduction focuses on costs:

> When students drink, many "binge," consuming large amounts of alcohol at one sitting until they pass out. _{destabilizing condition} **Bingeing is, tragically, far from harmless. In the last six months, it has been cited in three deaths from alcohol poisoning, two from falls, and one in a car crash.** _{costs} We can reduce bingeing through better education. _{solution}

This one focuses on benefits:

> When students drink, many "binge," consuming large amounts of alcohol at one sitting until they pass out. _{destabilizing condition} **Had certain universities reduced bingeing, they might have saved the lives of the six students who died in the last six months as a result of bingeing.** _{benefits} We can reduce bingeing through better education. _{solution}

You might think that this is just a stylistic choice, but research suggests that we fear a loss more than we are attracted to a gain, even when they are objectively identical. For example, the effect of a hole in the ozone is the same, whether we say its solution might *save* 10,000 lives or leaving it unsolved might *cost* 10,000 deaths. But we tend to react more keenly to the risk of 10,000 dead than to the chance of saving an equal number of lives.

So if you want to cite benefits, state the costs when you first introduce the problem and add the benefits after you state the solution:

> When students drink, many "binge," consuming large amounts of alcohol at one sitting until they pass out. _{destabilizing condition} **Bingeing is, tragically, far from harmless. In the last six months, it has been cited in three deaths from alcohol poisoning, two from falls, and one in a car crash.** _{costs} We can reduce bingeing through better education, _{solution} **and thereby not only save those who binge from injury or death, but mitigate the damage they do to those around them.** _{costs restated as benefits}

Articulating the Conditions and Consequences of a Conceptual Problem

Conditions. In a conceptual problem, the destabilizing condition is something your readers don't know, but want to. You can articulate that condition in different ways. You can tell readers that they or others have been just plain wrong:

> Many educators proclaim that on-line classes will usher in a new era of education. [relevant quotations] **But the facts have contradicted these promises of a golden age. Few students are motivated to learn** . . . .

You can also tell readers that others have made an error in methods of research (something academics love to point out):

> Critics of American education rightly argue that our high school students trail those in other countries in math and science. **But a study of the populations of students tested suggest sampling errors that put those criticisms in doubt.**

Or, more politely, you can tell readers that their knowledge and understanding are incomplete:

> Problem solving is a well-investigated aspect of cognitive behavior. [review of research] Despite this extensive research in problem solving, **cognitive science knows little about the issue of problem finding** . . . .

Or, more politely still, you can tell readers that questions they can answer point to another they can't:

> A question in the criticism of Flannery O'Connor is how her religious beliefs shaped her fiction. One of the newest has been O'Connor's response to racism. Both issues have been studied thoroughly. [summary of criticism] **But no one has yet asked how religion has shaped O'Connor's view of racism** . . . .

Although you can always state the condition of a conceptual problem as a question—*How did O'Connor's religion shape her view of racism?*—writers rarely do so in introductions. When you state your condition, put your question into the form of a statement of something your reader does not know.

Consequences: It is harder to express the consequences of that gap in understanding, the "why readers should want to know" part. We too easily assume that if we just say what is not known or understood, readers will think finding out is worth their time to read our argument. For example:

> When some critics charge that Flannery O'Connor does not appreciate the evil of racism, they ignore her religious beliefs. _{destabilizing condition} Her stories show that her treatment of racism as a spiritual crisis is sympathetic to equality and suggests an understanding of racism that set her apart from liberals of her time. _{answer/main claim}

If we are among those who criticize O'Connor or are fascinated with everything about her, we might read on to find out why this writer thinks her critics are wrong. But if we haven't thought much about O'Connor, we are likely to ask not *Why do you think that?* but *Why should I care that you do?*

You cannot count on readers to see the consequences of a conceptual problem, so you must state them explicitly: If you do not answer the specific question, what larger question remains unanswered? Just as with a pragmatic problem, you can state consequences of a conceptual problem twice, once as a negative consequence of not knowing, and again as the positive benefit of having the knowledge. For example:

> When some critics charge that Flannery O'Connor does not appreciate the evil of racism, they ignore her religious beliefs._{destabilizing condition} **If we fail to recognize** that O'Connor saw racism as a symptom of a larger spiritual and religious crisis, **we risk overlooking her insights into sources of racism that are deeper and more harmful than mere social or cultural causes.** _{consequence} Her stories show that her treatment of racism is more sympathetic to equality than is apparent and suggests an understanding of racism that sets her apart from liberals of her time. _{answer/main claim} **Once we recognize the spiritual basis of her thinking, we see that O'Connor's exploration of Southern culture is far more penetrating than her critics ever understood.** _{consequence restated as benefit}

By stating the consequences of understanding O'Connor's ideas on race *twice* in detail, the writer casts a much broader net: She makes a claim on the interest not just of readers who want to understand those specific ideas but also of those who care about O'Connor, her stories, Southern culture, sources of racism, and so on. She gives a rich and detailed answer to the question, *So what?*

Consequences and Costs in Framing Applied Conceptual Problems

We call a conceptual problem *applied* when we can trace its consequences to some ultimate tangible cost. But the immediate consequence of an applied conceptual problem is still something that we do not know.

Some students feel that tangible costs are more motivating than conceptual consequences. So when they state a problem, they jump right to those tangible costs:

> If we can't answer the question of how children respond to the fragmented structure of network TV programs, _{condition/first question} then we risk stunting their intellectual growth by letting them watch it. _{cost/tangible harm}

But that way of thinking about a problem jumps over the link between a conceptual condition and an ultimate pragmatic cost: *What must we understand before we know what to do?* To state an applied problem clearly, you have to state not just the conceptual condition and its ultimate pragmatic cost, but also the chain of conceptual consequences that connect them:

> If we can't answer the question of how children respond to the fragmented structure of network TV programs, _{condition/first question} then we can't answer a more important one: Does network TV affect children's ability to concentrate? _{consequence/larger question} If we can't answer that question, then we can't answer a more important one: Do we stunt children's intellectual growth by letting them watch network TV? _{cost/tangible harm}

So if you address an applied problem, clearly explain why we cannot know what to do until we understand some specific aspect of the problem.

The Outer Frame of Your
Introduction: Common Ground and Solution

Thus far, we've described the core of an introduction, the statement of a problem. Schematically, it looks like this:

INTRODUCTION
. . . . + [Destabilizing Condition + Costs] ~problem~ + ...

Most introductions, however, have two more parts that give readers a framework for understanding the problem.

- Before they read about a problem, readers are ready for an introductory contextualizing element that we call **common ground.**
- After they read about the problem, they look for its **solution,** your main claim (or at least a gesture toward it).

Thus a full introduction consists of these elements:

INTRODUCTION
Common Ground   +   Problem   +   Solution
[Destabilizing Condition + Costs]

We'll discuss the solution first, then common ground.

The Solution

After you pose your problem, readers usually look to the end of your introduction to find the gist of your solution. The solution of a pragmatic problem calls for or implies an action; the solution of a conceptual problem answers a question. For example, this introduction to the pragmatic problem of bingeing calls for an action—educate students:

> . . . Bingeing crosses the line from fun to reckless behavior that, if uncontrolled, will kill and injure still more students. ~costs~ We will never end bingeing entirely, but colleges must start educating students how to manage its risks, just as we now educate them about sexual harassment and other social problems. ~solution/main claim~

Though it is a bit of a cliché, a rhetorical question can achieve the same end:

> We will never end bingeing entirely, but is it possible to educate students in how to manage its risks, just as we now educate them about sexual harassment and other social problems? ~solution/main claim~

Some writers only hint at a solution, implying that they will not state it explicitly until their conclusion:

. . . Bingeing crosses the line from good times to reckless behavior that, if uncontrolled, will kill and injure still more students. _{costs} We will never end bingeing entirely, but it is a problem we cannot ignore. The solution is not obvious, but finding one must be part of our educational mission. _{promise of solution to come}

Notice, however, that while that last sentence only promises a solution, it introduces concepts—*part of our educational mission*—that suggest ideas that the writer will develop in the body of his argument.

Removing Causes Versus Ameliorating Costs

This book does not focus on problem solving, but to make effective arguments you should understand some aspects of it. One is knowing what part of a pragmatic problem your solution fixes: Does it remove the root causes, thereby eliminating the problem entirely, or does it only lessen its costs? For example, no one can cure AIDS, but physicians do know how to control its costs by removing some of its devastating symptoms and postponing death. People can thus be infected with HIV (the condition), but live with the problem, if its symptoms (costs) are ameliorated.

Suppose Sue convinces administrators at her school that students need more access to teachers outside of class, and they imagine two solutions. One would get at a root cause and eliminate the problem: require teachers to have more office hours. The other would ameliorate the costs of too few hours, thus making the problem seem a smaller one: make teachers available via e-mail. They might also find a solution that simply makes students not mind the consequences: give each student a $500 budget to spend on office hours at $50 an hour and tell them they can keep what they don't spend. That last solution is tongue-in-cheek, but it would give at least some students (not all, we would hope) reason to be happy about not meeting with teachers.

You can solve a problem in two ways: remove its cause or ameliorate its costs. The problem with ameliorating costs is that root causes have a way of sprouting new costs.

The Risks of Delay. Think twice before you decide only to promise a solution in your introduction. Readers may suspect you are hiding a solution they won't like, or that you don't have a solution at all. If you have reason to withhold a solution to a pragmatic problem but you want to avoid seeming to conceal it, express your problem so precisely that readers can infer its solution.

For example, we can infer a solution to the problem of binge drinking from this introduction, because its states the problem so explicitly:

> Increasingly, except for driving under the influence, college students are unaware of the risks of excessive alcohol consumption. First-year students in particular gravely underestimate the risks they face. Fewer than 40 percent even know about the toxic effects of alcohol, and most of them think it affects only long-term drinkers. Yet the university does nothing either during orientation or later to alert students to those risks and how to manage them. _{destabilizing condition} As a consequence, many students "binge," until they pass out or worse, injure or

even kill themselves. In the last six months, bingeing has been cited in three deaths from alcohol poisoning, two from falls, and one in a car crash. Bingeing injures not only drinkers but those around them. _{costs} We may never eliminate bingeing, but finding a way to lessen its risks must be part of our educational mission. _{promise of solution to come}

We can predict that the solution will involve educating first-year students about the risks of drinking, probably during orientation. So if you think you must withhold your main claim until the end of your argument, consider stating your problem so clearly that it implies its solution.

You can't do that with a conceptual problem, however, no matter how specifically you state it:

> Although excessive drinking has always been part of college life, we do not know why particular students engage in dangerous bingeing, whether they binge because of a psychological condition, or because of response to peer pressure. _{destabilizing condition} Lacking that knowledge, we do not know what kind of programs would . . . . _{consequence}

We know what gap in understanding is at stake in answering that question, but not at all what the answer will look like. In conceptual problems, you can help readers anticipate your answer only if you explicitly state or strongly imply it:

> Lacking that knowledge, we do not know what kind of programs would . . . _{consequence} We believe, however, that at least some bingeing is associated with a personality type that is attracted to risk taking . . . . _{solution}

EXAMPLE

A Problem That Forecasts Its Solution

> *Here is the skeleton of an argument about doing research on the Internet. Notice that at the end of the introduction, the writer does not specify a solution because it is so obvious.*

Does the Internet help college students learn? Enthusiasts proclaim it has made a world of information available to any freshman with a computer. Skeptics warn that cyberspace is so full of junk that research in it will never amount to anything more than garbage collecting . . . . I concede that the skeptics have a case. _{common ground} But the problem with doing research on the Internet is not about garbage. It's that, by doing all their homework on the Internet, _{destabilizing condition} students may develop a misunderstanding of research itself and even of the subjects they are studying. _{cost—end of introduction}

Historical research takes place in libraries and archives, but it is not a straightforward process of retrieving information. _{reason 1} You may open a box of manuscripts . . . but . . . every document . . . must be read between the lines and related to all the surrounding documents. . . .

Moreover, most documents never make it into archives. . . . _{reason 2}

[Moreover] . . . no digitized text can duplicate the original—its handwriting or typography, its layout, its paper. . . . _{reason 3}

[Finally d]igitizers often dump texts onto the Internet without considering their quality as sources, and students often fail to read those texts critically. . . . _{reason 4 end of body of argument}

Such thoughts touch off Luddite fantasies: smash all the computers and leave the Internet to drown in the ocean of its own junk. But that way madness lies, and my students have taught me that, if handled with care, the Internet can be an effective tool. . . . Instead of turning our backs on cyberspace, we need to take control of it—to set standards, develop quality controls and direct traffic. Our students will learn to navigate the Internet successfully if we set up warning signals and teach them to obey: Proceed with caution. Danger lies ahead. _{solution/main claim}

Source: From Robert Darnton, "No Computer Can Hold the Past," *New York Times,* June 12, 1999.

Common Ground

As we've seen, experienced writers motivate readers to read by describing the costs of a problem so that readers want to see it solved. But before they do that, writers often use another device to encourage readers to take their problem seriously. They open with a statement of what we call *common ground;* then they immediately upset it, something we did in opening this paragraph.

In that first sentence, we stated something we hoped you would accept as unproblematic because you already heard us say it:

> As we've seen, experienced writers motivate readers to read by describing the costs of a problem so that readers want to see it solved.

That was our common ground. In the next sentence we strongly qualified it with something we thought you did *not* know, implying that your knowledge was at least incomplete.

> As we've seen, experienced writers motivate readers to read by describing the costs of a problem so that readers want to see it solved. _{common ground} **But before they do that, writers often use another device to encourage readers to take their problem seriously.**

In that second sentence, we destabilized what we hoped you had taken as settled. To be sure you noticed, we opened with **But** *before they do that.* In other words, we began with stable common ground just so that we could upset it.

Common Ground in Pragmatic Problems. In pragmatic problems, you can use anything as common ground, so long as it can be upset by the condition of your problem. Here is a fact about drinking that most of us know:

> Drinking has been part of American college life for more than three centuries, and it has been accepted, even celebrated as part of growing up.

If you accept that as common knowledge, we can upset it by stating that something has changed. We signal that destabilization with a *but, however,* or other term warning that we are about to qualify what we just said:

> Drinking has been part of American college life for more than three centuries, and it has been accepted, even celebrated as part of growing up. _{common ground} **But recently,** a new, dangerous kind of drinking known as "binge" drinking has become increasingly widespread. _{destabilizing condition}

When writers address a well-known problem, they often omit common ground, beginning directly with the problem:

> The recent rise in college fatalities and injuries _{cost} caused by binge drinking _{destabilizing condition} has convinced many administrators that they must address the problem directly. Some have instituted rules regulating drinking on college property, one of which is claimed to work: ban alcohol entirely. _{solution}

If a writer simply wanted to echo that solution, she could go from there to her main claim:

> . . . one of which is claimed to work: ban alcohol entirely. _{solution} We support that position, for several reasons. _{main claim}

But if she disagreed, she could turn *all* of that into common ground with a *but* or *however* that introduces the real problem:

> . . . one of which is claimed to work: ban alcohol entirely. _{common ground} Such a blanket prohibition, **however,** will do more harm than good. _{destabilizing condition} It will cause students to. . . . _{costs} Therefore, we must seek. . . . _{solution}

In other words, in a pragmatic problem you can use *anything* as common ground, if readers accept it and you can upset it .

Common Ground in Conceptual Problems. Writers usually create common ground for a conceptual problem by sketching current knowledge that they then claim is incomplete or wrong. Skilled writers also use this statement to highlight those themes that the writer will take issue with. For example, the following introduction uses common ground to sketch what critics believe about Flannery O'Connor's views on racism. In it, the writer introduces three themes that she develops thereafter: southern culture, attitudes toward race, and religious beliefs (we highlight those themes in different ways):

> *"I write the way I do because . . . I am a Catholic*
> *peculiarly possessed of the modern consciousness."*

> Although Flannery O'Connor's stories give us deep insights into SOUTHERN CULTURE, some have criticized her attitude toward <u>race</u>, calling it the product of "an imperfectly developed sensibility" and claiming that "large SOCIAL ISSUES as such were never the subject of her writing." _{common ground} But that criticism ignores her *religious beliefs*._{destabilizing condition} If we fail to see that O'Connor treated <u>racism</u> as a symptom of a larger *spiritual* crisis, we risk overlooking her insight that the sources of <u>racism</u> run deeper than mere SOCIAL OR CULTURAL CAUSES. _{consequence} Her stories show that her treatment of <u>racism</u> as a *spiritual* crisis is more sympathetic to <u>equality</u> than is apparent and suggests an understanding of <u>racism</u> that sets her apart from liberals of her time. _{answer/main claim} Once we recognize the *spiritual* basis of her thinking, we see that O'Connor's exploration of SOUTHERN SOCIETY AND CULTURE is even more penetrating than her critics assumed. _{cost restated as benefit}

Literature Review as Common Ground. If you write a research paper for an advanced class, you will typically use as common ground a "literature review," a survey of research on the topic. But you'll irritate readers if you offer an endless list of every bit of published research remotely connected to the problem. Limit a literature review to work directly relevant to the problem you address. Cite only those articles whose claims you intend to extend or correct.

The most familiar common ground in academic writing is something widely believed by those in a field, a statement of prior research or "truth" that the destabilizing condition will disrupt and put into question. But the common ground that most academic readers find most interesting is not a statement of truth that turns out to be wrong, but a statement of a problem that turns out to be the wrong problem. Compare:

> The majority of Americans now support plans to administer regular achievement testing, end social promotions, and hold teachers and schools responsible for the performance of their students. _{statement of fact as common ground} **But more testing will be ineffective if school boards don't provide enough money to make it work.** _{destabilizing condition}

> The American public school system has been the foundation of this country's political and economic successes. But for decades, American students have scored lower than those in almost all the world's economic and political powers, largely because we have stopped holding all students to the standards of our best. The American people now seem to agree that we can stop this decline by administering regular achievement testing, ending social promotions, and holding teachers and schools responsible for the performance of their students. _{mistaken problem as common ground} **However, the real solutions won't be found in testing because the real problems are rooted not in our children's classrooms but in their living rooms and bedrooms, not in their teachers' lack of ability or commitment, but in their parents' lack of involvement.** _{destabilizing condition}

Because academic readers often value questions more than answers, they prefer problems that raise new questions to those that simply contradict old answers.

Prelude

There is one more element that writers use to introduce all these elements, particularly in popular journalism. You may recall being told to "catch your readers' attention" by opening with a catchy anecdote, fact, or quotation. What better catches our attention is a problem in need of a solution. But a catchy opening works when it vividly introduces key concepts related to the problem. To name this device, we've borrowed a musical term: *prelude.*

Here are three preludes to use to open an argument about bingeing.

1. A startling fact:

> A recent study reports that at most colleges three out of four students "binged" at least once in the previous thirty days, drinking more than five drinks at a sitting. Almost half binge once a week, and those who binge most are not just members of fraternities, but their officers. _{fact}

2. A quotation, familiar or not:

"If you're old enough to die for your country, you're old enough to drink to it."
How often have you heard that justification for allowing 18-year-olds to
drink? _{quotation}

3. An illustrative anecdote:

When Jim Shay, president of Omega Alpha, accepted a dare from his fraternity
brothers to down a pint of whiskey in one long swallow, he didn't plan to
become this year's eighth college fatality from alcohol poisoning. _{anecdote}

We can combine all three:

"If you're old enough to die for your country, you're old enough to drink to
it." _{quotation} Tragically, Jim Shay, president of Omega Alpha, won't have a chance
to do either. When he accepted a dare from his fraternity brothers to down a
pint of whiskey in one long swallow, he didn't expect to become this year's
eighth college fatality from alcohol poisoning. But he did. _{anecdote} According to
a recent study, at most colleges, three out of four students have, like Shay,
drunk five drinks at a sitting in the last thirty days. And those who drink the
most are not just members of fraternities, but, like Shay, officers. _{striking fact}
Drinking, of course, has been a part of American college life since the first
college opened. . . . _{common ground} But in recent years. . . . _{destabilizing condition}

Preludes are rare in writing in the natural and social sciences, more common in
the humanities, and most common in writing for the general public. You use a
prelude best when it introduces key themes that your argument will pursue,
particularly when it represents your problem in a vivid and concrete example.
Here now is the structure of the fullest introduction:

INTRODUCTION

Prelude   +   Common Ground   +   Problem   +   Gist/Promise of Solution
[Destabilizing Condition   +   Costs]

You don't need all five elements in every introduction. The only one you
always need is a destabilizing condition (if its cost is obvious). For a long argument, though, you can expand each element to a paragraph or more, creating
an introduction several pages long.

Problem-Posing Versus Problem-Solving Arguments

There is a kind of argument common in newspapers and magazines that
addresses a problem not to solve it, but only to show readers that a problem
exists. Instead of building the introduction around a full statement of a destabilizing condition and costs, concluded with a solution, the writer describes only
the condition, making that the main claim. For example:

Colleges are aware of the risks of binge drinking and its costs, _{common ground}
but there has recently appeared a new threat, one that seems more benign, but

could be worse. _{destabilizing condition} It is a drug called *Ecstasy*. Users report that it induces a sense of serenity and connection to others, but its long-term damage is only now beginning to emerge. _{end of introduction}
    First, . . . _{cost 1}

In the body of the argument, the writer goes on to prove the existence of the problem by describing its costs, turning each into a reason; he does not argue for a particular solution, only that some solution must be found.

These two outlines contrast the structure of problem-solving and problem-posing arguments.

Problem-Solving Argument	Problem-Posing Argument
Introduction	**Introduction**
(Prelude)	(Prelude)
(Common Ground)	(Common Ground)
Destabilizing Condition	Destabilizing Condition/**Claim**
Costs	
Gist of Solution/Claim	
Body	**Body**
(Warrants)	(Warrants)
Reasons supporting Solution	Costs as Reasons supporting Claim
Acknowledgment/Response	Acknowledgment/Response
Conclusion	**Conclusion**
Solution/Claim restated	(Gesture toward a Solution)

EXAMPLE

A Problem-Posing Argument

In this essay, the writer works harder to pose a problem than to solve it. He opens with common ground that he destabilizes by claiming that final papers he recently received were worse than those in past years because students did their research on the Internet.

Sometimes I look forward to the end-of-semester rush, when students' final papers come streaming into my office and mailbox. I could have hundreds of pages of original thought to read and evaluate. Once in a while, it is truly exciting, and brilliant words are typed across a page in response to a question I've asked the class to discuss. _{common ground}
    But this past semester was different. I noticed a disturbing decline in both the quality of the writing and the originality of the thoughts expressed. What had happened since last fall? Did I ask worse questions? Were my students unusually lazy? No. My class had fallen victim to the latest easy way of writing a paper: doing their research on the World Wide Web. _{destabilizing condition}

He then specifies the costs of that destabilizing condition, how they were worse:

It's easy to spot a research paper that is based primarily on information collected from the Web. First, the bibliography cites no books, just articles or pointers to places in that virtual land somewhere off any map: http://www. reason 1 Then a strange preponderance of material in the bibliography is curiously out of date. . . . reason 2 Another clue is the beautiful pictures and graphs that are inserted neatly into the body of the student's text. They look impressive . . . but actually they often bear little relation to the precise subject of the paper. reason 3

The author gestures toward a solution at the end, but nothing in his argument supports it, so it is just a way to bring his argument to a close.

I'd like [my students] to . . . ponder what it means to live in a world where some things get easier and easier so rapidly that we can hardly keep track of how easy they're getting, while other tasks remain as hard as ever—such as doing research and writing a good paper that teaches the writer something in the process. Knowledge does not emerge in a vacuum, but we do need silence and space for sustained thought. Next semester, I'm going to urge my students to turn off their glowing boxes and think, if only once in a while.

Source: From David Rothenberg, "How the Web Destroys the Quality of Students' Research Papers," *Chronicle of Higher Education,* August 15, 1997.

Conclusions

Conclusions vary more than introductions, but in a pinch, you can map their parts onto the parts of your introduction. Just reverse their order:

1. Open your conclusion by stating (or restating) the gist of your main claim.
2. Explain its significance by answering *So what?,* in a new way if you can, but if not, restate what you offered in the introduction, now as a benefit.
3. Suggest a further question or problem to be resolved, something still not known. Answer not *So what?* but *Now what?*
4. End with an anecdote, quotation, or fact that echoes your prelude. We'll call this the *coda.*

For example, here is a paraphrase of the introduction to that Flannery O'Connor paper on page 60.

1. "I write the way I do because . . . I am a Catholic peculiarly possessed of the modern consciousness." prelude
2. Critics say O'Connor had no social conscience. common ground
3. But she viewed racism not as a social issue but as a spiritual crisis. destabilizing condition *(So what?)*
4. If we ignore this, we miss her insights into the true sources of racism. consequence

5. Her treatment of racism is more sympathetic to equality than is apparent. _{answer/main claim}

To create a conclusion, the writer could first restate her main claim, then add a new consequence, raise a new question to pursue, and close with a coda in the form of another quotation from O'Connor that echoes the opening prelude:

> So those who claim that O'Connor was indifferent to racism fail to see how she saw past the surface of social conflict to a deeper crisis of faith—our failure to recognize the healing knowledge that comes from suffering. _{main claim restated} Indeed, these insights put her among a select few Southern writers who saw the failure of the modern world to deal with human differences not just as an economic or social problem, but as a spiritual one. For example, ... _{new consequence/significance} Seen in this light, a rereading of her private correspondence might reveal. . . . . _{new questions to pursue} As she said in one letter (May 4, 1955), "What I had in mind to suggest [in that story] was the redemptive quality of the Negro's suffering for us all . . . . I meant [a character in the story] in an almost physical way to suggest the mystery of existence." _{coda}

There are other plans for conclusions, but this one works when nothing better comes to mind.

Introductions and Conclusions as Ways of Thinking

Some think formal plans like these kill creativity; in fact, they encourage it:

- Preludes and codas force you to think about key concepts and how to encapsulate your problem in vivid language.
- Common ground forces you to think about what your readers believe that your problem will unsettle.
- A destabilizing condition forces you to think about the part of a troubling situation your solution will change.
- The question *So what?* forces you to think about costs that your readers are unwilling to pay and larger questions they want answered.

Some students fear that this pattern will become boring, but you can vary it so much that readers notice it only when they look for it.

WRITING PROCESS
Motivating Your Argument

THINKING-READING-TALKING

Use Problem Statements to Focus Your Reading

Read introductions carefully; they tell you what a writer thinks is important.

- The common ground provides context. What other writers does he respond to? What views does he claim his will replace? Literature reviews are particularly useful as bibliography for future reference.

- In a pragmatic problem, the destabilizing condition states what the solution will change; in a conceptual one, the gap in knowledge or understanding that the answer will close.

- The costs or consequences tell you why the problem is important.

- The solution tells you how to read what follows.

If you don't find a problem in the introduction, look in the conclusion.

PREPARING AND PLANNING

Exploring a Topic to Find a Problem

Most classroom arguments are based on assigned readings, but when you have to write a research paper from scratch, you must find a problem on your own. Here are four steps to help you do that: (1) find a topic, (2) narrow it, (3) question it, (4) turn the best questions into a problem.

Step 1: Find a Topic That Interests You

If your assignment doesn't specify a topic, look for one that interests you. Worry later whether it will interest others.

For General Topics

1. If you are free to explore any interest, what would you like to know more about? Think about its history, economics, and controversies.

2. What are politicians *not* talking about that they should? If your governor were to speak on campus, what issues should she address?

3. What public issues make you angry? Finish this sentence: *What bugs me about politics/teaching/movies/radio/TV/advertising is . . .*

4. Browse a big magazine rack for a title that grabs your interest. Skim the article to see if you'd like to know more.

5. Join an e-mail group or visit a Web site on a subject that interests you. Look for debates, questions, archived messages, and related sites.

6. What courses will you take next term? If you can find a topic related to one of them, you get a head start on your work.

For Topics in a Particular Field of Study

1. Ask your teacher which issues discussed in class are hotly contested.

2. Browse through a recent encyclopedia in the field you are studying, looking for open questions.

3. Ask a teacher or librarian for journals that review the year's work in your field.

We cannot exaggerate how important it is to find a topic that will hold your interest. If it bores you, you will surely bore your reader.

Step 2: Turn Your General Topic into a Specific One

A general topic is like an entry in an encyclopedia:

| AIDS | Balance of trade | Jefferson-Hemings debate |
| Homelessness | Evolution of birds | Campaign finance reform. |

Too often, inexperienced writers think that when they find a topic, they've found a problem. Not so. To find a problem, they must first turn their general topic into a specific one by adding relationships, connections, and qualities:

SIMPLE TOPIC

Territorial behavior in ground squirrels

SPECIFIC TOPIC

The **acquisition** of **territorial protection behavior** in ground squirrels and its similarity to behavior of **human children**

SIMPLE TOPIC

Calvinism in Lincoln's "Gettysburg Address"

SPECIFIC TOPIC

The **influence** of **Lincoln's Calvinist beliefs** about **destiny** on his **justification** and other speeches for the need for **political and personal sacrifice** in the "Gettysburg Address" and other speeches

We realize you might be puzzled after reading these suggestions: *How can I "add relationships, connections . . ." until I know something about the topic?* In truth, you can't. That's why it's hard to write a research paper in a course with no specialized content. You have to find a topic and read a lot about it, maybe aimlessly, before you can narrow it, much less find a question to answer.

Step 3: Question Your Topic

Once you narrow your topic, ask five kinds of questions about it. The first two break your topic into its parts so that you can see how it functions as a self-contained system of parts that relate to one another in different ways.

1. Identify the component concepts that constitute your specific topic. What are their parts and how do they relate to one another?

What are the elements of Lincoln's Calvinist beliefs about destiny? Did one of them in particular cause him to believe sacrifice was necessary? How did the element of destiny relate to the elements of punishment? What are the elements of punishment? Of sacrifice?

2. Turn your topic into a narrative of a process. How did it begin and how does it end? What are its historical stages, its evolution?

   How did Lincoln's ideas about fate, punishment, and sacrifice change? How does the Gettysburg Address relate to earlier and later addresses? How did Calvin's ideas reach Lincoln? How does Lincoln relate his ideas to those of the founding fathers? How were his speeches influenced by traditional patterns of oratory?

The next two questions ask you to look at your topic as a part of a larger whole, related to other parts:

3. Every thing is part of some larger thing. Put your topic into a larger system. How does it relate to other parts of the system?

   Were Lincoln's beliefs part of a larger philosophy? Were his calls for sacrifice similar to those of others? How did his understanding of destiny fit into a general religious outlook?

4. Everything has a larger history. What came before? What comes after?

   What did those before Lincoln think about destiny? How have those after him thought about it? How have they thought about his ideas?

The final question evaluates qualitative aspects of your topic:

5. Everything has qualities. What are the qualities of your topic?

   Is Lincoln's use of these ideas effective? Traditional? Innovative? Mistaken? Cruel? Wise?

After you ask lots of questions, ignore the ones you can answer easily, because they are probably not worth pursuing. Focus on those that both interest and perplex you. Now ask each of those questions, and imagine someone asking in return *So what? What if you never answer that question? What would you do with the answer? If you can answer that question, what bigger question can you answer?* It will be a frustrating but invaluable exercise because it will help you focus on the significance of your question, and it's the significance of a question that determines its potential for turning into a good research problem.

Step 4: Turn Questions into a Problem

The more you know about a topic, the better you can turn your best questions into a problem. Here is a formula to help you do that. Fill in the blanks in each of these three steps. These steps help you develop a pragmatic problem:

  1. I am working on the problem of _____
     2. In order to find out how to _____ (*So what if you don't?*)
        3. so that you/we/someone can avoid the cost/benefit from _____

For example:

  1. **I am working on the problem of** traffic congestion after football games,
     2. **in order to find out how to** move traffic more quickly, (*So what if you don't find out?*)
        3. **so that** businesses will not suffer from traffic gridlock.

For a conceptual problem, you depend even more on questions, because they define what you don't know. *Why* and *how* questions are most useful:

  1. I am working on the issue of _____
     2. in order to find out why/how/when/what _____ (*So what if you don't find out?*)
        3. so that I can understand better why/how/what _____

For example:

  1. **I am working on** the appeal that the Taj Mahal has in the West,
     2. **because I want to find out why** Europeans think of it as the only masterpiece of Indian architecture, (*So what? What if you never find out?*)
        3. **so that I can understand better why** we misunderstand the art of other cultures by focusing on a few notable but not representative works.

Some of us can't do that last step (. . . *so that I can understand better why* . . .) until we are close to the end of our work. If you are in the early stages of a research project, don't spend a lot of time trying to figure out what larger question you can answer. Work on the first question (. . . *in order to find out why* . . .). Have faith that once you answer that first question, you will discover how to answer the second one. It is usually late in the game that any of us sees the full significance of our work.

DRAFTING

The Language of Common Ground

If you have a problem imagining common ground, use one of these phrases to get you going:

   Most/many/some people have thought/believed . . .
   At first glance, it might appear/seem that . . .
   It is widely believed/reported/claimed/said . . .
   X (some authority) has claimed/asserted/stated . . .

Finish the sentence, then begin a new one with *but, however, in fact*, or other signal that you will qualify what you just wrote. Or try this: Recall what *you* thought about your topic before you started your research. How has your thinking changed? Describe your original, uninformed beliefs in your common ground. Start with something like *It is easy to think* . . . , complete it with what you thought before, then go on with a *but* or *however* to destabilize it with what you know now. You can develop ways to state common ground by skimming the first few paragraphs of editorials and articles in magazines, journals, and newspapers.

REVISING

Test Your Introduction and Conclusion

Once you finish a first draft, revisit your introduction to make sure it fully states your problem and accurately predicts the key concepts in your argument. Ask these questions:

1. If you have a prelude, does it introduce themes that you develop through the rest of the argument?
2. Does your common ground mention those themes? Does it state something readers believe and that you can correct?
3. Does the destabilizing condition contradict or qualify that common ground?
4. Do your costs or consequences answer the question *So what?*
5. (a) Does your introduction conclude with the solution to your problem or the answer to your question; that is, does it conclude with your main claim?

   (b) If you withhold your main claim until the conclusion, does your introduction end with a sentence that uses its key concepts?

Now check your conclusion:

1. Does the main claim there restate, complement, or at least not contradict the end of your introduction?
2. Have you suggested the significance of your main claim? In a pinch, restate the costs from the introduction as benefits.

Check for Common Themes in the Body of Your Argument

Once you are sure that the concepts in your introduction and conclusions cohere, test whether you have kept your readers on track by repeating those concepts through the body of your argument:

1. Find the sentences at the end of the introduction and beginning of your conclusion that promise, state, or restate your main claim. Circle three or four main concepts in them, especially ones that you contributed, that were not in the language of your assignment.

2. In the body of your argument, circle words you circled in (1).

3. Underline words in the body that closely relate to those you circled.

Now scan your argument:

1. If you have neither circled nor underlined many words in the body, you may have gotten off track.

2. If in the body you circled few words but underlined many different ones, change some of the underlined words to words you circled.

3. If words appear frequently in the body but not in the introduction or conclusion, revise your introduction and conclusion so that they do.

The point is to ensure that readers think your argument hangs together around a few key concepts announced in your introduction, developed in your body, and tied up in your conclusion.

Build a Title Out of Your Key Concepts

Your title should preview the key concepts in your argument, so build it from words that you circled in your introduction and conclusion. We suggest a title consisting of two parts, separated by a colon. Such titles may feel stiff, but they give you two chances to tell your reader what to expect. For example, the *least* useful title for that Flannery O'Connor paper (p. 60), would be this:

Flannery O'Connor's Attitudes Toward Race

Readers would get more from a title built out of key words:

Flannery O'Connor's Critique of Our Modern Spiritual Crisis:
Racial Suffering as Spiritual Redemption

If you are working in a field that encourages section headings, create one-line headings for each section based on words in the main point of that section.

 INQUIRIES

1. Pure researchers defend their work by arguing that without it we would still be in the Dark Ages. Does that seem a reasonable defense? Without tangible consequences to judge by, how do you know when pure

research is pointless and wasteful or worth the effort? For example, one researcher dug up the body of Jesse James to see whether he was actually shot in the back, as legends say. Is it worth disturbing the dead to find that out? Can you think of any good reason to dig up someone who died a century ago?

2. A skeleton was found in Washington State that may predate even the Native Americans who settled in the area and is said to have features of Caucasians. Native Americans in the area want to rebury the skeleton as one of their ancestors just as it is; the National Park Service wants to test the skeleton, claiming it might not be a Native American ancestor and, under any circumstances, is so unusual that it deserves further study. How should we settle this kind of question? On the one side are the religious beliefs of Native Americans, on the other scientific interest in a skeleton that could rewrite the prehistory of America. Native Americans frame this matter as a pragmatic problem, the National Park Service as a conceptual one. How would you decide what kind of problem it should be?

3. The film *Contact* is, among other things, a parable about the value of pure research. Watch the film with friends, if possible. How do you respond to its defense of pure research? What do your friends think? Is it reasonable for the movie to portray the National Science Advisor who is skeptical of pure research as a villain? What do you think of the way the movie uses the romance between the two main characters to contrast the scientist's faith in research with the religious leader's faith in God? What about the industrialist's claim that he funds pure research to "give something back" to humanity?

4. Some cultures avoid questioning established knowledge and beliefs. What do you make of a society that does not value new knowledge? Is it appropriate to make a value judgment about such societies? Is it possible to want to know too much? Are there some things we should not know?

5. Pick a pragmatic problem that affects you right now—crowding in the dorms, difficulties registering for classes, over-large classes, lack of Internet access, etc. List everyone who could conceivably help you solve it—friends, roommates, parents, teachers, school officials, etc. Then list the costs that might motivate each of them to act to solve the problem. Don't focus on the costs your problem exacts on you, but on those it exacts on them.

IN A NUTSHELL

About Your Argument . . .

We make arguments to solve two kinds of problems, pragmatic and conceptual. Both kinds of problems have the same structure:

Problem = Destabilizing Condition + Cost/Consequence

But what goes into that structure is different. For a pragmatic problem:

- The destabilizing condition can be, literally, any situation, condition, event at all, so long as it has a cost.
- The cost answers the question *So what?* The answer always points to some form of unhappiness, pain, loss, distress—something that you and your readers want to avoid.

For a purely conceptual problem:

- The destabilizing condition is always some gap in knowledge or lack of understanding.
- The consequence of that gap answers the question *So what?* The answer always points to another gap in knowledge or lack of understanding, but one that is more significant, more consequential than the first.

Introductions to conceptual and pragmatic problems have up to five elements:

- An opening prelude that offers an anecdote, fact, or quotation that forecasts or encapsulates the problem.
- Common ground, some belief or idea that your audience holds that is not quite right, or is at least incomplete.
- Your problem, which consists of two parts:
    a destabilizing condition
    a cost or consequence of that condition.
- The gist of your solution, or at least a sentence introducing some of the key concepts that the rest of the argument will use in getting to the solution.

Many introductions do not have all of these elements. Preludes are more common in journalistic or popular writing, less so in academic or professional writing. If the problem is well-known and on readers' minds, you don't need common ground. In some cases, the cost of the problem is so obvious that it's not necessary to state it.

You can map your conclusion onto your introduction:

- Recapitulate your main claim (or express it for the first time).
- Describe why your claim is significant.
- Add what is yet to be done, how your argument is incomplete.
- Close with a coda that echoes the prelude.

. . . and About Writing It

Your first job is to transform your topic into a problem.

- Narrow your topic by adding to it as many qualifiers and modifiers as you can.
- Ask questions about its relations to other things, about its own history, about its role in a larger history, and about its qualities.
- Focus on your problem by running through the following formula every so often. For a pragmatic problem:

    1. I am working on the issue of _____

       2. in order to find out how to change _____ (*So what?*)

          3. so that you/they/someone can avoid the cost/gain the benefit of
          _____.

For a conceptual problem:

    1. I am working on the issue of _____

       2. in order to find out why/how/when/what _____ (*So what?*)

       3. so that I can understand better why/how/when/what

          _____.

Be sure that throughout your introduction, but particularly in the last couple of sentences, you use concepts central to the rest of your argument. Do this:

- Circle the key words in your introduction and conclusion.
- In the body of your argument, underline those words or words related to them. Look for both synonyms and homonyms.

If you underline only a few words in the body of your argument, you may have gotten off track. Even if you haven't, your readers will think so. Insert those circled words and words related to them. If you can't do that easily, you have to start over. Now do the same thing for each major section.

Finally, create a title out of the most important words you have circled.

Part 2

Developing Your Argument

Chapter 4

∞

Articulating Claims

In this chapter, we look in detail at your main claim, the solution to your problem, the point that your argument supports. We show you how to develop a claim that readers will judge to be thoughtful and that can guide you through the process of drafting the rest of your argument.

At the heart of every argument is its main claim, the point you want to support, the solution to the problem that caused you to make an argument in the first place. *Claim,* though, has two meanings: When you claim *that* something is so, you also make a claim *on* your readers' time to consider what you've written in support of it. You justify that second claim only when you offer them something in return. That's why we stress that a claim is not just a statement you want readers to agree with, but the solution to a problem you think they should care about.

The tough part, of course, can be finding that good solution that your claim expresses. Sometimes you don't have to search. For example, if you believe human cloning is wrong, you know where you stand. But on other issues, you may have no ready answer: Should insurers do genetic screening for a tendency toward alcoholism? How have TV sit-coms changed our attitudes toward families in the last fifty years? We can't help you answer such questions, but we can suggest how to express those answers you find in a way that readers judge to be thoughtful.

Exploring Claims Without Rushing to Judgment

Whatever strategies you follow to solve your problem, you can't wait until you've looked at all the evidence before you come up with a solution to test. Expert problem solvers don't wait. They size up a problem quickly, then spin off a few tentative solutions that are compatible with the data they start with. Then they let those tentative solutions guide their search for more data, using those new data to test each hypothesis and, if one fits, to support it. Without those initial hypotheses, they would not know what evidence to look for or how to evaluate what they found.

Less successful problem solvers also jump to a quick solution, but then they cling to it, using it not to guide further research, but to close it down. They don't make that mistake intentionally; it's just that all our minds are built to make quick judgments that reflect what we want to be true and usually already believe. It's a habit of mind that, in the short run, helps us manage crises. But it's risky.

Think, for example, of those who propose the same solution to every problem. The next time a student shoots a classmate, no matter what the facts are, some will instantly point to the too easy availability of guns, others to a lack of family values, still others to violent movies and video games. The business world has a maxim about such people: *To a person with a hammer, every problem is a nail.* If profits are falling, the ad manager thinks the solution is more advertising; the operations manager thinks it is to modernize the plant; the personnel manager wants to invest in recruiting and training. Each might be partly right, but when they insist on their pet solution to the exclusion of others, they risk missing the best one, because all they see is a nail that matches their particular hammer.

Admittedly, our advice is hard to follow, but here it is: Formulate a few tentative solutions to a problem sooner rather than later, but hold them lightly as you test them against the evidence. Resist what most of us do: Jump into a simple conclusion that we can't climb out of. We can't change human nature, but you can deflect your own tendency toward hasty, superficial judgments by asking questions, by patiently reasoning, and especially by talking things over with others who disagree.

What Kind of Claim Does Your Problem Require?

In the last chapter, we discussed how a well-framed problem motivates readers to read. You motivate them further when you state at the end of your introduction a solution that is not self-evidently true, but seems clear, plausible, and thoughtful. As we said, we can't help you find the best claim; that requires research and testing. But we can suggest ways to evaluate and develop the best one you've found so that your readers will at least give it a fair hearing.

Is Your Claim Pragmatic or Conceptual?

Above all, you need to decide early whether you can solve your problem by getting readers to understand or to act, because we make arguments about conceptual and pragmatic problems differently. The solution to a conceptual problem asks readers only to *understand* or *believe* something, as this claim does:

> Not only do students whose first language is not English do better in class when they receive tutorial help, but in the long run they require less faculty time.

The solution to a pragmatic problem asks readers not only to understand but to *do* something (or endorse an action). Such claims are typically built on a *should* or *must:*

> State U. should increase the budget for tutorial help for students whose first language is not English.

If you trust readers to read between the lines, you can hope they will infer your solution, as we can from this claim:

> Since students whose first language is not English require less faculty time when they also receive tutorial help, State U. could save money by increasing the budget for tutors.

Most of us, though, think readers are able to infer more than they actually do. So when in doubt, *explicitly* state what you expect of them: to understand something, with no intent that they act, or to perform (or at least support) an action.

When you can, state your claims affirmatively. For pragmatic problems especially, a negative solution does not provide a plan of action; a positive one does. Compare:

> The university should stop using its teaching evaluation form because it does not reveal students' feelings about learning.

> The university should develop a new teaching evaluation form that tells faculty whether their students think they are learning useful skills.

If you cannot find a plausible solution and your assignment allows it, redefine the problem: decompose the bigger problem into subproblems, one of which you might be able to solve, or at least clarify. Suppose you start with the conceptual problem of how sit-com families have changed in the last fifty years, but decide that question is too large for you to answer. You can narrow it: How have the families changed in the highest-rated sit-coms in the first year of every decade since 1950? Or, suppose Elena thinks she cannot solve the problem of the university's failure to provide international students with enough help in English; she might instead address a smaller problem: international students do not know where to find the help that is available. You can also redefine a pragmatic problem as a conceptual one by identifying questions whose answers will eventually help solve the pragmatic problem.

Values Claims

Claims that assert something is right or wrong, good or bad, are often called "values" claims. Some values claims are covert pragmatic claims because they imply that readers should do something, without stating exactly what. For example, in a *Washington Times* newspaper column, restaurant owner Richard Berman complains about food recommendations he thinks are extremist, such as replacing the Thanksgiving turkey with turkey-shaped tofu. His main point states values that he implies readers should act on:

(continued on next page)

(continued from previous page)

> In an effort to change American eating habits to conform to their puritanical vision, groups such as the Center for Science in the Public Interest, the Vegetarian Society, and People for the Ethical Treatment of Animals are perverting the way Americans look at food.[a]

By not saying what we should do about those arguments—ignore extreme claims, cook a traditional Thanksgiving turkey, or eat in a restaurant—he relieves himself of the obligation to defend any solution.

On the other hand, a values claim is conceptual when it implies only that we should approve or disapprove, and nothing more:

> As president, John Kennedy was inspirational, but as a person, he was sexually corrupt.

That claim asks us only to disapprove of Kennedy's character. While it might imply, *Don't be like him!*, our negative judgment alone solves the conceptual problem posed by the writer: *You might be wrong about what you think of John Kennedy and therefore about the role of models in political life.*

Whether you assert a values claim that is pragmatic or conceptual, you still have to make an argument with reasons, based on evidence, governed by warrants. You still have to acknowledge and respond to other views. Values claims can be tricky, however, because they assume beliefs, definitions, and values that transcend the particular issue. We will agree that Kennedy was corrupt only if we already hold moral principles that a writer can appeal to. If not, a writer would have to lay down those principles, and then argue that they are true.

[a] "Turkey Police, Beware," *Washington Times*, p. A19.

What Degree of Acceptance Do You Seek for Your Claim?

Some writers think that agreement is all-or-nothing, win-or-lose, agree-or-die. But that's shortsighted. We might not accept a big claim about a big problem, but we might accept a modest one about part of it. For example, Elena might think her college devotes too few resources to helping international students with their English, but she also knows it is unlikely to spend lots of money on a new language center. If, however, she can get some administrator just to *consider* increasing the budget for language tutors, she will achieve an important interim outcome. Partial success is rarely total failure.

So as you formulate a claim, think how you want readers to take it. What do you want them to do?

- **Respect** your reasons for making your claim and, by extension, yourself.
- **Approve** of your claim and the argument supporting it.
- **Publicly endorse** your claim as worth consideration.
- **Believe** in your claim and in your argument supporting it.
- **Act** as you propose, or support someone else's action.

Only the last two count as complete success for those who see argument as a win-or-lose proposition. But those who do must fail more often than they succeed, because few arguments completely convince anybody of anything. Your argument is a total failure only when your readers scoff not only at it, but at you, rejecting both as not worth their time, much less their respect.

What Counts as a Claim Worth Considering?

A claim will not motivate readers to read the argument supporting it unless it seems on its face worth considering. So once you have a claim you think is worth your time supporting, ask three questions to determine whether your readers will think it worth their time reading.

Can Your Claim Be Contested?

Even if readers have no settled beliefs about a topic, they will—or should—adopt an amiably skeptical attitude: *Well, that's interesting, but let's see your support.* You are in trouble if instead they think, *That's obvious!* A claim is worth considering only if readers might *contest* it. You have no good reason to ask for their time if they already believe your claim or are indifferent to it. For example, how would readers respond to claims like these?

> 1a. Education is important to our society.
>
> 2a. We should not ridicule how people look.
>
> 3a. I will summarize current views on the disappearance of frogs.

Can you imagine a reader thinking, *If that's true, I'll have to change my mind about education/ridicule/frogs?* Not likely. Those claims don't need an argument, because no one would contest them.

Here's a quick way to assess whether a claim is contestable (another way of saying significant): Revise it into its negative form (or revise a negative claim into its affirmative). Then assess whether it still seems plausible or significant.

> 1b. Education is **not** important to our society.
>
> 2b. We **should** ridicule how people look.
>
> 3b. I will **not** summarize current views on the disappearance of frogs.

Claims (1b) and (2b) seem self-evidently implausible, so they fail the test. No one will reject a claim if no one believes its opposite. The negative claim (3b), on the other hand, seems trivial. If the negative is trivial, then the affirmative probably is too. In none of these cases is the claim worth supporting, because no one would contest any of them.

We must note, however, that human thought has been revolutionized when someone has proved false a claim that at the time seemed self-evidently true:

The sun does **not** go around the earth.

We do **not** consist of solid matter.

We cannot rule out as forever false the claim that education is not important (some groups in fact believe it). You would make your reputation if you could convince us of that, but it would take a powerful argument to do so.

Can Your Claim Be Proved Wrong?

At least in principle, state your claims so that they can be proved wrong (the technical term is *disconfirmed*). That may seem odd. Don't we make claims we can prove, not ones our readers can *dis*prove? In fact, a careful writer makes a claim only when he believes that someone could *at least in principle* find evidence that would prove the claim right or wrong and is willing to consider that evidence.

For example, suppose someone wants to argue that ghosts exist. Imagine someone asks that person,

What would it take to convince you that they don't?

And that person responds,

No conceivable argument or evidence could convince me that ghosts do not exist, because I just know they do and *nothing* can prove that souls do not survive death.

Both parties might learn from an exchange of views, but if the one making the argument believes the other can contribute nothing to the conversation *even in principle,* then that other will be an unwilling audience for the argument.

We make arguments most productively when both parties can imagine being wrong, when both see the issue in question as contingent, not forever settled, still open to question. That means all parties in an argument should agree to a first principle in the social contract of cooperative arguments: *Both reader and writer must be able to imagine that there could be evidence that might change their minds.* Now that principle does not disparage belief in ghosts or anything else we can't prove. We are entitled to believe whatever we please, for any reason, good or bad, or for no reason at all. But when we make public claims about a private belief in order to answer some significant question or solve some difficult problem, and we ask readers to *agree*, we must open our own minds to their arguments *against* our beliefs as much as we ask them to open their minds to ours.

Is Your Claim Reasonable on Its Face?

Once you have a claim that readers can contest and at least in principle disprove, you must start listening to that voice in the back of your mind asking questions your readers are likely to ask, questions like these:

- Is your solution **feasible**?

Tanya is unlikely to get a hearing from the dean if she suggests that the problem of weak teaching could be solved by shifting half the athletic budget to a Teaching Resource Center. But the dean might listen if she suggested a small tax on research grants to subsidize one.

- Is your solution **ethical** (or **legal, proper, fair,** etc.)?

She would be instantly rejected if she proposed that the administration secretly monitor classes, but she might get a hearing if she suggested that faculty be encouraged to observe one another's teaching.

- Is your solution **prudent?** Might it create a problem worse than the one it solves?

She would have no chance of getting the dean to cut the salary of faculty with poor teaching evaluations because they would rebel. But he might consider merit raises to reward good teaching.

What Counts as a Thoughtful Claim?

At some point—sooner better than later—you have to get a hypothesis out of the dark comfort of your mind into the cold light of print. Only then can you ask, *Will this claim encourage readers to judge it—and me—as thoughtful?* Sad to say, we cannot teach you how to be thoughtful. We can only describe what encourages readers to think you might be. Compare these claims:

> TV makes crime seem a bigger problem than it is.

> Though violent crime has fallen around the country, many believe it has increased in their own neighborhoods because night after night their local TV news shows open with graphic reports of murder and mayhem, making it seem that violence happens every night just outside their front door.

The second claim seems more interesting, because its verbal complexity reflects the complex situation it describes (and indirectly the mind that made it).

Now we are *not* asserting that a wordy claim must be better than a short one. Too many words can obscure issues, and a few well-chosen words can focus readers on what's important. But inexperienced writers commonly make claims that are too thin rather than too thick. So in what follows we will go overboard in encouraging you to make claims as detailed as you can, even too detailed. You can always revise them. So take what follows as an exercise in exploratory thinking, not as a plan for drafting what you will actually submit to your readers.

Is Your Claim Conceptually Rich?

When your claims include more concepts, you give your readers and yourself more to work with. Compare these claims:

> The **effects** of the Civil War are still **felt** today.

> The Civil War lives on in the **sunbelt axis** of the **federalist question.**

> The **ideological and social divisions** of the Civil War still **exert an historical influence** today on the **political discourse** of **North** and **South** (and the **West**), reflected in their **antithetical political theories** about the **relative scope** of **state** and **federal powers** and the **proper authority of government** over **free individuals**.

The first feels both thin and vague. It mentions unspecified *effects* that are *felt* in some general way. The second is specific, but still feels thin for readers unable to unpack the technical terms *sunbelt axis* and *federalist question*. The third expresses a richer set of concepts—in fact, too many for one claim, but remember we are exploring and developing claims, not writing final drafts yet.

A claim rich in concepts helps readers see the full implications of what you ask them to do or believe. A conceptually rich claim also helps you improve your argument in two ways:

- It obligates you to develop those concepts in your argument.
- When readers see you return to them in the body of your argument, they are more likely to think your argument is coherent (it might help to review pp. 70–71.)

So when you think you have the makings of a good claim, spend time adding more concepts than you think necessary. (We show you steps for doing that in the Writing Process section below.) If you add too many, apply the Goldilocks rule to find a happy medium (not too much, not too little, but just right):

> The **ideological divisions** of the Civil War still **shape** the **political discourse of North and South** today, reflected in their **antithetical theories** about **state** and **federal powers** and the **authority of government** over **individuals**.

Is Your Claim Logically Rich?

At the core of most claims is a simple proposition like this:

> State U. could do something about tuition. _{claim}

That claim borders on simplistic: What does *do something* mean? We can make its language richer:

> State U. could slow tuition increases to five percent a year. _{claim}

But we can also elaborate its logic in two ways:

1. Add a reason-clause beginning with *because* or *if*, or a phrase beginning with *by* or *in order to*.

Compare these two claims:

> State U. could slow tuition increases to five percent a year. _{claim}

> State U. could slow tuition increases to five percent a year _{claim} **because its administrative costs are significantly higher than comparable universities,** _{reason 1} **and its faculty teaches less than other state schools.** _{reason 2}

The first claim states a proposition that is logically thin. In the second, readers can see the gist of a solution in the *because*-clause and can thereby better anticipate the rest of the argument.

Note: Be aware that your real main claim may be in the *because*-clause if it focuses on causes. Suppose the writer and reader agree about the need to slow tuition increases. If so, the main claim would concern the two causes for high tuition stated in the *because*-clause. If your main claim is in a *because*-clause, revise it so that it appears in a main clause:

> State U.'s **administrative costs are significantly higher than comparable universities,** _{claim 1} **and its faculty teaches less than other state schools.** _{claim 2}

Then add a new because-clause that gives a reason:

> . . . and its faculty teaches less than other state schools, _{claim} **because the university has focused more on its internal needs than on the needs of its students.** _{reason}

2. Add a concession-clause beginning with *although, while,* or *even though* or a phrase beginning with *despite, regardless of,* or *notwithstanding.*

When you open with an *although*-clause, you acknowledge an alternative point of view. There are three common options:

• An alternative point of view contradicts your claim:

> **Although some argue that we must raise tuition to meet the rising costs of maintaining State U.'s physical plant and updating research facilities,** _{acknowledgment of alternative conclusion} State U. could slow tuition increases to five percent a year because its administrative costs are significantly higher than comparable universities and its faculty teaches less than other state schools.

• There is evidence that argues against your claim:

> **Although State U.'s administrative costs have not risen faster than inflation and it has hired no new faculty in three years,** _{acknowledgment of contradictory evidence} State U. could slow tuition increases to five percent a year because its administrative costs are still significantly higher than comparable universities and its faculty teaches less than other state schools.

• Something limits the scope of your claim:

> **Although college costs will always rise to reflect inflation,** _{acknowledgment of limited scope of claim} State U. could slow tuition increases to five percent a year because its administrative costs are significantly higher than comparable universities and its faculty teaches less than other state schools.

If your claim gets too long, divide it. Put a period after the *although*-clause and delete the *although*. Then begin the main claim with *but, however, even so, nevertheless,* etc. (It is *not* a grammatical error to begin a sentence with *but* or *however.*)

> The costs of maintaining State U.'s physical plant are rising, and scientific advances require it to update research facilities continually. **However,** State U. could slow tuition increases to five percent a year because its administrative costs are significantly higher than comparable universities and its faculty teaches less than other state schools.

Is Your Claim Appropriately Qualified?

When you state your main claim, allow for the possibility of doubt, because readers don't like flat-footed certainty like this:

> State U. would stop tuition increases if it just eliminated administrative waste and required faculty to teach enough classes.

When we read a claim so unqualified and certain, we feel a kind of visceral distrust. Thoughtful readers will wonder, *How can you be so sure? How can the problem be so simple?* Contrast that flat-footed certainty with a more modest, more nuanced claim:

> State U. **might be able** to **slow** its rates of tuition increases, if it **could reduce** administrative costs and get **more** of its faculty to teach **more** classes.

You invite readers to question your judgment when you imply that your claims are 100 percent right and all-inclusive. (You can find vocabulary for qualifying in the Writing Process section below.) Of course, if you overqualify, you give readers reason to doubt your confidence. In either case, your ethos suffers.

It's a balancing act. Compare these claims:

1. Research proves that people with a gun at home **will** use it to kill themselves or a family member rather than to protect themselves from intruders.

2. **Some recent** research **seems** to **suggest** there **may** be a **risk** that **some** people with a gun at home **could** be **more prone** to use it to kill themselves or a family member rather than to protect themselves from **potential** intruders.

3. **Recent** research **suggests** that people with a gun at home **more often** use it to kill themselves or a family member than to protect themselves from intruders.

Most academic and professional readers would reject (1) as too absolute and (2) as wishy-washy, but probably find (3) closer to confident yet temperate, because it comes closest to that Goldilocks rule: not too certain, not too uncertain, maybe not just right, but close. (How's that for hedging?)

Certainty in Eighteenth-Century Politics and Twentieth-Century Science

Those who think that hedging is mealymouthed might note Benjamin Franklin's account of how he deliberately created his ethos of judicious moderation by speaking

> ... in terms of modest diffidence, never using when I advance anything that may possibly be disputed, the words *certainly, undoubtedly,* or any others that gave the air of positiveness to an opinion; but rather say, *I conceive,* or *I apprehend a Thing to be so or so It appears as to me,* or *I should think it so or so for such and such Reasons,* or *I imagine it to be so,* or *it is so if I am not mistaken.* This habit I believe has been of great advantage to me ... To this habit (after my character of integrity) I think it principally owing that I had early so much weight with my fellow citizens when I proposed new institutions or alterations in the old, and so much influence in public councils when I became a member.

That advice is relevant today. Among those who make arguments for a living, scientists may distrust certainty the most because they know how fast scientific truths can change. You see this not only in the way they test claims, but in the language they use to make them. Here, a science journalist describes how scientists typically comment on published research:

> Notice the qualifiers on belief: "pretty much," "more or less," "don't particularly disbelieve." Scientists are great suspenders of belief. They know that their measurements often have large margins of error, their experimental devices are often relatively inadequate, and their own understanding incomplete. They know that the world is complex, interconnected, subtle and extremely easy to get wrong. Geologists once believed that the Sudbury mineral complex in Ontario, the source of most of the world's nickel, precipitated out of a melt formed when the liquid in the earth's middle rose up through the crust. But after finding shattered rock, microscopic mineral grains subjected to intense pressure, and other signs of a great impact, they now believe the nickel formed when a 6-mile-wide meteorite hit the Earth so hard that the crust melted ... Geologists will mostly believe that until more evidence comes along.

Source: From Ann Finkbeiner, "In Science, Seeing Is Not Believing," *USA Today,* October 21, 1997.

WRITING PROCESS
Finding and Articulating Claims

PREPARING AND PLANNING

Planning a Research Project

A research project is like diamond mining; you have to know what you are looking for and where to look; then you must process lots of dross to find a few gems; and even then the best finds need polishing. In the same way, when you address a problem that requires more than casual research, you need a systematic plan to guide your search. If you have only a topic to guide you, you may have to read widely before you find a problem worth pursuing. But as soon as that problem emerges and you generate one or more hypotheses for a tentative solution, you can plan your research systematically.

Once you select a tentative claim, focus your reading or other data collecting on the evidence you'll need to test and support it. You'll waste a lot of time if you just start collecting information randomly. Instead, invest some time planning your search:

1. Decide what kind of reasons and evidence readers expect in support of your claim. Your reasons must be relevant to your claim, and your evidence must be relevant to your reasons. But your evidence must also be the *kind* of evidence that your readers expect in support of your particular *kind* of claim. For example, what kind of data would convince your particular reader that extrasensory perception exists? Objective data generated by controlled experiments? Testimony from someone they trust? Only their own personal experience of it? Imagine that evidence, and then use what you imagine both to guide your search and to test what you find.

2. Weigh the cost of the search against the value of the evidence. You want the evidence that best tests and supports your claim, but second-best evidence is better than none. Decide how long it will take to find the best evidence. Is there a risk that you will find none? If the best evidence may prove too hard to find, limit your risk by gathering the most readily available evidence first. For example, if Elena had only a few weeks to prepare her argument supporting a Center for English Language Studies, she couldn't survey every college with a center. She would have to settle for a less reliable phone survey of a few she knew of.

3. Decide on the most likely source of evidence. You have many options.

- **Libraries:** A college library will provide most of the data you need. The trick is knowing how to find them. Every library has a tour, and most librarians are eager to help. An hour or two invested in learning how to find resources in different fields will pay off in time saved later.

- **The Internet:** The Internet is an important source of information, but for now it is like an undiscriminating library without librarians. The Internet has few gatekeepers that screen information for quality. While much of it is reliable, much is not. So it is a case of "browser beware." At least be sure you know who stands behind the information in a site. Until the Net develops the quality controls of libraries, use it for the following purposes, cautiously:

    To find out what your library has. Yours probably offers electronic access to articles, abstracts, and databases.

To get public materials. Most major newspapers and magazines maintain Web sites with information on recent articles, sometimes the articles themselves. You can purchase reprints of articles in the *New York Times* and other major newspapers.

To find information too recent to be found in libraries. Many government reports are released first on the Web, then in print.

To supplement information you find in libraries. Some journals conduct Net-based discussions among readers and authors. Others use the Web to archive data not included in printed texts.

To find information that libraries don't collect. For example, a student interested in steel pan music found that many steel bands have their own Web pages.

- **People:** You may need support beyond the written word. When you use people as sources, plan carefully to avoid wasting not just your time, but theirs.

  Prepare questions and bring them to the interview. Use them to avoid wasting time, but don't read them like a script.

  Record all identifying information—including the exact spelling of your source's full name. Record the date and place of the interview.

  Tape-record the interview if you can. If you can't, try to get the exact words.

  If you transcribe from a tape recorder, delete the *umm's* and *you know's,* but don't change anything else.

- **Direct Observation:** Many questions can be answered only through field studies or controlled experiments conducted in ways a discipline requires. In a writing class, it's not likely you'll have to collect such evidence, but you might construct a problem that needs it: How do instructors in different departments mark their papers? Do some bars encourage binge drinking more than others?

  Before you start observing, record the date and place of the observations and relevant circumstantial details. If the location is relevant, sketch a map.

  If you record quantitative data, create a blank data table or chart before you start; record data precisely, right then, not later from memory.

  In your argument, use only the data that your *records* support, not what you recall after you realize you failed to record information you should have. Be sure to tell readers how you collected the data. And if you have data that call your claim into question, you are obliged to report that as well.

4. Sample the evidence. Don't waste time looking for evidence that a source can't provide; sample sources first to determine their value. For a survey, test your questions in a trial run or focus group. For books or articles, skim a few introductions and abstracts to see whether they look promising. For direct observation, make a quick visit to the site to see what it offers.

5. Take stock as the evidence mounts. Some students turn off their judgment when they start gathering evidence, reading book after book, taking endless notes before they realize that most of what they have is irrelevant to any claim they might make. So from time to time, pause to consider the value of what you have collected. Avoid the common mistake of assuming that you have done your job when you have found any evidence at all. Teachers more often complain that students offer too little evidence than too much.

DRAFTING

Use Specific Language to State Claims

When you state your claims using specific words, readers can understand it better and then use it to help them anticipate how you will support it. Before you draft a claim, both your main claim and major subclaims, do the following:

1. List additional specific terms that might fit your claim. Concentrate on nouns and verbs; you'll have to ask different questions about each. For example, for the claim *The divisive effects of the Civil War are still felt today*, ask these two questions.

- For nouns, ask *What kind of?* Then ask it again for each of those terms. Add all the terms that might apply to your list.

  For example, for the term *effects*, ask, *What kind of* **effects**?—*political rivalry, regional prejudice, economic competition, ideological differences.* Then for the term *ideological differences*, ask, *What kind of* **differences**?—*theories of government, states' rights, individual freedom, right to work laws, Bible belt fundamentalism.*

- For verbs, ask *How?* Add all the terms that might apply to your list.

  For example, *How are effects* **felt**?—*by the regions mistrusting one another, by the South voting as a political bloc, by the South seeing federal efforts toward desegregation as an imposition from the North, by old divisions influencing new attitudes, by the politicians of each region advancing different theories of government.*

Once you have a list of specific terms relevant to your claim, look for related words that might express your ideas more precisely.

- For each term, ask the question *as opposed to?* If a new term expresses your ideas better than the old one, replace the old one.

  For example, **Differences** as opposed to *divisions, disruptions, disagreements*. **States' rights** as opposed to *federalism, the power of the federal government, the freedom of states to govern themselves*. **Influence** as opposed to *determine, shape*.

2. Write the claim using the most appropriate words on the list. Review your lists, picking out three or four terms that best express the key ideas of your claim (in bold). Then write a claim using those terms and any others that fit (in italics):

> *Relevant Kinds of Effects*
>
> **ideological divisions**, political rivalry, **theories of government**, *state vs. federal power, individual freedom*

> *Relevant Ways They are Felt*
>
> **old divisions shape new attitudes**, bloc voting in the South, *politicians of each region advance different theories of government*

> The **ideological divisions** of the Civil War still **shape** the *political discourse* of North and South today, reflected in their **antithetical theories** about *state and federal powers* and the *authority of government over individuals*.

REVISING

Qualify Claims That Are Too Certain

Readers often distrust claims and writers that express arrogant, unquestioning certainty, preferring ones that show civil diffidence. When you review the sentences in a completed draft, check the language of your main claim and major subclaims for too much certainty.

Watch out for sentences that overstate the scope of your claim by suggesting that something is *certainly* true *always* and *for everyone*:

- **Probability:** If you find *certainly, absolutely, without question*, etc., consider writing *probably, normally, likely, tend to, inclined to*, etc. If you find *impossible, inconceivable*, etc., consider writing *unlikely, improbable*, etc.

- **Frequency:** If you find *always, every time, without fail*, etc., consider writing *usually, frequently, predictably, habitually, almost always*, etc. If you find *never, not once*, etc., consider writing *seldom, rarely, infrequently, almost never*, etc.

- **Quantity:** If you find *all, every, each*, etc., consider writing *many, most, some, a majority, almost all*, etc. If you find *none, not one*, etc., consider writing *few, hardly any*, etc.

Remember that a claim may seem too certain even without any of these words. If you write the claim, "Readers distrust writers who are certain," readers may assume that you mean "*All* readers are *always certain* to distrust *all* writers who are certain."

But don't overqualify. You would seem wishy-washy if you wrote "Some readers are occasionally somewhat inclined to distrust writers who are certain." Usually, one qualification is enough: "Readers *are likely to* distrust . . . ," "Readers *often* distrust . . . ," "*Many* readers distrust . . . "

Even more than they distrust writers who make unqualified claims, readers distrust those who assert those claims too strongly. When you claim that your reasons or evidence support a claim, be moderate in asserting how strong your case really is:

- **Level of proof:** Unless you have the strongest possible evidence, avoid phrases like *X proves Y, X settles the question, Y is beyond question, without a doubt*, etc. If you find *X demonstrates, establishes*, or *shows* Y, consider writing X *suggests, points to, argues for, leads us to believe, indicates*, etc.

Here too, you don't want to diminish the real strength of your argument, but readers are likely to be suspicious if you exaggerate the level of your proof.

INQUIRIES

1. Are those who make conceptual arguments responsible for what others do with their claims? Is a scientist who discovers something that someone uses to create new weapons responsible for their consequences? Should a geneticist get credit when his discoveries help doctors save lives? If so, should he be blamed if those same discoveries are used in immoral ways? What about a political scientist whose ideas about limiting the power of government inspire someone to bomb a federal building? What principle might we use to make distinctions among these cases? Could you make a case that some claims should never be made? What about a discovery that makes it possible for anyone to build an atomic bomb in his kitchen? What might be the unintended consequences if researchers kept secret discoveries that they thought might be potentially dangerous?

2. Suppose you are a leader in a national student organization dedicated to reducing the costs of a college education. Sketch a plan of action for asking college presidents to support a policy that will lower tuition.

What role would negotiation or mediation have in your plan? What about propaganda (advertising, public relations, etc.)? Coercion (demonstrations, civil disobedience, lobbying legislators, etc.)? How would argument fit into your plans?

6. Look in your old papers for the qualities of good claims (pp. 83–87). Look especially for signals of cause and effect (*because, so, in order to,* and so on) and reservation (*despite, although, while,* and so on). If your claims seem thin, elaborate them in ways we've suggested.

IN A NUTSHELL

About Your Argument . . .

Claims are at the heart of every argument. They are your main point, the solution to your problem. Though you should try to formulate a tentative claim or hypothesis as soon as you can, you must also work hard to keep your mind open to giving it up in favor of a better one. That's why it's important to imagine a number of hypotheses and hold them all in mind as you work your way toward a best one.

Useful claims have these qualities:

- Your claim should be clearly **conceptual** or **pragmatic**. It should assert what readers should know or what they should do.

- Your claim should be something that readers will not accept without seeing your good reasons. It should be **contestable**.

- Your claim should in principle be capable of being proved wrong, because you can imagine evidence that would make you give it up. It should be **disconfirmable**.

- Your claim should be feasible, ethical, and prudent. It should be **reasonable**.

Be clear to yourself the degree of assent you seek. What do you want your readers to do?

- **Respect** your reasons for making your claim?

- **Approve** of your claim and the argument supporting it?

- **Publicly endorse** your claim as worth serious consideration?

- **Believe** in your claim and in the argument supporting it?

- **Act** as you propose, or support someone else's action?

. . . and About Writing It

Work toward a claim that has these qualities:

- Its language is explicit and specific. It previews the central concepts that you will develop in the rest of the argument.

- It is elaborated with clauses beginning with *although, because,* and *unless.* If you think that makes the claim too long and complex, then break it into shorter sentences.

- It is hedged with appropriate qualifiers such as *many, most, often, usually, probably,* and *unlikely* instead of *all, always,* and *certainly.*

Make a plan to gather evidence. Think about these questions:

- What kind of evidence do readers expect you to report?

- Will the cost of searching for specific evidence be greater than the benefit of finding it?

- Where are you most likely to find the evidence you need? Libraries? The Internet? Personal interview? Observation?

Follow these steps:

- Start by sampling the evidence from a source to see whether it is relevant and sufficient.

- Periodically take stock of the evidence as it mounts.

- Don't wait to get every shred of evidence before you start writing.

Chapter 5

Reasons and Evidence

In this chapter, we focus on the support that makes a claim seem credible and convincing. We distinguish three kinds of support you need to keep straight: reasons, evidence, and reports of evidence. We also show you how to arrange reasons into an order that is useful to readers.

Those who make a flat claim, expecting us to agree just because they say so, risk seeming at best uncivil. We expect at least one reason in its support and some qualification. Compare these examples:

> TV's obsession with sexuality damages the social and emotional development of our preteens. _{claim}

> **Though the TV industry has improved children's daytime programming,** _{acknowledgment} its prime-time obsession with sexuality **may** be damaging the social and emotional development of preteens _{claim} **because many of them model their behavior on what they see others do.** _{reason}

But careful readers expect more. A reader might accept that as a good reason, but only if the writer shows that preteens in fact base their behavior on TV. A reason can support a claim only if it is based on more than the writer's opinion. Thoughtful writers create a broader and deeper base of support by treating their reasons as subclaims, sometimes supported by still more reasons, but at bottom based on sound evidence. In this chapter, we explore what it means to support a claim with reasons and evidence.

Reasons and Evidence as Forms of Support

As we saw in Chapter 1, the language we use about *having* an argument makes us sound like combatants. But when we describe *making* one, we sound more like builders. We *support* claims with reasons that *rest on a firm base* of evidence. That *solid footing* should be so *unshakable* that critics cannot *topple* our argument by *undermining* its *foundation*. Such language portrays an argument like this:

Those metaphors are useful, but to understand how we actually plan and draft arguments, we need four more terms with more literal meanings: *fact, data, evidence,* and *reasons*. The first two we can define easily:

- A *fact* is a statement in words or symbols that readers accept as true, or at least will not contest: *The capital of Ohio is Columbus; 2 + 2 = 4.*

- *Data* (the singular is *datum*) are sets of facts. We can summarize data in words: *In 1980, Abco's market share was 19.4%; by 1990, it slipped to 11.7%, but has grown to 22%.* But more often, we present data in tables, graphs, and charts:

Abco Market Share (%)

1980	1990	2002
19.4	11.7	22.0

Facts and data, however, are inert information until we use them as *evidence* supporting *reasons* that in turn support claims. Here is a brief argument including data as evidence:

Although television has improved after-school programming, its prime-time shows may be undermining the social and emotional development of many preteens _{claim} by exposing them to sexually explicit behavior that encourages them to engage in sex play before they understand its consequences. _{reason} In his report on the relationship between TV watching and sexual experimentation, **Kahn (1996) studied children ages 10–13 who regularly (three times in four weeks) watch sexually oriented shows on television (more than five references to or images of sexual conduct). He found they are 40 percent more likely to engage in sexual play than those who do not watch such programs at all.** _{evidence}

That is the core of an argument in a standard form: Claim + Reason + Evidence.

Distinguishing Reasons and Evidence

The difference between reasons and evidence seems intuitively obvious, but it is more complex than it seems. We sometimes use those terms interchangeably:

> What *reasons* can you offer to support your claim?
>
> What *evidence* can you offer to support your claim?

But we also distinguish them in sentences like these:

> We need to think up *reasons* to support our request.
>
> We need to think up *evidence* to support our request.
>
> Before I accept your *reasons,* I have to see the *evidence* they rest on.
>
> Before I accept your *evidence,* I have to see the *reasons* it rests on.

Most of us find the first sentence in the pairs natural, the second a bit odd.

One source of the difference is the metaphorical images we associate with reasons and evidence. With evidence, we use metaphors like *solid* or *hard* that incline us to think that we can see evidence out in the world, "outside" our subjective experience. We feel that reasons, on the other hand, metaphorically come from "inside" our minds. We believe we could check your evidence if you told us where to look; we don't ask where to look for your reasons.

Since we assume evidence is at least in principle *public* and *sharable,* readers ask certain questions about it:

- Where did you find your evidence? What are your sources? Are they reliable?

- How did you collect it? What methods and devices did you use? Could I see it for myself?

Recall the conversation among Sue, Ann, and Raj (pp. 22–24): When Sue claimed that her school did not treat students well, she offered as a reason that teachers kept too few office hours. When asked to back up that reason, she reported the actual hours posted: *Prof. X, Monday, 4–5 P.M., Prof. Y, Friday 4–4:30 P.M.,* etc. Those names and numbers were not her reasons, not her judgments or opinions, but what she hoped her friends would accept as evidence, as facts independent of her beliefs. Figuratively, Sue's argument looked like this:

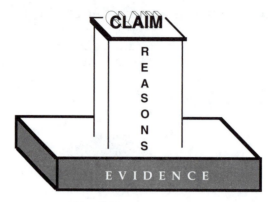

We judge reasons that lack a foundation of evidence as "mere opinion," and mere opinion is, to continue the construction metaphor, "too flimsy" to support "solid" claims about "weighty" problems.

Distinguishing Evidence and Reports of It

You can use that construction image as a loose way to think about the core of an argument, but when we examine it closely, it turns out to be a bit misleading. In what follows, we make a distinction that may seem academic hairsplitting, but that we think is important in understanding how arguments really work. We need the distinction because what we call evidence rarely is.

Primary and Reported Evidence

As unsettling as it may seem, what we call evidence is almost always just a *report* of it, or even a report of a report. Most evidence "itself" cannot be "in" an argument, if we define evidence as objective stuff we can find out in the world.

- In a murder trial, the evidence "itself" might be a bloody glove that a prosecutor can hold up for the jury to see, but in a written argument, she can only describe the glove or show a photograph of it.
- An economist making an argument about unemployment could point to actual individuals with no jobs, but in a written argument, he could only refer to those people in words or numbers.
- In an argument about the nature of matter, a physicist can't even point to the smallest particles he investigates. He can only refer to them in mathematical terms.

What we offer as evidence is almost always only a *report* that describes, pictures, represents, refers to, or enumerates the actual gloves, people, and particles.

Even when you've seen "real" evidence with your own eyes, you can bring it into a written argument only by representing it in words, numbers, or images. For the purposes of your argument, you have to ignore a multitude of details, because it is impossible to represent them all. When you report evidence, you smooth it out, tidy it up, make it more coherent, more regular than the "stuff out there" really is.

Representations as Evidence

Some students wonder about quoted words. Aren't they "the evidence itself"? Even when words are quoted correctly (which is often not the case), they are taken out of context, leading us to understand them in ways that their context may contradict. What about photographs? Even when we reproduce a photograph as exactly as possible, it is still seen on different paper, in a different context, with a different purpose. Remember that just as a picture of an apple is not an apple, so a report of evidence is not the evidence.

We emphasize this distinction because the word *evidence* carries so much authority and seems so weighty and objective. When we offer what we claim is "hard" evidence, we are likely to be half convinced that it has an objective reality that no reader could question. But a report is neither objective nor the real thing. What we call evidence is almost always a report of it shaped to fit an argument.

Once you grasp that distinction, you can see why careful readers care that your reports of evidence be reliable and from a good source, and why they expect you to tell them where you found the evidence, or others' reports of it, and who gathered it. They want to know how much it was shaped even before you found it. That's why readers look for footnotes to assure themselves that they could, if they wanted, track your reports back as close as they can get to the evidence "itself." Evidence is only as sound as the chain of reports leading to it.

Recall again that in the discussion among Sue, Ann, and Raj, the question of evidence turned on that very issue:

Sue: We pay a lot of money for our education, but we don't get anywhere near the attention customers do. _{reason}

Raj: Like how? [*i.e., What evidence do you base that reason on?*]

Sue: For one thing, we have trouble seeing teachers outside of class. Last week I went to every office on the first floor of the Arts and Sciences building and counted the hours posted on the doors. [She pulls a piece of paper out of her backpack.] They average less than an hour a week, most of them in the afternoon when a lot of us work. _{report of evidence}

Ann: Can I see?

Sue: Sure. [Sue hands the paper over.]

But when Ann looked at the numbers, she was still not looking at the evidence "itself": that was attached to doors. Ann must assume that Sue copied those hours accurately and reported them fairly.

If the distinction between evidence and reports reflects how most arguments really work, then Sue's argument does *not* look like this:

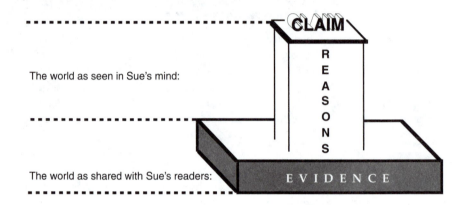

Instead, her argument must look like this:

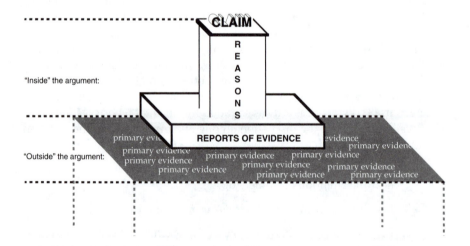

What Sue can offer as evidence *inside* her argument is only a report that she hopes Ann and Raj accept as reliably grounded on evidence *outside* the argument. But Ann and Raj won't go look at the hours posted on doors, so from their point of view, Sue's argument really looks like this:

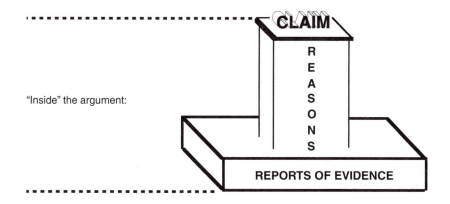

"Inside" the argument:

They have to trust that she got the numbers right. And that's why you must develop a reputation for reporting evidence accurately, without obviously self-interested spin, because the last person in the chain of trust is you. Betray that trust and you lose credibility, not just for your current argument, but possibly for the next one and the ones after that.

On the Evidence of Dinosaurs

Even when it seems we can hold evidence "itself" in our hands, we may be holding only nature's report of it. Not long ago, paleontologists announced that they had uncovered the heart of a dinosaur, the first ever found. After examination, they decided that it had two chambers, evidence, they said, that the dinosaur it came from may have been warm-blooded. The evidence they could point to, however, was not the actual heart of that dinosaur; it was a fossil stone casting created by natural processes—nature's "report" of the evidence. Moreover, what the scientists pointed to as evidence was not even the fossil casting but a series of two-dimensional CAT-scans of its internal structure that they assembled into a three-dimensional model. Their evidence that dinosaurs might have been warm-blooded is a three-dimensional model that reports on a series of two-dimensional images that report on a stone fossil that reports on an organ that no longer exists. The hard question is how much each of those reports distorts that once-beating heart (if in fact it is a heart, which some paleontologists doubt).

At this point you may have an uneasy feeling that reasons and reports of evidence are a lot alike, because both are the products of a subjective mind. They are alike, but here's one way to sort them out: Think of your reasons as the *outline* of your argument, its logical outline. Think of reports of evidence as what readers must accept as true to support its points.

Multiple Reasons

Even when you base a reason on reliable (reports of) evidence, readers may be reluctant to accept just one reason as sufficient support for a significant claim. So you usually have to offer more reasons that relate to your claim in two ways:

- You can offer parallel reasons, each one supporting a claim directly.
- You can offer "stacked" reasons, each one resting on the one before, the first one directly supporting your claim, the last one resting on evidence (or a report of it).

Reasons in Parallel

Parallel reasons supporting a claim look like this:

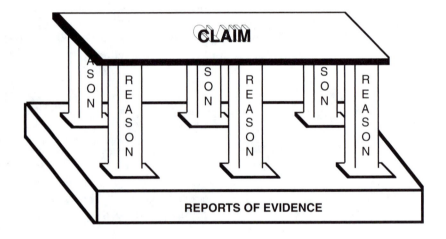

Each reason stands independently of the others. Take one away and the claim might slump, but the other reasons may be sufficient to prop it up. Take away more, and it might collapse.

Three reasons in parallel is the standard plan for the five-paragraph essay many of us learned in high school:

¶1 There are three reasons why we should curb binge drinking. claim

¶2 First, it gives the campus a bad image. reason 1 For example,...report of evidence

¶3 It also creates legal liability. reason 2 Four cases have been...report of evidence

¶4 Finally, it causes injury and even death. reason 3 Last month,...report of evidence

¶5 Therefore, we can see that bingeing has become,...repeated claim

Some good arguments actually have only three reasons, but so many bad arguments have been written in that form that the five-paragraph, three-reason essay has a bad image at the college level. So avoid three if you can.

Reasons in Sequence

You can also arrange reasons not separately in parallel, but "stacked," each reason resting on another, the first directly supporting the claim, the last resting on reports of evidence:

(You can also imagine these reasons sideways, as a chain or series of steps.)

For example, in this argument the writer bases a main claim on two stacked reasons resting on a report of evidence:

This nation needs a system of testing that will benchmark achievement in math and reading, so that we can measure educational performance consistently. claim

We must be confident that our children are developing the intellectual skills to face the challenges of the third millennium. reason 1 supporting claim

Without testing, taxpayers cannot judge how well their schools and children are doing compared not just to other schools in the United States, but more importantly in the world. reason 2 supporting reason 1

The National Association for Educational Excellence has recently reported that current test results are statistically unreliable at the national level, because different states give different tests that cannot be correlated, and some do little testing at all. report of evidence supporting reason 2

Only a system of national testing will provide us with that sound data. _{claim restated}

We could make the same argument beginning with the report of evidence and moving to the claim:

> The National Association for Educational Excellence has recently reported that current test results in math and reading are statistically unreliable at the national level, because different states give different tests that cannot be correlated, and some do little testing at all. _{report of evidence}
>
> Without these data, taxpayers cannot judge how well their schools and children are doing compared not just to other schools in the United States, but more importantly in the world. _{reason 1 based on evidence}
>
> As a result, we cannot be sure that our children are developing the intellectual skills to face the challenges of the third millennium. _{reason 2 based on reason 1}
>
> In short, this nation needs a system of national tests that will benchmark performance in secondary education so that we can measure educational performance consistently. _{claim}

Experienced writers create arguments like these by laying deeper and deeper foundations for their claims thereby thickening their arguments. The risk of such an argument is that if readers miss just one intermediate step, they can lose track of the logic, and the argument collapses.

The Deep Complexity of Serious Arguments

When we address an issue that requires more than two or three pages of argument, we build our case out of multiple reasons in parallel, each of which rests on multiple reasons in sequence, all of them based on evidence. In so doing, we create an argument of considerable complexity. Yet as complex as it might seem in writing, we create that kind of complex argument in conversation every day whenever we engage in a lot of back-and-forth about a serious issue. Our task in writing an equally complex argument is first to imagine such a conversation, then to translate it into a written argument by patiently organizing its reasons in parallel and in series, all based on evidence.

Using Reasons to Help Readers Understand Evidence

If evidence anchors an argument, why not just base a claim directly on reports of it? Sometimes we do, but reasons are essential. In sequence, they signal the structure of the argument, and it is that structure that helps us understand and remember the whole argument. Reasons also help us understand and interpret complex evidence more quickly and clearly. For example, this is unclear:

> The demographic future of semi-rural counties is predicted by their employment trends. _{claim}

County	Industry	Population by County			
		1985	1995	Change	% change
Tuttle	Farming	200,502	100,400	(100,102)	-50.7
Oswego	Farming	150,792	90,614	(60,178)	-39.1
Clark	Mnfctrng	120,651	250,266	129,615	100.2
Perko	Mnfctrng	92,047	276,890	184,843	300.1

reported evidence

A careful reader could figure out how the numbers support the claim—manufacturing means more population; farming means less. But a reason that interpreted the data before we read them would tell us both which data are most important and how they support the claim:

> The demographic future of semirural counties is predicted by their employment trends. _{claim} **Primarily agricultural counties are losing population, while Clark and Perko, with a strong manufacturing base, have doubled and even tripled in population.** _{reason}

County	Industry	Population by County			
		1985	1995	Change	% change
Tuttle	Farming	200,502	100,400	(100,102)	-50.7

reported evidence

Some writers fear that they insult readers when they spell out in a reason what readers can figure out for themselves. And it is true that no one wants to read the obvious. But all writers, experienced and inexperienced alike, overestimate what readers can figure out on their own. So you usually do readers a service when you add a reason that points out what is important in a report of evidence, making clear how it supports your claim.

Readers need the same help when the evidence is a quotation. Here is a claim about Hamlet that rests directly on the evidence of a quotation:

> As Hamlet stands behind his stepfather Claudius while he is at prayer, he demonstrates a cool and logical mind. _{claim}

> > Now might I do it [kill him] pat, now he is praying:
> > And now I'll do't; and so he goes to heaven;
> > And so am I reveng'd...[Hamlet pauses to think]
> > [But this] villain kills my father; and for that,
> > I, his sole son, do this same villain send to heaven[?]
> > Why, this is hire and salary, not revenge. _{report of evidence}

Many readers find that argument a bit hard to follow. Nothing in the quotation seems obviously to support a claim about Hamlet's cool reason. Lacking a reason, we have to figure it out on our own. Compare this version:

> As Hamlet stands behind his stepfather Claudius while he is at prayer, he demonstrates a cool and logical mind. _{claim} **At first he impulsively wants to kill Claudius on the spot, but he pauses to reflect. If he kills Claudius while praying, he sends his soul to heaven. But Hamlet wants him damned to hell forever. So he coolly decides to kill him later:** _{reason}

Now might I do it [kill him] pat, now he is praying:

And now I'll do't; and so... _{report of evidence}

That reason tells us what to see in the quotation that relates it to the claim.

In short, a detailed report of evidence seldom speaks for itself. Without a reason to explain it, readers may struggle to understand what it signifies. They work less hard when you add a reason that both supports the claim *and* explains the evidence. Visually, it looks like this:

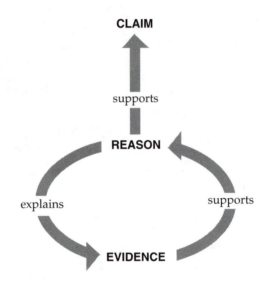

When you offer evidence in the form of quotations, images, tables or charts, don't just attach it to a claim. Add a reason that tells your readers what to look for.

WRITING PROCESS
Reasons and Evidence

PREPARING AND PLANNING

What Your Reasons Imply About Your Claim (and You)

Once you assemble your reasons, consider what they imply about both you and your readers. Since every reason implies a principle of reasoning (warrant), each one tells readers something about your values and what you think of theirs. Even if a reason is true and supports your claim, it could poison your argument and your ethos if readers reject the values it rests on.

Suppose Jorge claims that plagiarism from the Internet should be curbed, offering these reasons:

R1: Plagiarism prevents good students from standing out.
R2: It erodes the foundations of trust that a community depends on.
R3: If the public learns about it, it will make the university look bad.
R4: It makes students think they can get something for nothing.

Each reason casts a different light on both Jorge and on the kind of person he imagines his reader to be. Most of us would rather be identified with preserving the social foundations of trust than protecting the university from bad press.

Once you have a list of reasons, test each for what it implies about your ethos and your image of your reader. If you can't tell, ask someone.

Ordering Multiple Reasons

Once you have a list of reasons, decide how to order them. Too many writers put their reasons in the order they thought of them, which is rarely the best order.

Parallel Reasons

If you have parallel reasons supporting a claim, arrange them in an order that readers will think is coherent and helpful.

Ordering Parallel Reasons by Their Substance

You might find a principle of order based on the ideas or things the reasons refer to. The most obvious choice is to group them based on who or what the reasons are mostly about. For example, in these three reasons supporting the claim that even small "social" lies should be avoided, two are about liars and one is about the person lied to:

R1: Once you get used to little lies, you tell bigger ones more easily.
R2: The person you lie to suffers from not knowing the truth.
R3: You eventually lose credibility.

So, we should probably put (1) and (3) together, before or after (2).

You can also order reasons on the basis of their relation to preexisting order, such as chronology and geography, or one specific to your particular claim, such as least-to-most controllable cause. For example, to explain the causes of the Holocaust someone might offer these five parallel reasons:

R1: Allied leaders did not try to stop the Holocaust for political reasons.
R2: Germany had a long history of anti-Semitism.
R3: Many societies have practiced other versions of ethnic cleansing.
R4: Hitler and those around him were uniquely evil.
R5: Jews did not resist soon enough.

It's hard to see any principle in that order. To emphasize the Holocaust as an historical event, an order based on time, earliest to latest (or vice versa) would be clearer:

(3) society in general
(2) German history
(4) Hitler's evil
(5) weak Jewish resistance early
(1) failure of allied leaders

Or to emphasize the difference between personal and social causes, an order that arranged reasons from most personal to most social would be better:

(4) Hitler's personal evil
(1) failure of individual allied leaders
(5) weak Jewish resistance early
(2) German society
(3) society in general

Ordering Parallel Reasons by Readers' Responses

A better way to order parallel reasons is by how you want readers to respond to them. One principle of order is relative *strength*. For example, the reasons for the Holocaust might be ordered from what readers should take to be weakest to strongest, or vice versa, depending on whether we want to make a quick impact or to build toward a climax. (Of course, readers differ in which reasons they judge strong or weak.)

A second principle of order based on readers' responses is relative *acceptability*. Even when readers think a reason is strong, they may still not like hearing it. For example, it is likely that Jews, Germans, and those associated with the Allies would each resist most strongly the reason that assigns responsibility to each of them. Each group would probably want to see other causes acknowledged before considering their own responsibility.

Another principle of readers' order is relative *complexity*. Readers grasp simpler reasons more easily than complex ones. (What is easier or more difficult, of course, depends on what they know.) For example, to argue that our ability to learn language is not like our ability to learn chess or algebra but is based on a genetically determined competence, we could offer three reasons:

R1: All human languages share the same complex principles of grammatical organization.

R2: Children all over the world learn to talk at about the same age.

R3: Chimpanzees can't learn the grammatical structures that two-year-olds master easily.

The first reason is very difficult to grasp; the second easier; and the third easiest of all. If so, we would understand the argument better if those reasons were in reverse order, because that would allow us to build some "momentum" in understanding the argument.

Finally, reasons can be ordered by *familiarity*. (This too varies by readers.) Readers understand familiar reasons more readily than unfamiliar ones. For example, of the three reasons about learning language, the first is least familiar to most of us, the second most familiar for those of us who have been around children. So for them, the best order is 2-3-1.

If these principles of order conflict, the simplest principle is to put your strongest reasons last, or at least the ones you want to emphasize, but only if you are sure your reader will read to the end of your argument. If you fear your reader may not read to the end, put your strongest reason first. Under any circumstances, *choose some* principle of order and *make clear* to your readers what it is.

Reasons in Series

When you offer reasons in a series, only one reason supports the claim directly. The others support that reason, the "bottom" one resting on evidence. You have two basic choices in how you order the reasons. The first is a default order—claim first, followed by support:

Claim $_{based on}$ Reason 1 $_{based on}$ Reason 2 $_{based on}$ Reason 3 . . . $_{based on}$ Evidence

The second is a "discovery" order, starting with facts and moving to an inference:

Evidence $_{supports}$ . . . Reason 3 $_{supports}$ Reason 2 $_{supports}$ Reason 1 $_{supports}$ Claim

Those two orders can reflect the process of cause-and-effect or of reasoning.

Process Orders

If your reasons reflect some external process like cause and effect, you can order them to reflect its sequence. Begin at the beginning of the process and move to its outcome, like this:

> When buyers are satisfied with the quality of a product and the quality of service when it breaks down, $_{step 1}$ they are likely to become loyal customers. $_{step 2}$ Loyal customers are important, because they don't need advertising or a high-powered sales force to buy that product again. $_{step 3}$ So the more loyal users a product has, the more profits a company can expect. $_{claim}$

Or you can begin with the outcome and move back to its beginning, like this:

> Manufacturers increase profits and sales $_{step 3}$ when they create loyal customers who buy their product once and return to buy it a second time, $_{step 2}$ without the need of advertising or a high-powered sales force. Customers become loyal when they are satisfied with the quality of service they get on the product when it breaks down, but more importantly with the product's intrinsic quality. $_{step 1}$ Therefore, while manufacturers should focus on both service and product quality, they should emphasize product quality. $_{claim}$

Both orders make sense. Which you choose depends on how you want readers to think about the process. The step they read last is the one they will focus on.

Reasoning Orders

You can order sequential reasons to follow not an external process but the internal process of your readers' logic. In the next example, the writer reports Thomas Jefferson's order of reasoning. The second reason depends on the logical principle stated in the first, and the third reason depends on the second (and the writer bases it all on the reported evidence of Jefferson's words):

> When Jefferson wrote "all men are created equal" with "certain inalienable rights," _{evidence} he laid down the first principle of civil society—we all have intrinsic rights that cannot be taken away. _{reason 1} To protect those rights, we establish government, _{reason 2} but when government tries to take those rights away, we have the duty to replace it with one that will protect us. _{reason 3} In a democracy, we do that by the vote. But when ·a government is a ruthless tyranny, we have the duty to throw off its rule by force, if necessary. _{claim}

The reverse order is possible, but harder to follow.

We can't tell you how to choose from among these orders: that depends on your argument, on your situation, but most of all on your readers. In general, though, arrange your reasons so that the one you want your readers to focus on comes last, so long as you are certain they will read attentively to the end; if you are not, put your important reasons first. Under any circumstances, assume that the order in which you happened to write them down is probably *not* the order that best helps readers grasp them. In fact, try out different orders on surrogate readers to see how they respond.

REVISING

Balance Reasons and Evidence

Beware the data dump. Readers want reliable reports of relevant evidence, not all the data you can find. If you find the best evidence to support a reason, don't confuse the issue with less relevant evidence. If your evidence is less than best, you'll need more, but no careful reader will be convinced by tons of undigested data and quotations. So as painful as it will feel, cut data that do not support your claim.

Beware as well the opinion piece. Readers want your reasons, but they expect you to back them up with evidence. If you can't find reliable evidence to support a reason, drop it and find another reason you can support. If you can't support most of your reasons with at least some evidence, then your claim is shaky and so not worth an argument.

To diagnose whether you have done either, highlight every quotation and statement of data:

- If you highlight more than two-thirds of your paper, you may have a data dump.
- If you highlight less than one-third, you may not have enough evidence to support your reasons.

INQUIRIES

1. How close to the primary evidence itself are these: (a) a musical score; (b) musical recordings made from that score; (c) color reproductions of oil paintings in art history books; (d) full-size exact reproductions of etchings in art books; (e) a videotape of an automobile accident; (f) a tape recording of a meeting; (g) a transcription of that tape recording; (h) a drawing of a witness in a courtroom; (i) a photograph of a witness in a courtroom? What question must you ask and answer before you can answer this question?

2. What counts as evidence for being in love? For sexual fidelity? For God directly telling someone to do something? For pain that disables someone from working?

3. Some people refuse to judge any reason good or bad, because any reason is a good one for the person offering it. If so, then all reasons are equally good. They are in effect just opinions, and everyone's opinion is as good as anyone else's. Do you agree that all opinions are equally good? If you do, then some philosophers would claim that you have contradicted yourself. Have you?

4. Analyze a magazine ad as an argument. (Select one that's half a page or larger.) Assume that the main claim is an unexpressed *Therefore you should buy this product.* What does the ad offer as reasons for buying the product? What does it offer as a report of the evidence? If it is a picture, how did the ad "spin" that report?

5. Look at the advertising in four or five magazines that appeal to people with different demographic profiles. For example, a teen magazine, a techie magazine, an intellectual magazine, a sports magazine, a woman's magazine, etc. How do they differ in the ways advertisers try to get their particular readers to buy products? Do the ads in the same publications use similar kinds of evidence even for different readers?

IN A NUTSHELL

About Your Argument ...

You rest claims on reasons and reasons on reports of evidence. When you report evidence that you yourself observed or that someone else has reported, report it accurately and cite your sources so that readers can check it for themselves.

Since readers usually need more than one reason before they will agree to a claim, don't be satisfied with only one.

Except for the simplest, most obvious cases, don't cite reports of evidence without also stating a reason that connects those reports to the claim. Reasons not only support claims, they also interpret evidence. The reason should tell readers what to see in the evidence that is relevant to your claim.

... and About Writing It

When you have multiple reasons, select an order that helps readers:

- If reasons are parallel, order them on the basis of strength, acceptability, complexity, or familiarity.
- If your reasons are linked, decide whether you want them to follow some external process or an internal process of reasoning.

Keep a balance between reasons and reports of evidence:

- Beware the argument that is made up mostly of quotations or data.
- Conversely, be certain that you have at least tried to find evidence for every reason.

Chapter 6

Reporting Evidence

In this chapter, we discuss different kinds of evidence, with a special focus on how to evaluate what you have and decide what more you need.

You take a big step toward good arguments when you understand that

- careful readers look for both reasons and evidence;
- you can give them not the evidence itself, but only reports of it; and
- they judge your argument as stronger and your ethos as more credible when the evidence you report is the kind they expect, gathered from sources they consider reliable.

But we risk misleading ourselves when we speak of "gathering" evidence (or reports of it), as if it were scattered around, waiting to be picked up. Getting evidence is closer to hunting down a specific quarry. Colomb spent five years, on and off, hunting for the address of a doctor who practiced in London at the end of the seventeenth century. You probably can't spend weeks, much less months, hunting for evidence, but you'll still need to do some sleuthing. (From here on, we use the term *evidence* to refer to both the *evidence* itself and your reports of it. When we have to distinguish them, we will.)

Even after you find evidence, you have to evaluate it as your readers are likely to. They will think of objections that you may not, and they are likely to think of evidence you didn't find. Or they may not think your evidence is as relevant to your reasons as you do. Asking these questions will be hard; we all tend to seize on evidence that confirms what we want to believe and tend to ignore, reject, or even distort evidence that contradicts it. So to meet your burden of evidence, you have to anticipate the questions your readers may ask, which means seeing your reports of evidence through their eyes.

Weigh Your Burden of Evidence

In conversation, you know you have to provide enough evidence when the other person doesn't ask for more. But when you write, you don't have readers there to tell you when they do. You have to judge each case individually, but three questions will help you decide what kind of evidence you need and how good it has to be.

1. **What kind of evidence do your readers expect?** Readers in different academic or professional communities accept only certain kinds of evidence. An environmental science teacher will expect you to draw toxicology data about a local lake from technical reports, not a newspaper; a history teacher will expect you to work with primary documents, not textbook accounts of them. Disciplines vary too much to give you a general rule other than this: When you write in a new community, ask an experienced member to show you what counts as evidence in that field. The first question is whether your readers will want empirical evidence (numbers, controlled observations, etc.) or "softer" forms of evidence (personal narratives, eyewitness reports, etc.). You also have to match the kind of evidence you report to the problem you address. In an argument about binge drinking, for example, you would need one kind of evidence to argue that it is caused by the psychology of late adolescence, another by our culture of addiction, and another yet by a genetic predisposition to risk taking. Each new argument presents new demands that you have to puzzle out case by case.

   Don't assume that the evidence you need is the evidence you can get most easily. Resist the temptation to rely only on what you happen to have experienced—the striking event you witnessed, the memorable person you knew, that one time you talked with a binge drinker. A "for instance" is not proof.

   If your problem requires personal evidence or if that's all you can get, don't settle for anecdotes you have told and retold: search the details of your own memory, and when you can, seek corroboration from records or other participants. Memory is a poor witness; it needs all the help you can give it.

2. **How strongly will readers resist your claim?** The more readers resist a claim, the more evidence they want. Assume your readers will want more evidence when you ask them to

   - accept a claim that contradicts what they deeply believe,
   - do something that costs them time or effort,
   - do or think something that creates new problems, such as the loss of something they like, the disapproval of others, etc.

In those situations, their feelings matter as much as your logic. Suppose you found evidence that a famous political figure knowingly included false stories in a book that made her famous. Her political opponents will snap up any evidence against her, while her admirers will demand more and better evidence before they agree that she is a fraud.

3. **How fully do you want your readers to accept your claim?** If you ask readers to accept a strong claim wholeheartedly, they will expect your best reports of the best evidence. But they may be satisfied with less if you ask less of them—for example, to approve a claim rather than act on it, or only to understand and respect your reasons for making it. If Harry asks the dean to extend library hours to accommodate students with day jobs, the dean will want more than anecdotal evidence about dissatisfied students. But she may be receptive to a few good stories if Harry wants her only to ask her assistant to find out whether students have a reasonable complaint.

The Four Maxims of Quality

Once you think you can meet your readers' expectations with sufficient evidence of the right kind, evaluate its quality, but again from their point of view. Readers judge evidence by four criteria: (1) accuracy, (2) precision, (3) representativeness, and (4) reliability. How severely they apply those criteria depends on their stake in your claim. For instance, for a claim that some natural herb improves Alzheimer's symptoms, FDA researchers responsible for testing such cures will demand multiple studies that meet all four criteria; family members caring for an Alzheimer's sufferer are likely to accept a lower threshold of evidence; and the producers of the herb a lower one yet. Imagine your readers asking these questions about your evidence:

1. **Is your report of evidence accurate?**
   This is the prime maxim. Get one fact wrong and readers may distrust everything else you say—and you, as well.

2. **Is your report of evidence precise enough?**
   It is 100 percent accurate to say that the population of Ohio is between a million and a billion, but not precise enough for most purposes. What counts as precise, though, differs by both use and field. A physicist measures the life of a particle in millionths of a second; a paleontologist might be happy to date the appearance of a new species give or take half a million years.

3. **Is the evidence you report representative?**
   This depends on your kind of problem. If you generalize about how people get off welfare, you need a huge sample. But if you are studying a new chemical compound, you can make big generalizations from tiny samples. Human populations vary a lot; samples of a chemical

compound little or not at all. These days, representative sampling depends on statistical methods whose principles every educated person should understand.

4. **Are your reports of evidence from reliable sources?**
The problem of reliable sources turns on four issues: currency, reputation, disinterestedness, and level of source.

• **Currency:** Is your source up-to-date? Again, this varies by field. In computer science, a year-old research report is probably out-of-date; in philosophy, ancient authorities are always relevant. In general, look for the most recent work in a field.

• **Reputation:** Readers are more likely to trust evidence from people with good reputations, strong credentials, and name recognition. They will be suspicious at best of data that you pull from the Web site of someone no one has ever heard of. But even expert credentials do not ensure reliability: Linus Pauling won a Nobel Prize in chemistry, but he was judged to be a flake when he began to tout vitamin C as a cure for most ills known to medicine.

• **Disinterestedness:** Will readers be confident that, however expert your sources, they are not tainted by self-interest? Not long ago, a government study of the safety of silicone breast implants was almost wholly discredited when it was discovered that one scientist on the panel had received research funds from a company making implants. Even if that scientist had been utterly objective, the critics were right to charge that the mere appearance of a conflict of interest was enough to undermine the image of integrity of the whole panel.

• **Level of source:** Generally, you should get as close as you can to the evidence itself. The closest are primary sources. If you are studying texts, primary sources are the original books, letters, diaries, and so on. If you are studying physical phenomena, primary sources are the notebooks and the reports based directly on them of those who observed and collected the evidence "itself." For textual evidence, use a recent edition by a reputable publisher; for physical evidence, use the original article (not just the abstract or, worse, someone's report of it). Be aware that some journals have better reputations for publishing sound research than others. Find out which journals are most (and least) respected before you cite evidence from one.

If you can't find primary sources, look for reliable secondary sources—scholarly journals and books that report on primary sources. Tertiary sources report work found in secondary sources; they include textbooks, articles in encyclopedias, and mass publications like the *Reader's Digest*. If these are the only sources available, so be it, but assume that careful readers will not accept them as authoritative.

Trustworthy Reports of Evidence

We've emphasized that what you offer as evidence is almost always a report of it, and that a report predictably shapes evidence to suit a writer's own goals and interests. So when you gather evidence from the reports of others, be aware not only that your source has already shaped it, but that you will again. Even when you report your own observations of the evidence "itself," you cannot avoid giving it some "spin." To report evidence responsibly, you have to understand its different kinds, how we predictably distort it, and the best ways to present it.

Reports of Memories

As you read these words, you can feel the heft of this book, the texture of its pages. You can close the book and hear it snap; you can sniff it, even nibble at a page to taste it. Your nerve endings are reporting on the data from "out there," data that support your belief that this book exists. Now put the book down for a moment and look away. [_____] The instant you did that, the "self"-evidence of this book vanished, leaving you with nothing but mental traces—a lingering taste, perhaps; a visual or tactile memory. At that moment your memory was reconstructing those sense data, reporting the reports of your senses.

  Memories often feel like the most trustworthy evidence, a record of our "direct" experience through our senses. But in fact, memory is one of the least reliable forms of evidence. When we construct a memory of an event, our minds unconsciously give it a form to make it easy to store and recall. We shape it into a coherent story, eliminating some details, enhancing others, even inventing elements to fill out a plot. And the more impressive the event, the more our memories are likely to change it. Even when we try not to embellish a memory, it's too late because our mind has already reshaped it for us. So use evidence from memory cautiously and corroborate it with other evidence.

Never Trust Eyewitnesses

In one study, people recalling a videotape of a car accident estimated the speed of the cars differently, depending on whether they were asked how fast the cars were going when they either bumped or smashed into each other. Depending on the words, the subjects even "remembered" different amounts of broken glass, though the videotape showed none at all!

Source: Elizabeth F. Loftus and John C. Palmer, "Reconstruction of Automobile Destruction: An Example of the Interaction Between Language and Memory," Journal of Verbal Learning and Verbal Behavior 13 (1974), pp. 585–589.

Anecdotes

An anecdote is a report of memory designed for public consumption. Even if we try to stick only to known facts (and many of us don't), we reshape our already storylike memory into an even better story, adding and deleting still more details, reorganizing them to make the story funnier, more dramatic, more pointed to support whatever reason we had for telling the story in the first place. After we tell it a few times, we have turned that anecdote into a finely honed short story with a beginning, middle, and end—likely to have little relationship to the event it reports.

That's why especially persuasive anecdotes can be so treacherous, especially when we use one to dress up "objective" numerical data. When readers see pallid statistics enlivened by a vivid anecdote, the numbers take on the quality of evidence from "out there" because we seem to experience what they represent in our mind's eye. Compare these examples:

> Fifty-three percent of Americans over the age of 65 have an annual income above $30,000, but 15 percent have incomes of less than $7,000 a year.

> Around 9 A.M., the cabin attendant on TWA flight 1643 to San Francisco asked Oliver and Sarah Peters whether they wanted the western omelet or the fruit plate for breakfast. Recently retired, they were on their way to visit their children and grandchildren in San Diego, happy to be escaping the below-zero windchill in Chicago. At about the same time, 85-year-old Amanda Wilson was sitting at her kitchen table on Chicago's southside, staring at two five-dollar bills, a quarter, and a dime, trying to figure out one more time how to get through the next two weeks on 85¢ a day. She lives on $565 a month Social Security, most of which goes for heat, light, and rent on her one-room apartment. She had a daughter once, but . . .

The anecdote is a good illustration, but bad evidence.

Although all anecdotes are too far from the original event to be reliable evidence, personal anecdotes can undermine a sound argument in a special way. When you offer a personal experience to support a claim, you discourage others from asking you hard questions about it, because they would seem to challenge your truthfulness. How can someone doubt what you actually experienced, actually saw, actually felt? It feels like calling you a liar. We can challenge evidence politely when it is in the form of data from "out there," but the truth of your personal experience is in your mind, a place that is socially protected from public skepticism.

Some writers claim that personal experience is truer to the spirit of Truth than objective data. But it is not the kind of public truth that readers want as a basis for a contestable claim. So be aware that if you do use a personal anecdote as evidence, readers may be too polite to question it openly, but will silently dismiss it as they think to themselves, *Anecdotal*. Acknowledge the limits of personal evidence, *This is only my experience, but. . . .* But more importantly, look for other evidence to corroborate it.

Reports from Authorities

Some students think they offer evidence when they quote an authority. But what they usually offer is only that authority's own report of evidence, or more often, just their own reason stated in that more authoritative voice. For example, Mai might think she is supporting her claim with evidence in the form of a quotation, but here she only restates her reason in words more authoritative than her own:

> Teachers should be required to respond to their teaching evaluations $_{claim}$ because those who read them are more likely to improve their teaching than those who don't.$_{reason}$ According to J. Wills, for example, teachers who study their evaluations "profit from their openness to criticism" (*The Art of Teaching*, 330). $_{reason\ restated}$

Mai may be right that the teachers who respond to evaluations are more likely to improve, but the quoted words only restate her own reason: they are evidence only that Wills has said the same thing. Mai could strengthen her claim if she reported not just Wills's claim but his evidence as well:

> Teachers should be required to respond to their teaching evaluations $_{claim}$ because those who read them are more likely to improve their teaching than those who don't.$_{reason}$ According to J. Wills, for example, teachers who study their evaluations "profit from their openness to criticism" (*The Art of Teaching*, 330). $_{reason\ restated}$ He studied 200 teachers who spent at least an hour reviewing their evaluations. The next term, they achieved 15 percent higher evaluations than those who circulated teaching evaluations but did not read them (*The Art of Teaching*, 333–335). $_{reported\ evidence}$

When you quote authorities, you do two useful things:

- If your authority is credible, you make your position more credible.
- If your authority gathered evidence you report, you bring readers as close as they can get, short of reading the authority itself.

Of course, you still have to show that the authority has based her reasons on sound evidence.

Why Question Others' Reports?

If you need reason to suspect the reports of evidence that you find in your sources, consider some research by Robert P. Newman and Keith R. Sanders. They studied the transcripts of a National College Debate Tournament to identify every instance where a debater cited specific testimony (quotations, numbers, etc.). They then compared each citation with its source to determine how accurately the debaters reported it.. They found that more than half of the reports of reports of evidence were wrong! (Of course, we have to trust that Newman and Sanders collected their evidence accurately.)

Source: "A Study in the Integrity of Evidence," *Journal of the American Forensic Association* 2 (1965): 7–13.

Photographs, Films, and Videotapes

"Ocular proof" is compelling, because it makes us vividly feel "what really happened." For example, NATO attacked Serbia for many reasons, but only after images of refugees and massacred civilians translated abstract moral imperatives into stark images. And terrorism has become a reality in this country not just because on 9/11 it killed more than 3,000 people, but because photographs and video tapes have seared into our national memory images of the planes exploding into the World Trade Center, of people jumping hand-in-hand to their deaths, and of the collapse of the towers into a cloud of dust and rubble.

We might think that videotapes, films, photographs, and recordings are more reliable than memories, but as we all know, they can all be fabricated so convincingly that even experts can't distinguish fakes from the real thing. (Always distrust images you find on the Web.) But even when they are not doctored, images and recordings reshape what they record. That's why you must tell your readers who took the pictures or made the recording that you offer as evidence, and under what circumstances.

Quantitative Data

For some readers, numbers are the most compelling evidence, in fact the only acceptable evidence, partly because numbers seem most objective, partly because they are recorded by exacting types like scientists and accountants. If any evidence feels as though it is from "out there" in the world, it is what we can count, and what we can count we can objectively quantify.

But of course numbers, just like any other report of evidence, are shaped by the aims and interests of those who record them. When researchers gather data for an argument about the safety of air bags, the counters have to decide what to count—fatalities, serious injuries (what counts as serious?), people brought to hospitals, insurance claims, etc. They also have to decide how to organize the numbers—total fatalities, fatalities per year, per thousand, per miles driven, per trip, etc.

We might think that a table of numbers is most "objective," but that apparent objectivity is itself a rhetorical choice. While we get from these reports of evidence the same factual data, we are affected by them in different ways. The right choice depends partly on the kind of evidence your readers expect, but also on how you want them to respond.

Our Misplaced Trust in Numbers

Here's why one expert tells us to be wary of others' statistics, taken from an interview with Joel Best, author of *Damned Lies and Statistics: Untangling Numbers from the Media, Politicians, and Activists* (2001).

What do you mean when you say in your book that facts don't speak for themselves?

We all talk about facts as though they're rocks you pick up and they have an independent existence, and they don't. When you hear a statistic, someone has created that. You cannot take that number and assume that is a pure reflection of reality.

Take me through the process of how an accurate number gets transformed into an inaccurate one.

An article appears in the newsletter for the American Anorexia/Bulimia Association, and they quote a physician who says perhaps 150,000 people have anorexia, it's very serious and some people die. This was transformed, I think, first in a scholarly book, where someone said 150,000 people die from anorexia every year. You can see how this happens, maybe sloppy note-taking. Once the figure is out there, it's very hard to take back.

What's the biggest trap people fall into when hearing a number?

I think the biggest error is that we hear a number, and we automatically assume we know what is being counted. When we hear an estimate for the number of missing children, we imagine these are children abducted by strangers; we hear numbers for child abuse, and what pops into our mind is the worst possible case, and I think what people don't understand is how broadly these phenomena are being defined in order to generate these big numbers.

Source: New York Times, May 26, 2001, p. A17.

Negotiating What Counts as Evidence

When we accept a report of evidence as evidence, we tacitly agree not to question it further. For example, imagine having this exchange with Sam:

Sam: Why don't you take a course in statistics? claim

You: Why should I?

Sam: Employers are looking for people who can crunch numbers. reason

If you believe that Sam is reliable, you might accept what he says without asking for the evidence behind his reason. It doesn't matter whether his statement is really a reason or really evidence. All Sam cares about is whether you take what he says as reliable and sufficient grounds for believing his claim.

But suppose you don't quite trust him, so you ask what he bases his reason on:

Sam: Employers are looking for people who can crunch numbers. reason

You: What do you base that on?

Sam: Business magazines say that personnel directors can't find liberal arts grads who can deal with numerical data. reported evidence

Sam's response looks like reported evidence. But if you still have doubts, you might treat what he says not as a report of evidence, but only as one more subordinate reason, still in need of its own evidence.

> Sam: Business magazines say that personnel directors can't find liberal arts grads who can deal with numerical data. ~reason~
>
> You: Which ones say that?
>
> Sam: I've researched this. *Business Today* says, "According to 100 personnel directors from Fortune 500 companies, companies can't find enough liberal arts grads who can deal with complex numerical data." ~quoted~
>
> ~primary evidence~

You could question even that, asking

> You: Well, have you seen the actual survey?

(At this point, of course, Sam is probably thinking he made a mistake offering you advice in the first place.)

In the first exchange, you accepted as a basis for Sam's claim a statement that you agreed to treat as a fact. But in the longer exchanges, you and Sam negotiated what you would agree to count as a final report of evidence. Sam offered what he thought was a reliable report of evidence, but you kept treating it as just one more reason. Once Sam reads the words on the page and you question them too, the negotiation must end, because Sam has nowhere to go from there.

In much the same way, you and your reader have to agree on what to count as "true" before you can go on to agree or disagree about reasons and claims. So try to anticipate when a reader might reject what you offer as evidence as not evidence at all, but as just another reason in need of its own evidence. Imagine a conversation like the one with Sam, your reader asking again and again, *But what do you base that on?* You can't doubt everything, of course. But if you ask that question more than you think you need to, you are more likely to find a solid base of shared truth on which you and your readers can agree as a first step toward a solution to your problem.

WRITING PROCESS
Evidence

THINKING-READING-TALKING

Use Sources to Learn
What Kind of Evidence Readers Trust

As you move through your academic career, note the kinds of evidence that arguments in different fields offer: Is it quantitative data? Quotations? Field observations? Anecdotes? Interviews? Note whether sources explain how the evidence was collected. Use what you find to guide you in making your own arguments, with this qualification: Teachers usually want more evidence from their students than they do from their colleagues, not (just) because they don't trust you, but because they want to see how you think.

PREPARING AND PLANNING

Taking Notes

When you assemble an argument based on sources, your most important preparation is taking notes. Unlike the writing you do when you talk back to your readings, you have to record accurately what you may need later. When you take notes, keep several things in mind:

Notes from Written Sources
• Record all bibliographic information:

For a book, record the full title, author, and publication date, plus the name of the publisher and city. If you photocopy the title page, write down the year of publication from the back side of the title page. Include the library call number, because you may need your source again.

For a journal article, record the author, full title, volume number, date, and page numbers. Record the call number of the journal.

For an Internet source, record the URL (Uniform Resource Locator) and any information you can find about the author of the text and the date it was posted and last changed. Record the date you accessed the site.

• Summarize and paraphrase when the information is important, but its particular form of expression is not.

• Quote the exact words when they are striking or complex. If the passage or data table is long, photocopy it.

In your notes, distinguish what you quote directly from what you summarize or paraphrase, and without fail distinguish what you paraphrase from your own thinking. (Use different colored ink or cards; on a computer, use different fonts.) A week later, it's easy to think that what you took as notes are your own ideas in your own words, when in fact they belong to someone else.

• Record the context. Note whether the quote is a main point, a minor aside, a concession, etc. It is unfair to your source and reader to treat what a writer says in passing as something she would stand behind.

Notes from Interviews
• Record all identifying information—including the exact spelling of your source's name. Record the date and place of the interview.

- Tape-record the interview if you can. If you can't, try to get the exact words. If you transcribe from a tape recorder, edit out the *umm's* and *you know's*, but don't change anything else to make it sound better.

- Prepare your questions and bring them to the interview. Don't read them like a script, but use them to avoid wasting the time of whomever you are interviewing. Before you leave, glance over your questions to see if you have missed any important ones.

Notes from Observation

- Record the date and place of the observations and any relevant circumstantial details before you start. If the location is relevant, sketch a map.

- Record data precisely. If you record quantitative data, create a blank data table or chart before you start.

DRAFTING

Quoting and Paraphrasing

When you report written evidence, you have to quote directly, paraphrase, or summarize. The difference is not one of degree:

- When you quote directly, you reproduce the original text word-for-word, punctuation mark-for-punctuation mark.

- When you paraphrase, you substitute your words for the authors' in order to make a statement clearer or fit its context better. A paraphrase is usually shorter than the original, but it need not be. Readers should be able to say, "This sentence matches the one on page X."

- When you summarize, you reword and condense the original text to less than its original length. Readers should not be able to say, "This sentence matches the one on page X."

Paraphrasing or Summarizing in Disciplines that Focus on Data

In the natural sciences and the "harder" social sciences, writers draw on sources for one or more of three reasons:

- to review previous work in the common ground

- to acknowledge alternative positions

- to use the source's findings (main claim) or data to support their own claims and reasons

In these cases, readers care more about results than the words reporting them, so writers seldom quote sources; instead, they paraphrase or summarize.

Quoting in Disciplines that Focus on Words

In the humanities, writers both quote and paraphrase. Use direct quotations to

- cite the work of others as primary evidence;

- focus on the specific words of a source because they have been important in other arguments; they are especially vivid or significant; you want to focus on exactly how a source says something; you dispute the source and want to avoid seeming to create a straw man.

Paraphrase or summarize

- when you are more interested in the substance of reasons and evidence than in how they are expressed, and

- when you can say the same thing more clearly.

Don't quote just because it's easier or because you don't trust yourself to report a source fairly.

Integrating Quotations into Your Sentences

When you offer quotations as evidence, follow the conventions in your field. They differ, but here are some common ones:

- Introduce a quotation with a colon or introductory phrase.

  Plumber describes the accident that took Princess Diana's life in terms that reflect the cost of too little government regulation: "People like Diana believe they are immune from ordinary dangers and so don't bother with things like seat-belts. But everyone who died was not belted, and the one who survived was" (343).

- Weave the quotation into your own sentence (be sure the quotation fits the grammar of your sentence):

  Plumber speaks in terms that remind us of the cost of too little government regulation when he points out that "everyone who died [in that crash] was not belted, and the one who survived was" (343).

(Note that when this writer changed the original, she used square brackets to indicate the change.)

- Set off quotations of three or more lines in indented "block quote":

  After Oldenberg's balloon crashed into the ocean on his fifth failed attempt to circumnavigate the globe, his wife began to suspect there was more to his obsession than the "desire to achieve." She thought she found an answer in evolutionary biology:

> The brain of the human male evolved under circumstances where caution was essential because risk was ever-present. When civilization reduced the risk, men began to feel that their natural, evolved impulse toward caution made them weak and unmanly. When men create situations of extreme risk, it's not the risk they crave but a worthy reason to exercise their caution. (Idlewild, 135)

Avoiding Inadvertent Plagiarism

Don't paraphrase so closely that you seem to follow a source word for word. For example, the following paraphrase would plagiarize this paragraph:

> If you paraphrase, avoid language so similar to the source that your words correspond to its words. For instance, this plagiarizes what you just read.

To avoid inadvertent plagiarism, read the original; sit back and think what it means; then express it in your own words without looking back. You are too close to the original if you can run your finger along a paraphrase and recognize the same sequence of concepts (not words). The following would not be plagiarism of this paragraph:

> Williams and Colomb suggest that to keep from plagiarizing, digest the meaning of a passage, summarize it in your own words, then compare the sequence of ideas in your summary with the source. (126).

Our advice applies to most fields in the humanities, but practice differs in different fields. In the law, for example, writers regularly use the exact words of a judge's ruling without quotation marks. In some social sciences, researchers closely paraphrase the main finding of an experiment. Learn and follow the practice in your field.

INQUIRIES

1. Invent three or four plausible scenarios in which others will feel you are being rude to ask them to justify a report of evidence they have just offered. What makes your question impolite?

2. In the early history of science, experimenters would invite other scientists to witness an experiment so that they could testify to the accuracy of the data gathered. Would it seem reasonable today for a scientist to insist on watching data being collected before she accepted it as sound? Why not? How then do we today get "testimony" concerning the reliability of reports of research?

3. Should reproductions count as primary evidence? How about a videotape of an event? An audiotape of a speech? A photograph? Would you trust a tape or photo more or less if you knew the person who offered it was technologically naïve? What if that person were a technological whiz? Why

should that matter? Would it help to have witnesses who could testify about the circumstances in which the tape or photo was produced?

4. A recent book that uses stories as evidence is *I, Rigoberta Menchú*, a searing account of atrocities allegedly committed by the Guatemalan army. Written by Rigoberta Menchú Tum, the human rights activist and winner of the Nobel Peace Prize, the book has become highly controversial required reading on hundreds of campuses because it sparks a debate over the "higher value" of falsehood over truth. The controversy began when prestigious schools like Stanford required the book in general education courses, in some cases replacing writers like Shakespeare. Then in 1998, David Stoll, a specialist in Mayan history, showed that Menchú had fabricated some of her most sensational stories:

    - She described herself as a child working in near-slave conditions, unable to speak Spanish until adulthood, but she had actually attended Catholic boarding schools.

    - She describes acts of violence as though she witnessed them; in fact, she was away at school most of the time.

    - She says she watched the Guatemalan military burn her brother alive, but she wasn't there when it happened and the military probably did not do it.

    - She says another brother starved to death, but she had no such brother.

    - She says that her family lands were confiscated by wealthy landowners; in fact, they were lost to her father's in-laws.

Menchú at first denied that she had committed "purposeful inaccuracies," adding, "I didn't find anything in these reports that changes the fact that my people are dead. And that is my truth" (*New York Times*, January 21, 1999). Later, she admitted some inaccuracies, but has yet to recant her story.

Her critics were severe: one nominated her for the "Nobel Prize for Lying." Most of her supporters echoed her defense that she told a "larger truth." Some attacked Stoll for valuing mere fact over a "higher" truth. Others suggested that facts don't even matter: "Menchú made it clear from the outset that [she] had a political purpose, . . . to expose the atrocities committed by the Guatemalan army. This was not the fruit of some judicial investigation striving to be fair" (*Guardian*, December 16, 1998). But even before Stoll had exposed Menchú, her admirers had argued that an oppressed person has an authenticity that lets her speak for all her people; that what matters is not truth, but personal, ethical, and economic motives that break the "silence of the oppressed."

Suppose that Menchú's critics are right: What she says she saw, she did not. In fact, some of the things she said happened never happened at all. But also suppose that in a sense she is right: things like those she described did happen to people like her and her family. Should she have described her work as a work of fiction? Would it have had the same impact? Would it have been effective to add incidents that happened to others without pretending they happened to her? List reasons for accepting or rejecting her "larger truth" defense. Which weigh more with you?

5. The Greek philosopher Aristotle argued that fiction describes events more truthfully than a history. A history, he said, has to stick to the facts, whereas fiction can describe things more plausibly—as they should have occurred, not just as they happened to. Can you think of a way to defend Menchú's book based on Aristotle's idea of truthfulness? Sketch the major steps in such an argument. Would *you* accept such a defense?

IN A NUTSHELL

About Your Argument . . .

No skill is more useful than distinguishing reasons, evidence, and reports of evidence from your readers' point of view. You need more and better evidence when you want readers to change important beliefs, to do something costly or difficult, or to accept a solution that may create new problems. Your biggest challenge will be to find enough evidence to satisfy your readers, because as writers we all tend to be satisfied with less evidence than our readers want.

Once you think you have enough evidence, evaluate it in terms of the four maxims of quality: Is it accurate, precise, representative, and reliable? Use each kind of evidence only in the ways it is most reliable:

- Memories are always unreliable, because our minds shape them into a storylike structure influenced by what we believe or want to be true. Always try to find corroborating evidence.

- Anecdotes are even less reliable, because we impose on them an even more shapely story structure. Anecdotes can be good illustrations, but they are never the best evidence.

- Reports from authorities may be evidence only of what they believe. Distinguish what they offer as reasons from the evidence they report.

- Photographs and recordings are never objective. Even when they haven't been doctored, they depict just a slice of what they seem to represent.

- Quantitative data can be represented in different ways, and each gives it a "spin."

Remember that you ask readers to accept reports of evidence in lieu of the evidence itself, so they must be confident that you report it accurately. Along with warrants, evidence is one of the two anchors that readers must agree on before you can even make an argument.

. . . and About Writing It

When you report what a written source says, ask whether your readers expect the exact words or a paraphrase. In general, those in the humanities are more likely to expect the exact words; those in other fields will accept close paraphrases.

When you copy notes into your argument, be aware of how easy it is to forget that what you copy is not your own words, but those of your sources. You can avoid that by scrupulously distinguishing in your notes between your own words and those from a source. If you take notes on a computer, use a distinctive font; if you write them out, use colored ink or cards—whatever will help you distinguish your own words from those of your sources. You can afford to be wrong; you cannot afford to be accused of plagiarism.

Warranting Claims and Reasons

In this chapter we address the difficult task of deciding whether you have connected reasons and claims soundly. Even when reasons are true and based on reliable evidence, readers have to believe that each one is relevant to the claim it supports. When that relevance is in question, you show it through warrants.

Once readers see why your problem matters and understand your solution, they look for reasons that support it and for the evidence on which you base them. If readers don't see your reasons, they won't see the shape of your argument. But even if they do, they may still reject your claim if they do not see how your reasons are relevant to it. For example,

> **Tarik:** You should buy a gun _{claim} because you live alone. _{reason}
>
> **Leah:** Why is the fact that I live alone relevant to buying a gun?

How could Tarik respond? He might assert a general principle:

> **Tarik:** When you live in an isolated place, you need protection. _{warrant}

If Leah accepts this principle and believes it applies to her situation, then Tarik has shown her why his reason is relevant to his claim. If not, Tarik has to defend his principle.

When you think your readers might question not the truth of a reason, but its *relevance* to your claim, you have to offer them one more element of argument to convince them that your reasoning is sound—a general principle that connects your reason to your claim, a warrant. In this chapter, we explain how warrants guarantee that relevance.

How Warrants Connect Reasons and Claims

Consider this exchange:

Maude: It's just so tragic when someone like Princess Diana dies so young.

Harry: Well, her death wasn't a big tragedy _{claim} because her image was created by press agents and the media. _{reason}

Maude: Her image was certainly a media creation, but why does that mean her death was not tragic? It doesn't follow.

That question asks Harry to think not about his facts but about his reasoning.

Harry: Her death may have been sad, but you don't have a real tragedy when the person who dies is not a substantial person, but just the image of one. _{warrant} Di was mostly a media creation, _{reason} so her death was not really a tragedy. _{claim}

Maude did not ask Harry for evidence (though she could have: *What evidence do you have that Di was just a media creation?*). She seems to accept that. Instead, she asked him about his reasoning: *How is your reason relevant to your claim?*

In response, Harry offered Maude not more facts about Princess Di, but a warrant, a general principle applying to *any* such person. That general principle explains why he thinks his reason is relevant to his claim. If Maude accepts the warrant and reason, she must accept the claim, because it logically follows.

We also use warrants to explain how evidence connects to a reason. Suppose Harry does offer evidence to support his reason:

Harry: Her death was not really a tragedy _{claim} because she was mostly a media creation. _{reason} Di was never known for her accomplishments. **The public knows so much about her only because the press published more words about her lovelife than any other woman in the world.** _{evidence}

If Maude questioned not the truth but the relevance of that evidence, Harry would have to explain it with a warrant:

Maude: That may be true. But how does that make her a media creation? She was also a wife and mother and a good person.

Harry: Anyone who is famous, not for what she accomplished, but only because the press makes her private life public, is mostly a media creation. _{warrant}

What Warrants Look Like

Warrants come in all shapes and sizes, but they always have or imply two parts. One part names a general circumstance:

Someone is a media creation with no substance.

The second part states a general conclusion that we can infer from that circumstance:

> Such a person's death might be sad, but is no tragedy.

Put together, the two parts explicitly state a general principle of reasoning:

> When a person is only a media creation, _{part 1} that person's death might be sad, but is no tragedy. _{part 2}

> When dogs scratch _{part 1} they may have fleas. _{part 2}

> When someone has cold hands, _{part 1} that person has a warm heart. _{part 2}

We can also state those warrants in ways that only imply the connection between the parts:

> The death of a media creation, _{part 1} is sad but no tragedy. _{part 2}

> Scratching dogs _{part 1} may have fleas. _{part 2}

> Cold hands, _{part 1} warm heart. _{part 2}

There is no one right way to state a warrant, but for our purposes we will state them in the same way every time, not because that's how you should too, but because it is the clearest way for us to explain how they work. We will follow this formula:

> Whenever X, Y.

Sometimes, we might choose other introductory words: *if, when, if and only if.* But *whenever* is especially useful because it encourages us to consider how widely we can apply the warrant. *Whenever* implies that a warrant is true under all circumstances, something that is rarely so.

Warrants are most familiar to us as proverbs:

> When the cat's away the mice will play.

Schematically, we can represent that warrant like this:

> The authority is absent —[so we infer]→ those under that authority will slack off.

If you believe that *general* principle, then you can link a *specific* instance of authority being absent to a *specific* instance of those under that authority slacking off. Schematically, the link looks like this:

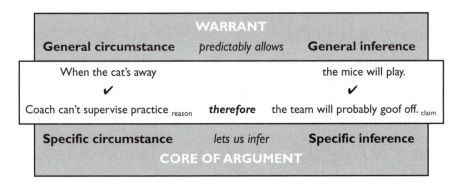

The check marks indicate that we think the specific circumstance qualifies as a legitimate instance of the general circumstance in the warrant, and the specific inference qualifies as a legitimate example of the warrant's general inference. (We'll see cases where they don't.)

We can reverse the order, if we choose:

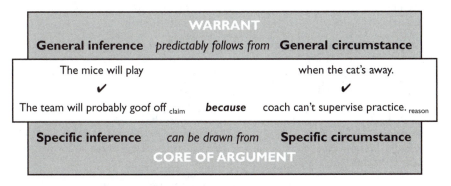

Warrants are the glue of arguments. They attach reasons to claims.

Warrants as Expressions of Cultural Codes

Warrants help us understand why people of different cultures struggle to make good arguments together. We all reason alike, but different cultures start from different assumptions. Those assumptions are not just static beliefs, but dynamic principles that tell us how to reason about specific facts. We often express them in proverbs that reveal much about how we think and what we value. For example, suppose we say of a child, *She really stands out from the crowd because she thinks for herself and says what she thinks.* We might then conclude, *When she grows up, she'll get her way,* because we have a cultural assumption reflected in a familiar proverb:

The squeaky wheel gets the grease.

(continued on next page)

(continued from previous page)
But the Japanese have a proverb that warns people not to stand out:

The nail that sticks up gets hammered down.

In other words, when someone stands out from the crowd, that person will be—rightly—forced to conform. So we agree on the same fact, a child standing out from the rest, but our different communities justify different inferences from it because they reason from different assumptions. Such differences cause many cultural conflicts. Expressing them clearly as warrants is difficult, but lets us at least understand, if not always resolve, our differences.

Distinguishing Reasons and Warrants

At first glance a warrant seems a lot like a reason, and so it's easy to confuse them. Consider this argument:

Though Franklin Roosevelt would not appear in public in his wheelchair or be photographed in it, his federal monument should depict him in his chair. claim He overcame a great disability to become a great leader, statement of support 1 and a great leader should be remembered as much for the challenges he overcame as for his achievements. statement of support 2

Those two supporting statements both feel like reasons. In fact, in ordinary conversation, that's what we might call them both:

The Federal monument dedicated to Franklin Roosevelt should depict him in his wheelchair. claim *The first reason* is that he overcame a great disability to become a great leader. statement of support 1 *The second reason* is that any great leader should be remembered as much for the challenges he overcame as for his achievements. statement of support 2

But those two statements support the claim in such different ways that to understand how arguments work we have to use different terms to name them.

- The first statement refers specifically to Roosevelt and to Roosevelt alone. It is a *specific* reason to support the *specific* claim that a monument should depict Roosevelt in his wheelchair.
- The second statement has nothing specifically to do with Roosevelt or his monument. It is a *general* principle stating that we should remember *any* great leader for overcoming a challenge *of any kind.* If we believe that Roosevelt was a great leader who overcame great obstacles, then he's covered by that generalization we call a warrant.

Warrants Versus Reasons

In ordinary talk, it does no harm to call a warrant a reason. Warrants are, after all, reasons for connecting a reason and a claim. One of our students called warrants *extended reasons.* And in fact, that captures a bit of what a warrant does: it "extends" over a reason and claim, holding them together. Other students have asked us, *Doesn't a warrant just say the same thing as the reason and claim, but in a different way?* Not quite. A warrant covers the same conceptual territory as the reason and claim, but a much wider territory as well, one that includes an indefinite number of other reasons and claims, involving not only leaders and challenges we know of, but countless others we don't, even those still to be born.

The Challenge of Using Warrants

Your challenge is not just to understand warrants; it's also to know how to use them—and when. To decide when and how to state warrants, ask yourself four questions:

- Will readers think of my warrant without my stating it?
- Will they think it is true?
- If they think it is true, will they think it applies to the reason and claim?
- If they think it is true and applicable, will they think it appropriate to their community?

1. Can Readers Recognize Your Warrant on Their Own?

In any argument, we state very few warrants, often none at all. The more we share assumptions, beliefs, and values with readers, the fewer warrants we need to state. In fact, if you and your readers are on culturally intimate terms, they may feel you are talking down to them if you state warrants they think should go without saying (imagine someone who keeps quoting proverbs). On the other hand, when your basic experiences and values differ from those of your readers, you usually have to state as warrants many of your important assumptions, values, and definitions.

Most cases fall somewhere between, forcing us to decide on a case by case which principles to state and which not. To do that, you have to anticipate when readers cannot imagine a principle for connecting your reason and claim or might imagine one different from yours. Consider this little argument:

Our school needs more writing tutors _{claim} because we are unsure our education is worth our rising tuition costs. _{reason 1} Tuition has gone up faster than inflation. _{reason 2} In 1997, inflation was 2.4%, but tuition rose 5.1%; in 1998, inflation was 2.1%, but tuition rose 6.7%. _{report of evidence}

The dean might respond:

True, tuition has gone up faster than inflation. You may even be right that we need more writing tutors. But why do you think we need them *because* you are not sure you are getting your money's worth? Why does your reason—you're not sure you're getting your money's worth—*have anything to do with your claim*—that we need more tutors? It's not relevant.

That is a hard question. The dean is not saying that she rejects either the reason or the claim, but that she can't imagine any principle that would make the reason relevant to it.

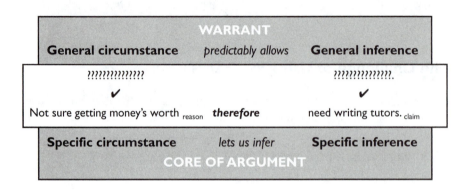

If you can immediately think of warrants that connect each important reason to your main claim, ask whether your readers will think of the same ones as quickly. If so, you don't need to state them. But be aware that we are all likely to assume that readers think more like us than they really do.

If you can't think of a warrant connecting a reason to your main claim, your readers probably can't either. In that case, you need to find one and state it explicitly. Here is a way to do that.

First, replace the specific terms in your reason and claim with general ones:

> We are not sure we are getting our **money's worth** from our **tuition**, so we need more **writing tutors**.

> We are not sure we are getting a **benefit equal to** our **cost**, so we are entitled to more **services**.

Then rephrase the general version with a *whenever*:

> Whenever we are uncertain that we are getting value equal to our cost, we are entitled to more services.

You can know whether your readers will accept a warrant only after you state it for yourself. That one seems dubious: Why should uncertainty about value for cost entitle a person to demand more?

2. Is Your Warrant True?

As does that one about uncertain benefits calling for more services, a warrant fails when we reject it as false. Here is an argument about gangsta rap:

The lyrics of gangsta rap are so vulgar _{reason} that they should be banned from radio. _{claim} Whenever language is degrading, it should not be allowed to circulate in public. _{warrant}

We can rephrase that warrant into our standard form, *Whenever X, Y:*

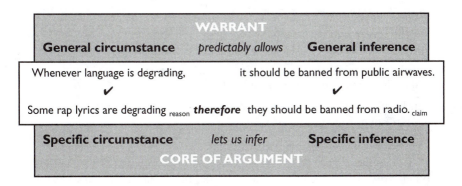

If we accept the warrant and reason, then the claim follows. But someone might reject the warrant because it is factually untrue or because another warrant trumps it:

> I can't agree, because whenever we express our ideas, the Constitution bars anyone from interfering with that right. _{competing warrant} So even though you might not like the lyrics in gangsta rap, they have the same constitutional protection as any expression of ideas.

Or that person might also respond with a counterexample that implies the original warrant is not always true:

> I can't agree. According to the Supreme Court, the First Amendment protects sexually explicit movies that are degrading to women. _{counterexample} So even though you may not like the degrading language in gangsta rap, it has the same constitutional protection.

If the counterexample is relevant, it should make us doubt the original warrant. Schematically, the counterargument looks like this:

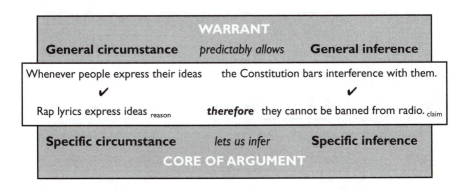

Now the question of banning such lyrics turns into a question of which warrant is more important in our system of beliefs. To settle that, the person making that argument would have to make another argument treating those dueling warrants as claims needing their own reasons, evidence, and yet more warrants.

Overreaching Warrants

We might accept some warrants as true *in general,* but not when people try to use them to justify extreme cases. What about the following argument?

> I helped you wash your car, _{reason} so you should help me paint my house. _{claim}
> After all, one good turn deserves another. _{warrant}

If your friend did help you wash your car, you might feel you owed him something, but not as much as he asks:

> You did help me wash my car, and in general one good turn deserves another, but only when the magnitude of the returned favor is proportional to the original one.

In other words, the warrant is generally true, but it has limits. And once you think of one limit, you can think of more:

> . . . and so long as I am capable of doing it, and so long as the favor is requested reasonably close to the first good turn, and so long as . . .

When we state a warrant like *One good turn deserves another,* we rarely, if ever, add the obvious limitations: *Of course you can do only what you are able to; of course you expect that a returned favor won't be asked for thirty years later.* All that goes without saying, so we don't say it. What's tricky about using warrants is not just that we usually take them for granted; even when we do state them, we take for granted their default limitations as well.

3. Does Your Warrant Actually Apply to the Reason and Claim?

This next problem is the most difficult to grasp. Consider this argument:

> I helped you wash your car, _{reason} so you should help me cheat on my test. _{claim}
> After all, one good turn deserves another. _{warrant}

Represented graphically, it looks like this:

The warrant is true, and helping you wash your car is a legitimate example of doing a good turn. So if your friend did help you wash your car, how could you refuse to help him cheat? You might say this:

> True, one good turn deserves another, but in this case, helping you cheat on a test *does not count as* a legitimate example of "a good turn." In fact, it would be a bad turn. So your reason is not relevant to your claim.

The warrant just does not apply to the claim, because the claim is not a legitimate example of the warrant.

We know this point is not easy to grasp, so here is another example, with Tarik still trying to get Leah to buy a gun:

Tarik: You should buy a gun. _{claim}

Leah: Why is that?

Tarik: The crime rate is up. _{reason}

Leah: Why should the fact that crime is up mean I should buy a gun?

Tarik: When your personal security is threatened, you should take reasonable precautions to protect yourself. _{warrant}

Leah: I agree that when we are threatened we should take reasonable precautions to protect ourselves, and maybe the crime rate is up. And maybe I should even buy a gun. But first, the crime rate being up *does not count for me as* an instance of my security being threatened, and second, even if it did, buying a gun *would not count for me as* a reasonable precaution.

Leah is saying that for her neither Tarik's reason nor his claim *count as* an example of being threatened or taking reasonable precautions. Schematically, it looks like this (the **X**s indicate Leah does not consider the specific circumstance or inference to be legitimate examples of the warrant):

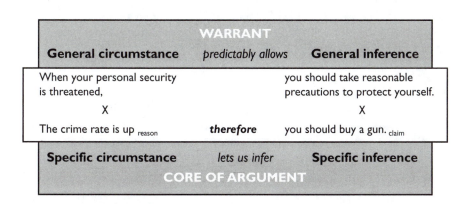

It might seem that warrants are too abstract to feel strongly about. But they express our deepest values. It is easier to change the facts we believe than to change something as entrenched as our values and definitions.

4. Is Your Warrant Appropriate to Your Readers' Community?

Warrants can fail in one more way, having less to do with truth or reasoning, than with their appropriateness. Some warrants are shared by most of us:

> When people tell many lies, we eventually distrust what they say.

Other warrants reflect the beliefs of different historical times. A change between these two warrants marked a change from one period in European history to another:

> When evidence contradicts traditional beliefs and authorities, ignore the evidence.

> When evidence contradicts traditional authority, question the authority.

The second characterizes what some call the modern skeptical mind.

There are also beliefs shared by most in the United States, but not by all Western societies:

> When an action is protected by a constitution, government may not interfere with it.

As communities become smaller, they share increasingly specialized warrants. Here's one shared by only a few specialists in animal behavior:

> When creatures engage in complex behavior they have not learned, that behavior is probably innate.

Those new to a field often find its arguments baffling, because professionals writing to professionals leave only glimpses of their assumptions, enough for other experts, but not for newcomers. None of us can avoid moments in our education when we feel baffled because those at home in a community we are just entering do not feel obligated to justify their reasoning. We learn those unstated ways of reasoning only from experience.

Information Overload?

If you are reacting as have many students using this book, you may be feeling overwhelmed with detail. We've given you a lot to think about and, what's harder, to put into practice. So don't be discouraged if you are feeling like the student who said this:

> Why do I feel less in control of making arguments as I read more about them? I feel like I'm writing worse, not better.

What we told him may encourage you: Several years ago some researchers tested new medical students to learn how well they could read X-rays for lung cancer. They found something odd. New med students quickly learned to do it pretty well, but as they gained more experience, they got worse. Then they got better at it again. The researchers concluded that at first, medical students saw exactly what they were told to see. But as they learned more about lungs, chests, and everything else that casts an X-ray shadow, they got confused: The more they learned, the less able they were to sort it out. But once they did learn to sort it out, they could see what was relevant and got better at reading X-rays again.

That's probably what's making you feel less in control of making arguments. You have more to think about than you did a few weeks ago. But it's not just that: you are probably demanding more of yourself, because you see more clearly what you must do. So as paradoxical as it may seem, your temporary confusion is a sign of progress.

Warranting Evidence as Relevant

Readers expect evidence to be relevant to reasons in the same way that they expect reasons to be relevant to claims. And for the most part, you warrant that connection in the same way:

> People condemn gangsta rap but I think it should be accepted as legitimate artistic expression $_{claim}$ because it reflects the experience of many who listen to it. $_{reason}$ Every teen-ager I know has at some time felt anger and rage against authorities. $_{report\ of\ evidence}$ When a lot of people share an emotion, then whatever expresses those emotions reflects their experience. $_{warrant}$

What gets tricky is warranting a body of evidence consisting of numerical data, quotations, pictures, and drawings as relevant to some reason. For example:

> As Hamlet stands behind his stepfather Claudius while he is at prayer, he demonstrates a cool and rational mind. $_{claim}$ He impulsively wants to kill Claudius on the spot, but he pauses to reflect. **If he kills Claudius while praying, he sends his soul to heaven. But Hamlet wants him damned to hell forever. So he coolly decides to kill him later:** $_{reason}$
>
>> Now might I do it [kill him] pat, now he is praying:
>> And now I'll do't; and so he goes to heaven;
>> And so am I reveng'd . . . [Hamlet pauses to think]
>> [But this] villain kills my father; and for that,
>> I, his sole son, do this same villain send to heaven[?]
>> Why, this is hire and salary, not revenge. $_{report\ of\ evidence}$

Someone might question the relevance of that report of evidence to the reason:

> I don't see how those words show that Hamlet "coolly decides to kill his father later."

If so, we'd have to describe the quotation in words that make its evidence match the evidence side of the warrant:

> Here, Hamlet carefully considers the consequences of killing Claudius step by step, which is a sign of a man who has put aside passion, at least temporarily, in favor of cool reason.

The same is true with tables, charts, graphs, pictures, and musical scores: describe what you see in the evidence that matches the evidence side of your warrant.

Arguing by Evidence Versus Arguing by Warrants

We make arguments in two common ways: We support claims with reasons based on evidence or we derive claims from reasons covered by warrants. Most academic and professional arguments rest on evidence, which puts a premium on fact; some civic and many personal arguments rest on warrants, which puts a premium on principle.

For example, suppose a sociologist opposed a needle-exchange program by making this argument from evidence:

> We should abolish the Southport needle-exchange program. _{claim} It has made the drug problem worse, _{reason 1} because it causes people to use more drugs. _{reason 2} A study of those who have participated in it shows that 70 percent have increased their use of drugs; the average rate has grown from 5.7 to 9.2 injections per week. _{evidence}

This argument rests on its evidence, without bothering to state its warrants. Someone who disagreed might question the source or soundness of the evidence, but she would not question its warrants because the relevance of the reasons to the claim seems obvious: *of course* we should abolish a program that increases drug use and makes the drug problem worse.

But suppose a politician made this argument opposing the same program:

> We all know that when you make risky behavior safer, you encourage more people to engage in it. _{warrant} Since the Southport needle-exchange program makes drug use safer, _{reason 1} it encourages people to use more drugs _{reason 2} and so makes the drug problem worse. _{reason 3} We should therefore abolish the program. _{claim}

This argument rests on its warrant, without bothering to cite any evidence. Few of us would ask for evidence supporting reason 1 (that the program makes drug use safer), because that's what such programs are intended to do. Here, it's the reason that seems self-evidently true. So, to accept this claim, we have only to decide whether the stated warrant is true and applicable.

That is an argument from a *principle expressed as a warrant*. When we make that kind of argument, we feel relieved of the burden of providing any evidence at all, because we have to show only that our general principle applies to the case at hand. In fact, this one is an all-purpose warrant that could be used against *any* program intended to reduce the cost of *any form of risky behavior*, from automobile seat belts to the distribution of condoms in schools.

Most thoughtful readers are skeptical of arguments from principle because they ask us to accept a claim based only on doctrinal truths rather than the facts of the matter. They are more likely than arguments from evidence to seem openly ideological. The danger in making them is that your entire argument falls if readers either reject the principle or deny that it applies. You may not have to offer evidence to support your reasons, but readers are likely to demand entire arguments to defend your principle.

```
┌─────────────────────────────────────────────────┐
│                 WRITING PROCESS                   │
│                    Warrants                       │
└─────────────────────────────────────────────────┘
```

PREPARING AND PLANNING

Identify Your Key Assumptions

When you plan an argument, don't focus only on your key points; you also have to understand the assumptions that go without saying for you, but may not for your reader: *What do I believe that my readers must also believe (but may not) before they will think that my reasons are relevant to my claims?* You'll find this one of the hardest questions to answer, because we all take our deepest beliefs for granted, rarely questioning them from someone else's point of view.

Suppose you want to argue that the drinking age should be lowered to eighteen because eighteen-year-olds are subject to the draft: What general principle must your readers *already* believe before they will accept that argument?

> When you're old enough to vote, marry, or die for your country, you're old enough to drink.

But is that true? If so, it's perhaps because you believe a more general warrant:

> When a person is old enough to assume basic civic responsibilities, then that person is old enough to engage in all adult activities.

But is that true? Why do you think so?

Before they agree that eighteen-year-olds should be allowed to drink, some readers would also have to hold other beliefs unconnected to drinking in particular but still relevant to the issue:

> When we determine maturity of judgment, we cannot decide on the basis of age alone.

> When we want to prevent bad consequences of overindulging in an activity, we should not ban the activity but try to prevent excess.

> When we criminalize behavior that many people approve of, we do not prevent that behavior, we just make it more attractive.

None of those beliefs directly concerns drinking, but if you favor drinking by eighteen-year-olds, you have to hope that your readers would not reject those assumptions out of hand. Or if you think they would, then you have to make an argument supporting them. You must also think about their limits: Are those principles true under any and all circumstances? You might finally decide not to state any of these warrants explicitly in your argument, but you benefit from the discipline of trying to think what they are.

Locate Warrants Where They Do the Most Good

Finding the best place for warrants is tricky, but here are two reliable principles:

1. Lay out important warrants before you offer claims and reasons. If you think readers might reject them, make an argument supporting them.

    For example, suppose you want to argue that schools should teach not facts, but skills. Rather than jumping straight into the reasons and evidence, you might lay down some general principles that you intend to argue from:

    > **When we educate young people in a democracy, our first job is to help them become productive citizens who can make the good decisions necessary for living in a dynamic democratic system.** _{warrant} [Add reasons and evidence supporting this assertion.] Given that responsibility, _{reason} our schools should focus on more than transmitting facts; they should develop children's ability to analyze those facts critically. _{claim}

2. State warrants that readers are unlikely to contest as a logical flourish after you've offered a specific claim and supporting reasons, like a punch line that leaves readers with a sense that the conclusion was inevitable.

    > We can no longer be objective about Senator Z's private behavior. _{claim} There are too many reports of unsavory incidents to think that he is innocent of everything he's been charged with. _{reason} **After all, where there's smoke, there's fire.** _{warrant}

Use Analogies as Surrogate Warrants

You can imply a warrant using analogies. This claim is based on a warrant (the reason is implied):

> Don't worry if you begin to feel less in control of making arguments as this book goes on. **When people learn a difficult skill requiring complex knowledge, they almost always perform worse when they first learn that knowledge but improve as they gain experience using it.** _{warrant} So you'll have a period of confusion before you master the craft of argument. _{claim}

We can base the same claim on an analogy:

> Don't worry if you begin to feel less in control of making arguments as this book goes on. **Just as medical students predictably get worse at reading X-rays before they become experts, so you'll have a period of confusion before you master the craft of argument.** _{analogy}

The analogy implies that an unstated warrant covers both cases and connects a claim known to be true (the *just as* part) to a claim in question (the *so* part).

And, of course, you can combine them:

> Don't worry if you begin to feel less in control of making arguments as this book goes on. When people learn a difficult skill requiring complex knowledge, they almost always perform worse when they first learn that knowledge but improve as they gain experience using it. _{warrant} Just as medical students predictably get worse at reading X-rays before they become experts, so you'll have a period of confusion before you fully master the craft of argument. _{analogy}

Readers judge analogies as they do warrants. They must first believe that your point of comparison (the *just as* part) is true—med students do in fact read X-rays worse as they first gain experience but then get better. Then they must believe that your analogy matches the claim and reason you are trying to connect—that *getting worse at reading X-rays* matches the unstated *being confused about arguments* and that *becoming expert at reading X-rays* matches *mastering the craft of argument.*

Use analogies

- when you think readers will respond better to a vivid concrete example than to a general statement of a principle;
- when you can't think of a way to state the warrant convincingly;
- when you have stated several warrants and don't want to overdo it.

Avoid analogies

- when readers might question your comparison;
- when they might not see how it applies to the reason and claim;
- when they might infer a warrant different from yours.

EXAMPLE

Analogy

In this passage, the movie critic Michael Medved uses analogy to defend a proposal to require age identification before young people can see movies rated PG-13 and R.

Skeptics raise substantive objections to nearly all the current reform proposals. In today's multiplexes, a resourceful kid might easily buy a ticket to *Tarzan,* but then quietly slip into the theater that's showing *The Matrix.* Serious new policies might also give rise to a flourishing new market for fake IDs. Meanwhile, the "forbidden fruit" effect may well kick in. By making adult material more difficult to see, we may succeed only in making it seem more alluring and desirable.

Such arguments might also be deployed, however, against long-standing age-based restrictions on the purchase of tobacco and alcohol. Yet no one doubts that these restrictions reduce the levels of youthful indulgence. We don't let twelve-year-olds legally buy cigarettes even though some of them are wily enough to circumvent the rules.

Source: Michael Medved, "Hollywood Murdered Innocence," *Wall Street Journal,* June 16, 1999.

INQUIRIES

1. Is it possible for two people to agree that some reason supports some claim, even though they are relying on completely different warrants? For example, here's a reason and claim that two people might agree on:

   Grades should be assigned on a curve _{claim} because then we would know who are the most deserving students. _{reason}

   But here are two different warrants that would "cover" that claim and reason:

   When society wants to identify its future elite, it should do so in a way that makes sharp distinctions in quality of performance.

   Whenever you want to make teachers objectively identify the hardest-working students, you should force them to rely on the statistically sound assignment of grades.

   Imagine two people who accepted the claim, but each on the basis of a different warrant. Would they stop agreeing if they learned about the other's warrant? In other words, are some agreements too shallow to survive shared knowledge?

2. Suppose two people agree to the following:

   Whenever you want to make teachers objectively identify the hardest-working students, you should force them to rely on statistically sound assignment of grades. _{warrant} Grades should therefore be assigned on a curve. _{claim}

   Can we conclude that the two people have deeper agreement because they agree on a shared warrant? Suppose they had these two reasons:

   We need to prevent teachers from judging students on superficial matters of personality, _{reason} so grades should be assigned on a curve. _{claim}

   We need to make sure teachers identify students who do not work hard, _{reason} so grades should be assigned on a curve. _{claim}

   Both reasons would count as good examples of the reason side of the warrant. But do these two people really agree? Would they feel that they agreed? Maybe when we agree, we don't agree as much as we think. Are there times when we should be satisfied with shallow agreement? Are there times when we should not?

3. The warrant about good turns is one that we might describe as signaling obligation: "When X is the case, we should do Y." Look at the popular proverbs listed below. Turn them into "When, then" warrants, then decide what kind of relationship they signal. Is it cause-effect, effect-cause, appearance-reality, etc.?

   Where there's smoke there's fire.

   One rotten apple spoils the barrel.

   You can't tell a book by its cover.

   Look before you leap.

   If you've seen one, you've seen them all.

   What sorts of limitations apply to these?

4. From a dictionary of proverbs, select a dozen or so that you find odd, puzzling, untrue. For each one, try to construct a little story in which someone follows the proverb. Here's an example:

   Alana wanted to go dancing on Saturday with her friend Tanya, who already had a date. So Tanya tells Alana, "There's a guy in my chem lab this afternoon who would love to go with you. Want me to talk to him?" "Maybe," says Alana, "but first I want to come by the lab." "Why?" asks Tanya. Replies Alana, "Look before you leap."

   Do you find it hard to invent stories in which people would follow a puzzling or untrue proverb? What does that tell you about your ability to understand the warrants of others? Can you imagine yourself acting in the way the characters in your stories do? What does that tell you about your ability to accept the warrants of others?

IN A NUTSHELL

About Your Argument . . .

Warrants are difficult to understand, so if you're not entirely certain about them, don't feel that you are alone. A warrant is a general statement that explicitly or implicitly relates a set of general conditions to a set of general consequences. We've expressed warrants in this regular way:

> When children behave in violent ways, it is because they have been influenced by violent movies, TV, and computer games.

But that can be expressed in a less explicit way:

> Violent movies, TV, and computer games cause violent children.

However we express a warrant, it serves to link a reason to a claim:

> More children are playing Mortal Kombat than ever before. ~reason~ We will see more children attacking other children ~claim~ since violent movies, TV, and computer games cause violent children. ~warrant~

If we believe the warrant and the reason, we have to believe the claim.

... and About Writing It

Your readers might have problems with warrants in five ways:

- They might not see your warrant.
- They might think it's not true.
- They might think that it is true, but needs to be limited.
- They might think the warrant does not "cover" the reason or the claim.
- The warrant might not be appropriate to your audience.

When you address highly contested issues, step back and ask yourself what you think your readers must believe *in general* about your issue *before* they will accept your specific reasons as relevant to your specific claims. If you think that your readers do not share those warrants, then you have to make them the center of their own argument, making them claims that need their own reasons, evidence, and warrants.

Chapter 8

Acknowledgments and Responses

In this chapter we discuss the kinds of questions, reservations, and objections that you can expect readers to raise about your arguments. We show you how to anticipate them and decide which to acknowledge and how to respond to them.

You can build complex arguments by answering just the first four of the five questions of argument:

What are you **claiming?**

What are your **reasons** on which you base your claim?

What is your **evidence** on which you base your reasons?

How do your **warrants** connect your reasons to your claims?

But when an issue is contestable, you can seem arrogant or even ignorant if you fail to imagine and acknowledge the fifth question readers are certain to ask:

But what about these alternatives, reservations and objections? How would you respond to someone who said . . . ?

It can be hard to answer questions like that, because we don't like to acknowledge that we might be, if not wrong, then not completely right. Our impulse is to become defensive, to counterattack (two more argument-as-warfare metaphors), fighting off (again) our adversaries' objections (yet again). But when you can imagine and then calmly answer such questions, not just once but throughout your argument, you deepen and broaden it and project a judicious and thoughtful ethos, something that eventually takes on an independent existence as your reputation.

The Importance of Other Viewpoints

When we say, *There are two sides to every question,* we underestimate how complex most issues are because the sides are more often three or four, and they differ not just over claims, but what counts as reasons, evidence, warrants, even the existence of a problem at all. How many sides are there on the question of whether Congress should apologize for slavery?

In conversation, those who offer endless alternatives and objections seem willfully obstructive—and sometimes they are. But in arguments about serious issues, you serve others badly if, to avoid seeming obstructive, you offer only mindless agreement or, worse, silent dissent. All parties to an argument have a duty to air alternatives and to raise objections in a spirit not of contention but of collaboration, to create the soundest argument possible.

Most of us find it hard to engage with alternatives and objections for four reasons:

- We don't know them, because we overlooked or never looked for them.
- We can't imagine that even in principle there exist other views to consider. Recall the research we reported on page 5 on how few people could think of even one argument as an alternative to their own.
- Even when we can imagine other views, we feel defensive about acknowledging that we might be wrong.
- And some of us fear that we undermine our own argument when we acknowledge uncertainty in it or strength in the arguments of others. But for most readers, the truth is the opposite.

Readers tend to distrust those who lack the knowledge—or confidence—to acknowledge that others might think differently.

Regardless of age, education, intelligence, and even experience, we all have to resist the most common flaw in human thinking: We hold tight to our own beliefs, seeking only evidence that supports them, ignoring contradictory evidence, or twisting what we do find until it supports our position. We don't do it knowingly. It's just what we are all inclined to do.

You can compensate for that bias if you actively seek out views that contradict your own and study them until you understand why someone could believe them. If you are making an argument about an issue without well-known contradictory views, imagine a skeptical but helpful friend questioning two aspects of your argument:

- Your friend might challenge the intrinsic soundness of your argument, objecting that your claims, reasons, evidence, or warrants are wrong.
- She might acknowledge that your argument is not intrinsically flawed, but offer alternatives: other claims, reasons, evidence or warrants that complicate or qualify your argument.

When you can imagine and then answer the views of others calmly and candidly, not just once but throughout your argument, you deepen and broaden it as well as project a judicious ethos. To help you imagine that friend raising objections or alternatives, we offer a checklist of questions in the next two sections.

Questioning Your Problem and Its Solution

At the most general level, readers may question how you frame your problem and solution, even whether there is a problem at all. Recall the conversation about students as customers among Sue, Ann, and Raj (p. 22). If Sue raised with her dean the lack of convenient office hours, the dean might ask some blunt questions (most questioners would be more tactful):

1. **What makes you think there is a problem?** *How many students in fact can't see their instructors when they have to?*

2. **Why have you posed the problem that way?** *Could the problem be not office hours but the willingness of students to make an effort to see teachers?*

3. **Exactly what kind of solution are you asking me to accept?** *How should we treat you like customers? What exactly should we do?*

4. **Have you considered limits on your claim?** *Are you saying that every instructor in every department keeps too few office hours? Most? Some?*

5. **Why do you think your solution is better than the alternatives?** *Why isn't the student as client model better than the student as customer model?*

Most important, though, are two objections that every solution to a pragmatic problem must overcome:

6. **How do you know your solution won't cost more to implement than the problem costs?** *To treat you like customers, we'll have to retrain everyone, which will take resources from current programs.*

7. **How do you know your solution won't make things worse by creating a bigger problem?** *If we treat you like customers, we will erode the teacher-student relationship that a sound education depends on.*

Questioning Your Support

After your readers question your problem and solution, they are likely to question its support. They will probably start by questioning whether you have enough evidence. Imagine the dean responding to Sue's charges with this:

1. **Your evidence is not sufficient.** *You gathered office hours from a single floor in one building. That can't be more than twenty offices. I need more evidence to take your claims seriously.*

The dean may next question the quality of Sue's (reports of) evidence:

2. **Your evidence is not accurate.** *I looked at those offices, and you counted three faculty who are on leave.*

3. **Your evidence is not precise.** *You said faculty average "about" an office hour a week. What's the exact figure?*

4. **Your evidence is not current.** *Are those hours from this semester or the last one?*

5. **Your evidence is not representative.** *You looked at offices from the same department. What about other departments? Are they all about the same or do most faculty keep more with only a few keeping much less?*

6. **Your evidence is not authoritative.** *How do you know the posted hours are the only times teachers see students? Have you asked the teachers?*

Finally, the dean might respond with the possible objections we reviewed in Chapter 7 concerning warrants:

7. **Your warrant is not true.** *You say someone who pays money for something is a customer. Why should I believe that?*

8. **Your warrant is too sweeping.** *You say that anyone who pays money for something is a customer, but that's too broad. Employers pay employees.*

9. **Your warrant does not apply.** *What students pay for is nothing like what a customer buys. An education is not a stove, so paying tuition is not like buying appliances.*

10. **Your warrant is inappropriate.** *The idea of applying the principle of buying and selling in higher education is simply unacceptable.*

We have phrased these responses bluntly, not to make Sue's dean seem antagonistic, but to encourage you to be honest with yourself. Face-to-face, readers may not put questions so harshly, but they are likely to ask them at least as directly in the privacy of their minds. In whatever spirit they ask them, though, they are meeting a responsibility we all must accept: the duty to engage actively to find the best solution to a problem, and that always means asking questions that most of us don't much like answering.

Questioning Your Consistency

Readers will look for one other weakness in your argument—that you contradict yourself or have failed to consider obvious counterexamples.

Senator, how can you condemn me for accepting contributions from the National Rifle Association when you accept contributions from the Ban Handguns Alliance?

How can you say that children's moral growth is harmed by sexually explicit movies when you also say that it is not harmed by violence on TV?

Readers will think you contradict yourself when you seem to apply a warrant selectively, using it when it suits your purposes and ignoring it when it does not. For example, if you claim that children are harmed by sex in the movies, readers will infer that the claim is based on a general principle of reasoning something like this:

> Whenever children experience vivid representations of glorified behavior, they are more likely to approve of and imitate it.

But that warrant does not give us a basis for distinguishing between sex in the movies and violence on TV. If we believe one is harmful, then we must believe that the other is as well—unless you can show that a more narrow warrant applies—perhaps that older children are *more* influenced by representations of sex than of violence because their awakening sexuality makes them respond to sexual images more intensely. But, of course, you would have to state that more narrow warrant explicitly and, since it is not obvious, support it.

If a critic can show that what you claim in one case contradicts what you claim in another or that you have ignored an obvious counterexample, you will seem to be guilty of intellectual inconsistency—a charge profoundly damaging to your ethos, especially when the inconsistency seems self-interested. The specific judgment depends on your kind of problem:

- In a pragmatic argument about what to do, you seem *unfair* when you expect others to follow a principle that you ignore.

- In a conceptual argument about what to believe, you seem *intellectually dishonest* (or at least careless) when you apply a principle selectively to get an answer you want.

So in planning your argument, ask whether your readers can apply the principle behind the case at hand to all similar cases. If not, you have to formulate a more narrow principle that distinguishes your case from the others.

EXAMPLE

How to Use a Response to Restate Your Argument

The excerpt below is from an argument claiming that undergraduate majors should be abolished because students do not benefit from specialized studies and need more general education. The writer acknowledges and responds to possible objections while simultaneously restating both the gist of his main claim and its support. Here, in outline, are the steps he follows:

1. He imagines that those who raise the objection already accept part of his claim, *Students need more general education,* thus reinforcing it.
2. He states the objection as an alternative solution, but one that partially agrees with his proposed action: *Majors should be, not abolished, but reduced.*
3. In response to that alternative, he indirectly restates the remaining part of his claim: *Specialization does not benefit students.*

4. Then, to support that response/claim, he restates his three reasons why specialization is not a benefit.
5. Finally, he acknowledges a qualification to his claim, *Some students might benefit from specialization,* but then restates his claim again: *Other students should not be forced to specialize.*

Here's the passage:

Another objection I anticipate [to my argument that majors should be abolished] is from people who would agree that the basic liberal arts learning students get today is inadequate, and who would buy into the idea of an expanded general education program _{restatement of part of main claim} ··· [but who would still argue for] a minimally sized major. Students could have the best of both worlds: the advantages of specialism along with the advantages of generalism._{alternative solution}

Certainly a curriculum like this would be preferable to what we have now; more, it would be a great improvement. _{benefits of alternative solution} But there is still a difficulty. It is still assumed that having a specialization, regardless of its size, is truly an advantage for students. And that is precisely what I am throwing into question. _{response/restatement of part of main claim} I have suggested that there is no more rigor in forcing the mind toward the greater depth of a major than there is in forcing it toward the lesser but significant depths of several different fields. _{restatement of reason 1 supporting response/main claim} And I have suggested that the way in which a major fine-tunes the mind may end up as a limitation more than an asset—inclining a student to see things from the narrows of one perspective alone. _{restatement of reason 2} Add to this the fact that many students' interests aren't strongly enough defined to make a commitment to a major, and the fact that many others don't need one for the vocational preparation they desire since they will be getting that in graduate school. _{restatement of reason 3} These are all telling reasons for questioning the practice of requiring students to have a major, and together they form a powerful and sensible rationale.

All of this isn't to say that no student should have a major._{acknowledgement of limitation} But it is to say that we should not require it of all students. _{restatement of main claim} Those in fields like engineering and architecture, those who have an obvious and strong inclination in other fields, should take majors . . . [But] for other students, there is no good reason for forcing them to specialize.

Source: William Casement, "Do College Students Need a Major?" *Academic Questions,* Summer 1998. Reprinted by permission of Transaction Publishers.

Responses as Subordinate Arguments

As you respond to questions, reservations, and alternative views, you create an argument that readers judge thoughtful, especially if you support your responses with additional reasons and evidence. By so doing, you enhance your credibility, a crucial component in creating your ethos. For example, here is part of an argument claiming that a university should invest more resources in course evaluations beyond simple in-class surveys:

> . . . Faculty can continue to improve if they get as much information as we can give them about our responses to their teaching.
>
> Some students may ask "If faculty aren't interested enough to improve their teaching on their own, why would they respond to our criticisms?" ₐcknowledgment of objection We think that view is cynical and that most teachers do care about our education. partial rebuttal of objection But even if they have a point, partial concession to objection the new information we propose to gather will include more than just student gripes. Once the information is part of the record, teachers will not ignore it. response/claim This happens in many professions. When doctors, airlines, or car manufacturers learn about problems with their products or services, they try to improve. reason For example, when data about the quality of the university hospital were made public, hospital officials tried to do better because they were concerned about loss of business. Now the hospital advertises its standings in surveys on TV. report of evidence When the shortcomings of a profession become public, they take action to improve. warrant

This writer explicitly acknowledges an objection that she imagines her colleagues might have, conceding they might be partly right. But she then responds to that objection with reasons, evidence, and a warrant to show why it would not apply in this case.

The writer might anticipate, however, that her readers will in turn question her response. For example, she might imagine that her most cynical readers would reject the comparison between teachers and airlines:

> But teachers are not like airlines; they have tenure and can't be fired, and colleges are not out to make money, so your analogy doesn't hold.

If she imagines that objection, she must respond with another argument:

> Of course, tenured professors differ from doctors and airlines because they don't need the approval of customers to stay in business. ₐcknowledgment of limitation But most professors are responsible professionals who understand that colleges have to attract students. response/claim Even state universities depend on tuition, especially higher out-of-state tuition. reason Last year, out-of-state students saved us from a deficit that threatened faculty raises. report of evidence Students have many choices and can shop around. reason When they research schools, they consider the quality of teaching in deciding where to go. warrant

We can imagine someone criticizing that response too, but at some point enough is enough. Life and papers are too short to answer every objection. But you don't have to answer every one to show you have been thoughtful enough to consider some.

What if you can't answer a question? Our recommendation may seem naive, but it is realistic: If you believe your argument has flaws but none so serious as to defeat it, concede them. Then assert that the balance of your argument compensates for its imperfections:

> We must admit that not every teacher will take these evaluations seriously. But even so, if we can get a substantial number to . . .

Conceding what cannot be denied is how thoughtful arguers respond to legitimate uncertainty.

Nothing reveals more clearly the kind of mind you have, indeed the kind of *person* you are, than your ability to imagine and then respond to alternatives, objections, and reservations. Few of us consistently do it well. But when you do it even occasionally, not only will your argument gain credibility, so will you, particularly when you respond to objections and reservations that are not simply wrong, but groundless.

WRITING PROCESS
Acknowledgment and Responses

THINKING-READING-TALKING

Use Acknowledgments to Understand Context

When you read an argument in a new field, you may not see what is at stake in every part of it. But you can infer some of that from the common ground, especially if the writer reviews research leading up to her question. You can find more context in the objections and alternatives that she acknowledges and responds to. She defines the limits of debate in her field in what she acknowledges or dismisses and defines what she thinks is relevant to her position in what she concedes or responds to at length.

PREPARING AND PLANNING

Collect Alternatives as You Read

When it is hard to imagine alternatives, start by making a master list of pros and cons, especially cons, and add to it as you prepare your argument. Don't forget to look for help in your sources.

- Take notes on positions your sources respond to. If you disagree with the source, those objections may support your own position and suggest further reading. If you agree with the source, you can acknowledge and respond to some of those alternatives and objections (after you look at them for yourself, of course).

- Don't record only claims that support your position; also record those that contradict it, along with the reasons and evidence offered in support. If you decide to acknowledge and respond to it, you will need a full argument to respond well.

• When you collect evidence to support your reasons, keep track of what may limit or contradict them. You may decide not to acknowledge those reservations, but they may help you imagine others.

Add Acknowledgments to Your Post-Draft Outline

When you sketch an outline, focus not on the alternatives or objections you intend to acknowledge, but on your own argument. You invite writer's block if before you start drafting you try to imagine every objection a reader might raise. After you have a draft of your core argument, work through your outline point by point, imagining questions readers might ask.

You might even include objections that you can imagine but that readers might not. They don't want to follow you down every blind alley, but they benefit when you share alternatives you pursued but ultimately rejected. They will also like your candor. We know this advice seems disingenuous—being candid about failure as a rhetorical strategy to ensure success. Nevertheless, readers judge your ethos by how open you are to alternatives, and they will know that only if you show them which ones you considered.

Locate Acknowledgments and Responses Where Readers Are Likely To Think of Them

Once you identify alternatives to acknowledge, think of a response, outline it, and decide where to put it. Acknowledge alternatives early if they are well established and relate to your whole argument:

• If your whole argument directly counters another, acknowledge that other argument in your introduction and again early in the body of yours.

• If an alternative bears on the whole argument but is one you want to drop quickly, acknowledge it in the common ground of your introduction:

Many teachers believe that the most important skill they can teach is the ability to solve problems. _{acknowledgment/common ground} But as important as that skill is, it is less important than the ability to discover, then articulate a problem clearly. As Einstein said, "A problem well put is half solved." _{response/destabilizing condition}

• Acknowledge an alternative right after your introduction, as background, if it bears on the whole argument and will occur to readers once they understand your problem and have a sense of its solution:

. . . The most valuable skill for students is the ability to discover and articulate problems clearly. _{claim} The issue of problem formulation, however, has been ignored by teachers. Their traditional focus has been on teaching students to analyze problems in order to . . . _{acknowledgment}

• Respond to incidental alternatives as they become relevant.

> There is a Web site that rates colleges based on students' reports of their experience. That may not be a reliable source, _{acknowledgment} but it is one that students check. _{response/claim} For example, . . .

Building a Whole Argument Around Alternatives

If you know that readers will think of more than one alternative to your solution, organize your argument by sequentially eliminating those alternatives, leaving your solution as the last one standing.

> How then should we respond to global warming? It has been suggested that we just ignore it. [explanation] But that won't work because . . .

> Others suggested that we exploit it by adapting our lives and agriculture to warmer conditions. [explanation] But that won't work either because . . .

> At the other extreme, some argue that we should end all atmosphere emissions immediately. [explanation] But that idea is impractical because . . .

> None of these responses addresses the problem in a responsible way. The only reasonable way to deal with global warming is . . .

DRAFTING

The Vocabulary of Acknowledgment and Response

Writers fail to acknowledge and respond to alternatives usually because they don't know and cannot imagine any or because they think that by acknowledging them, they weaken their argument. But a more mundane reason is that they simply don't know the expressions experienced writers use to introduce alternatives and responses.

We offer here that lexicon of words and phrases. To be sure (there is one of them right there), your first efforts may feel clumsy (*may* is common in acknowledgments), _{acknowledgment} but (a response usually begins with *but* or *however*) as you use them, they will come to seem more natural. _{response/claim}

Acknowledging

When you respond to an anticipated question or objection, give it the weight that readers are likely to. You can mention and dismiss it, or address it at length. We order these expressions in that order, from dismissive to respectful.

1. You can downplay an objection or alternative by summarizing it briefly in a short phrase introduced with *despite, regardless of,* or *notwithstanding*:

Despite Congress' claims that it wants to cut taxes, _{acknowledgment} the public believes that . . . _{response}

Regardless of problems in Hong Kong, _{acknowledgment} Southeast Asia remains a strong . . . _{response}

Notwithstanding declining crime rates, _{acknowledgment} there is still a need for vigorous enforcement of . . . _{response}

You can use *although,* and *while,* and *even though* in the same way:

Although Congress claims it wants to cut taxes, _{acknowledgment} the public believes that . . . _{response}

While there are problems in Hong Kong, _{acknowledgment} Southeast Asia remains a strong . . . _{response}

Even though crime has declined, _{acknowledgment} there is still a need for vigorous enforcement of . . . _{response}

2. You can indirectly signal an objection or alternative with *seem* or *appear,* or with a qualifying adverb, such as *plausibly, justifiably, reasonably, accurately, understandably, surprisingly, foolishly,* or even *certainly.*

   In his letters, Lincoln expresses what *seems* to be depression. _{acknowledgment} But those who observed him . . . _{response}

   Smith's data *appear* to support these claims. _{acknowledgment} However, on closer examination . . . _{response}

   This proposal *may* have some merit, _{acknowledgment} but we . . . _{response}

   Liberals have made a *plausible* case that the arts ought to be supported by taxes. _{acknowledgment} But they ignore the moral objections of . . . _{response}

3. You can acknowledge alternatives by attributing them to unnamed sources or to no source at all. That gives a little weight to the objection. In these examples, brackets and slashes indicate choices:

   It is easy to [*think/imagine/say/claim/argue*] that taxes should . . .

   There is [*another/alternative/possible/standard*] [*explanation/line of argument/ account/possibility*].

   Some evidence [*might/may/can/could/would/does*] [*suggest/indicate/point to/ lead some to think*] that we should . . .

4. You can acknowledge an alternative by attributing it to a more specific source. This construction gives more weight to the position you acknowledge:

   There are some [*many / few*] who [*might/may/could/would*] [*say/think/argue/ claim/charge/object*] that Cuba is not . . .

[*Most/Many/Some/A few*] knowledgeable college administrators [*say/think/ argue/claim/charge/object*] that researchers . . .

One advocate of collaboration, Ken Bruffee, [*says/thinks/argues/claims/ charges/objects*] that students . . .

5. You can acknowledge an alternative in your own voice or with a passive verb or concessive adverb such as *admittedly, granted, to be sure,* and so on. You concede the alternative has some validity, but by changing the words, you can qualify how much validity you acknowledge:

I [*understand/know/realize/appreciate*] that liberals believe in . . .

It is [*true/possible/likely/certain*] that no good evidence proves that coffee causes cancer . . .

It [*must/should/can*] be [*admitted/acknowledged/noted/conceded*] that no good evidence proves that coffee causes cancer . . .

[*Granted/admittedly/true/to be sure/certainly/of course*], Adams stated . . .

We [*could/can/might/may/would*] [*say/argue/claim/think*] that spending on the arts supports pornographic . . .

We have to [*consider/raise*] the [*question/possibility/probability*] that further study [*could/might/will*] show crime has not . . .

We cannot [*overlook/ignore/dismiss/reject*] the fact that Cuba was . . .

What X [*says/states/writes/claims/asserts/argues/suggests/shows*] may [*be true/make sense/be a good point*]: Perhaps Lincoln did suffer . . .

Responding

You signal a response with *but, however,* or *on the other hand.* Remember that after you state your response, readers may expect reasons and evidence supporting it, because they will take that response to be a claim needing its own support. You can respond in ways that range from tactfully indirect to blunt:

1. You can state that *you* don't entirely understand:

   But I do not understand . . ./I find it difficult to see . . ./It is not clear that . . .

2. Or you can state that there are unsettled issues:

   But there are other issues . . ./There remains the problem of . . .

3. You can respond more bluntly by claiming the acknowledged position is irrelevant or unreliable:

   But as insightful as that point may be, it [*ignores/is irrelevant to/does not bear on/was formulated for other situations than*] the issue at hand.

   But the evidence is [*unreliable/shaky/thin/not the best available*].

   But the argument is [*untenable/wrong/weak/confused/simplistic*].

But that view [*overlooks/ignores/misses*] key factors . . .

But that position is based on [*unreliable/faulty/weak/confused*] [*reasoning/ thinking/evidence*].

Addressing Logical Error

When you differ with a reader because you are reasonably sure the reader might not have thought through the issues as carefully as you, you need a few phrases to introduce your point of view in a civil way. Here are a few:

That evidence is certainly important, but we have to look at all the evidence available.

That explains some of the problem, but it is so complex that no single explanation is enough.

That principle holds in many cases, but we must consider exceptions.

You get the idea. Acknowledge the value of a particular view, but suggest that there is more to consider.

INQUIRIES

1. In most academic and professional situations, we make arguments stronger by acknowledging their limitations. But different standards apply in some professional situations—a lawyer defending a client in court, for example. Can you think of other circumstances in which you should not acknowledge any weakness in your argument? How do those circumstances differ from those that you normally find in academic and professional arguments?

2. Suppose that just before you turn in a paper for a class, you discover an objection to your argument that substantially weakens it. You cannot think how to counter the objection. In fact, you now think your argument is wrong. What should you do? This question is both ethical and practical. Are you ethically obligated to reveal this objection? Why or why not? Practically speaking, would it be wise to tell your teacher that you recognized the objection, but too late to do anything about it? Or should you just keep quiet and hope for the best? Which response do you think will project the best ethos?

3. Look at the editorial and op-ed pages of your local newspaper. Identify all the acknowledgments and responses. Which pieces use them best? Do those acknowledgments make those arguments persuasive? Do the same with some TV talk shows. Do the participants acknowledge and respond to other points of view as often? If not, why not?

IN A NUTSHELL

About Your Argument ...

You communicate the quality of your thinking by how candidly you acknowledge and respond to views different from your own. Admittedly, nothing is harder than finding those views, so you need a list of questions to ask yourself on behalf of your readers. Anticipate questions and objections about two aspects of your argument:

- Readers question the quality of your claims, reasons, evidence, or warrants. They assert that you are just wrong.
- They find nothing wrong with your argument per se, but think of alternative claims, reasons, and evidence, even ways to frame the issue.

Readers may question how you frame the problem:

1. Why do you think your problem is a serious one?
2. Why did you pose the problem this way rather than that?
3. Exactly what claim are you are asking me to accept?
4. Have you considered these exceptions to your claim?
5. Why do you think your solution is better than an alternative one?
6. How do you know your solution won't cost more than the problem?
7. How do you know your solution won't create new problems?

Readers also question evidence: They question whether it is sufficient, current, accurate, precise, representative and authoritative. They might also question whether your warrants are true, too broad, inapplicable to your reasons and claims, or inappropriate for your readers.

... and About Writing It

When you acknowledge and respond to an imagined objection or question, you can follow a well-established formula:

- Begin with a phrase such as *to be sure, admittedly, some have claimed*, etc.
- Follow with *but, however, on the other hand*, etc., and go on with the response.

When you respond to these kinds of objections and alternatives, you have an opportunity to thicken your argument by supporting your response with reasons, evidence, warrants, and yet more acknowledgments and responses to your response.

Part 3

Thinking About
Thinking in Arguments

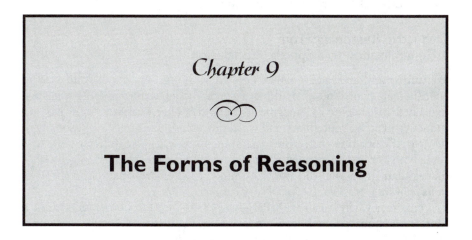

Chapter 9

The Forms of Reasoning

In this chapter, we discuss three kinds of reasoning: inductive, deductive, and abductive. We show you how these kinds of reasoning are commonly distorted by "cognitive biases," predictable habits of mind that keep you from thinking as well as you can. Finally, we offer strategies for avoiding them.

W e've told you how to plan and write sound arguments, but we haven't said much about the quality of reasoning that you put into them. In this chapter, we explain three general forms of reasoning—inductive, deductive, and abductive—and the flaws that can afflict them. As you prepare your argument, you must not only guard against those flaws in your own thinking, but construct your argument to anticipate how those same flaws might distort the reasoning of your readers.

Three Forms of Reasoning

If you have studied reasoning, you probably know about two kinds: *inductive* and *deductive*. It's a distinction philosophers have made for about 2,500 years, but one that does not reflect how most of us really think. The more common kind of reasoning is called *abductive*.

Inductive Reasoning: From Specifics to a General Conclusion

You reason inductively when you begin with specifics and then draw a general conclusion about them. Imagine that over the years Professor Stein records which students wrote papers on a word processor or on a typewriter, because she is studying trends in computer usage. One day as she looks over her records, she notices that those who used word processors tended to get higher grades. In reaching that conclusion, she reasoned inductively, from specific instances to a general claim that she did not have in mind until it occurred to her. That's pure induction: from specifics to an unanticipated general claim.

Deductive Reasoning: From a Generalization to a Specific Conclusion

We call reasoning *deductive* when we start with a generalization, add a more specific statement, and then draw a specific conclusion (roughly what we explained in Chapter 7). Imagine that the day after Professor Stein has her inductive insight about grades and word processors, she meets Professor Chen, who, for the first time, is requiring his students to write on computers. She tells him about her insight: Students who wrote on computers tended to get higher grades than those who did not. He thinks, *Since I now require my students to write on word processors, I'll probably give higher grades.*

Professor Chen began with Professor's Stein generalization, added to it a more specific reason, and drew a conclusion; that's pure deductive reasoning. (We should note that most philosophers define *inductive* and *deductive* somewhat differently. For them, deductive reasoning leads to a conclusion that *must* be true; inductive reasoning leads to a conclusion that is only *probably* true.)

Abductive Reasoning: From Problem to Hypothesis to Confirmation

Those examples, however, are misleading because we invented two implausible stories in which conclusions seemed to jump out of the blue without anyone looking for them. In fact, we rarely reason like that when we are planning an argument. Almost always, we begin thinking about claims not because we happen to have a lot of data or a warrant and reason lying about, waiting to lead us to a new and surprising insight, but because we have a problem.

When we engage in that kind of thinking we typically come up with a hunch about a possible solution—call it a probationary *hypothesis*—that plausibly might solve the problem. Then to test that hypothesis, we look for more data relevant to the problem, data that both support and contradict our hypothesis. If our hunch/hypothesis explains the data we started with and the new data we find better than any competing one, we accept it as the best available solution to our problem.

For example, imagine that after noticing that most of her students who wrote on computers got better grades than those who didn't, Professor Stein asks herself (that is, she poses a problem) whether writing on computers could be a *cause* of better grades. To test that hypothesis, she collects more data about students in other classes and discovers that most of those who wrote on computers also got higher grades. So she tentatively accepts her hypothesis—writing on computers causes better grades. But she thinks of an alternative explanation: Maybe those who *choose* to write on computers are more diligent students. If that's so, then computers don't *cause* better grades; both using computers and getting better grades are caused by something else: greater diligence.

So she now poses a more challenging problem: If *all* students are required to write on computers, will they get better grades? To test her hypotheses, she collects yet more data about students in other classes and other schools, including those who are required to use computers, those who choose to use them, and those who choose not to.

Assume her new data support her hypothesis: Writing on computers is indeed a significant factor in getting higher grades. If so, she has confirmed her hypothesis abductively. She began with a problem that motivated a hypothesis that accounted for the data she had; she used that hypothesis to look for more data; then she used those data to test and confirm her hypothesis.

There is, however, one thing she can never do. She can never *prove* her hypothesis/claim true, once and for all. She knows that tomorrow someone might come up with data that disconfirm her claim. And that's true of every inductive claim: They are only more or less probable. Even if every bird ever seen by the human eye has had feathers, it is only probably true that all birds have feathers, because somewhere there may be a featherless bird.

Real-Life Barriers to Thinking Clearly

Sad to say, real thinking is rarely so simple, because all of us have inherited habits of mind that lead our thinking astray, habits called *cognitive biases*. These biases don't reflect age, intelligence, education, or expertise. They are chronic and incurable. But once you know them, you can be self-critical of your thinking and use the discipline of good argument to guard against them, in your own thinking and in that of your readers.

Bias in Abductive Thinking

We've urged you to think abductively, to articulate your problem as carefully but as quickly as you can and then formulate a few tentative hypotheses to guide your thinking toward its solution. If you start by randomly gathering data on some topic, hoping a problem and maybe even a solution will turn up, you depend too much on luck. It would be as if Professor Stein collected data on students who pierced their noses or wore black to see if by chance those variables correlated with the quality of their writing. She needed a question and a plausible hypothesis to test before she could know what data to gather and how to evaluate it.

But that's also the point where we fall prey to the most treacherous bias in abductive thinking: We hit on a quick hypothesis, then hunker down on it, usually because it serves our purposes or fits our picture of the world—it's what we *want* to be true. Once we have our answer, we anchor our thinking to it, even when the best evidence tells us we should let it go. Anchoring happens to just about all of us, in ways that are both trivial and significant.

- *A trivial example:* Would you guess the area of France is more or less than 250,000 square miles? OK, now guess the area of Nigeria. Whatever you guess about Nigeria, it will probably be closer to 250,000 than if we had *first* asked you whether the area of France is more or less than 50,000 square miles (it is, in fact, 211,207 square miles). Whatever number you hear first tends to anchor your thinking to roughly that number.

- *A more significant example:* When a business starts losing money and its CEO frames the problem in terms of production costs, that formulation can permanently exclude consideration of a better solution, like too little advertising or a changing market.

We need a hypothesis to start, but instead of trying to poke holes in our first idea, we too often harden our thinking around it, until it ossifies into an impregnable truth. Here are some strategies to avoid anchoring.

Deliberately Seek Disconfirming Evidence

Once a belief is anchored, we are more likely to seek evidence that supports it than evidence that contradicts it. For example, here is a disconcerting finding about the way many doctors diagnose illnesses. When a patient describes symptoms, doctors are likely to make a quick diagnosis, then order tests to see if they are right. If the results are uncertain, they order more tests that they hope will confirm their diagnosis, and if those don't, still more. But as studies show, doctors seem less inclined to order tests that would *prove their first diagnosis wrong,* even though that would test their judgment more efficiently. They are more committed to proving themselves right than finding out they are wrong.

What Automobile Ads Do You Read?

What car ads are you most likely to read—those for your own car or for another make? Market studies show that most of us read more ads about our own car because we don't want to see evidence that another car might be better. None of us likes to think we might have bought the wrong car.

Source: Stuart Sutherland. *Irrationality: Why We Don't Think Straight!* New Brunswick, NJ: Rutgers University Press, 1992, p. 141.

Interpret Evidence Objectively

Even when we try to gather evidence objectively, we tend to reshape what we find to fit our hypothesis. A good example is reported by Stephen J. Gould in

The Mismeasure of Man (New York: Norton, 1981). Gould writes about Samuel Morton, an early nineteenth-century scientist with a good reputation for gathering objective data, who set out to prove that Caucasians were smarter than other races because they had bigger brains. To measure the size of brains, he filled skulls from different races with mustard seeds, then weighed the seeds, assuming their weight would correlate with the volume of the skull and therefore the size of the brain. He found that, indeed, the seeds that filled Caucasian skulls weighed more than those from non-Caucasian skulls, and so he concluded that Caucasians have larger skulls and therefore larger brains (and therefore greater intelligence).

He later repeated his work with lead shot, because it gave more consistent measurements. But when he did, he found—to his surprise—much less difference in the sizes of the skulls. Morton himself reported the puzzle, so he was trying to be objective. What apparently happened was this: To fill a skull completely with the small, light mustard seeds, he had to pat them down, and he seems to have unconsciously patted down the seeds in the skulls of Caucasians more tightly than he did in others. He thereby increased their density and total weight, thereby biasing his evidence to support the conclusion he wanted to reach: greater volume for Caucasian skulls.

This bias toward confirmation is what forces medical researchers to do "double-blind" experiments. When they test a new drug, they do not tell patients whether they are getting the drug or a placebo, because patients so much want a treatment to work that they tend to report they are getting better even when they aren't. But researchers also keep themselves in the dark, because if they knew which patients were getting the drug, they might persuade themselves that those patients had improved, because they too want the treatment to work.

Don't Dismiss Contrary Evidence

Not only do we tend to gather and interpret evidence in ways that fit our hypothesis; we tend to resist evidence that undermines it. In one study, researchers assembled two groups of students with opposing views on the death penalty and established how strongly they held those views. Each group then read two articles, one in favor of the death penalty, the other against. We might expect that after reading an argument opposing their respective beliefs, both sides would moderate their views and end up closer together. In fact, the opposite occurred. After reading the articles, the two sides were *further* apart. Apparently, both sides put more weight on the article that supported their views and rejected the one that refuted them, entrenching themselves in their prior beliefs even more firmly.

The Power of a Settled Belief

How strongly do we hold a belief, even when we have evidence we are wrong? More than we should. Researchers gave students invented suicide notes, saying that some were fake and some were real, and asked them to pick out the real ones. As they did so, some students were told they were doing a good job, others that they were not. At the end, the students were told all the notes were fake. Then they were asked how well they thought they would do with a set of real notes. Those who had been told (falsely) that they had done well tended to be more confident that they would do well with real notes than those told (also falsely) that they had done badly, even though all of them knew they had been lied to.

Source: L. Ross, M. R. Lepper, and M. Hubbard, "Perseverance in Self-Perception and Social Perception: Biased Attributional Processes in the Debriefing Paradigm," *Journal of Personality and Social Psychology* 32 (1975): 880–892.

Don't Be So Sure of Yourself

Another reason we hunker down on a claim is overconfidence. For example, do you think you are an above average, average, or below average driver? More than 90 percent of those tested think they are above average. Our over-confidence is not a sign of stupidity or immaturity. If we lightly changed our beliefs at the first hint of contrary evidence, we would fail to see the deeper regularities in our physical and social worlds. We need settled beliefs to live settled lives. But the cost of that confidence is becoming so entrenched in a belief that we don't change it when we should. It is behavior that is cost-effective in the short run, which is, after all, where most of us live. In the academic and professional world, however, we are expected to take a longer view.

The Cautious Language of Good Problem Solvers

A researcher who studied the language of good and bad problem solvers found that weaker problem solvers tend to use words that express certainty and totality: *constantly, every time, all, without exception, absolutely, entirely, completely, totally, unequivocally, undeniably, without question, certainly, solely, only, neither-nor, must, have to.* Stronger problem solvers more often use words that express uncertainty and qualification: *now and then, in general, sometimes, often, ordinarily, a bit, in particular, somewhat, to a degree, perhaps, conceivable, questionable, among other things, on the other hand, may, can.*

Source: From Dietrich Doerner, *The Logic of Failure: Recognizing and Avoiding Error in Complex Situations.* New York: Addison-Wesley, 1997.

Bias in Inductive Thinking

Our most common bias in inductive reasoning is jumping to a conclusion from too little evidence. Starting with the hypothesis that global warming is a myth, someone seizes on a record cold January as proof (or a proponent of warming seizes on a record hot August). Readers judge inductive reasoning sound only when they think you have considered *more* than enough data. The problem is not just to know what your readers will think is enough. You must also know whether they hold contrary beliefs based on their own insufficient, unrepresentative, imprecise, or even inaccurate evidence. If so, acknowledge that they may have some evidence for their belief, but suggest, carefully, that there is more out there than they know.

The Costs of Biased Evidence Gathering

David Irving, a historian who has written about Nazi Germany, has a superb reputation for unearthing obscure evidence. He has also denied that the Holocaust happened. When he was called irresponsible, he sued his accuser. After spending millions on his case, he lost both it and his reputation. Here is what one observer wrote the day after the verdict:

> [Some] otherwise responsible historians [have] made [an argument] to separate a "good" David Irving, the fact gatherer who has been able to unearth vast amounts of original documents and eyewitness testimony ... from the not-so-good David Irving who may get some of his interpretations wrong ... Perhaps the London verdict [against him] might be an occasion for historians who argue that you can defend Mr. Irving by separating "fact gathering" from interpretation to reconsider, [t]o learn the lesson that fact gathering can be prejudiced by what one is looking for—and by what one is not looking for. Can one praise a fact gatherer who somehow has failed to find the facts of mass murder? ... Unlike Mr. Irving himself, they are not guilty of Holocaust denial. But in their naivete about the relationship between fact and interpretation, they might fairly be charged with David Irving denial.

Source: Ron Rosenbaum, "The Roots of Holocaust Denial," *Wall Street Journal,* April 12, 2000.

Bias in Deductive Thinking

The risk in deductive reasoning is that we ignore evidence and rely entirely on general principles. Recall the argument about DNA evidence proving that someone in Thomas Jefferson's bloodline fathered a child by his slave Sally Hemings (p. 47). Some historians tested their hypothesis abductively, against a lot of individual bits of evidence:

- DNA evidence showed that someone in Jefferson's family fathered a son by Hemings.
- The son in question looked like Jefferson.
- Jefferson took Hemings with him when he went to Paris as ambassador.
- Some contemporaries accused him of having children by Hemings.
- Stories about Hemings and Jefferson passed down in her family for 200 years.

- Hemings's children were the only slaves Jefferson freed in his lifetime.

None of these items proves that Jefferson had a child by Hemings, but collectively they lead many historians to conclude that he probably did.

Historians on the other side dismiss that evidence, basing their argument on a warrant and reason that makes the evidence irrelevant:

> When a person devotes his life to freedom and equality, that person's character excludes doing something as immoral as having sex with a slave. _{warrant} Jefferson devoted his life to freedom and equality, _{reason} so he could not have had sex with Hemings. _{claim/conclusion}

Those historians ignore the evidence about Jefferson and Hemings because they put greater trust in their warrant and reason.

When you reason deductively, from a principle to a claim, guard against overgeneralizing. Think about the limitations and provisos that you leave unsaid. For example, the anti-Hemings historians have to acknowledge that their warrant has limits:

> People do not act against their fundamental character *unless they are under great stress, or they face great temptation, or they are coerced, etc.*

Even the staunchest Jeffersonian would have to acknowledge at least the possibility that after his wife died, he might have been drawn to Hemings, who was her half-sister.

How do we resist an unjustified adherence to the One True Principle? Engage with others to seek out different points of view, in person and in your imagination. Make time to question your claims and encourage that voice in the back (or front) of your mind to keep asking *But what would you say to someone who asked . . . ?* If you suspect your readers hold fast to One True Principle, you are unlikely to dislodge them. But you might be able to lessen their certainty, if you can show that the matter is more complex than it seems and that your case shows the limits of their rule.

WRITING PROCESS
The Forms of Reasoning

PREPARING AND PLANNING

Guard Against Leaping to a Conclusion

1. Consider all the solutions you can think of.
2. Imagine what would disconfirm your hypothesis, then look for it.
3. If you can't imagine disconfirming evidence that you can find quickly, watch for it as you do your research.

4. Gather data objectively. Ask, *What would I see in this if I opposed my solution/claim?*

5. Interpret data objectively. Ask, *How would I interpret this evidence if I opposed this solution/claim?*

6. Gather more evidence than you think you need.

Follow steps 2–6 even if you begin with a solution/claim that you fully intend to support. You may not change your mind (though you should stay open to that possibility), but you will better anticipate readers' objections.

Imagine the Biases of Your Readers

It is not enough to be a good critical thinker to make a good argument. You must also anticipate how your readers might not be. How will they receive evidence that contradicts their beliefs? What kinds of overgeneralizations have they made? What will it take to dislodge them from their favorite explanations? Since it is unlikely that you will be able to shake them loose from their deepest and most staunchly defended beliefs, you must find ways to help them see that their beliefs are less than 100 percent true in all contexts at all times. You must acknowledge their beliefs and perhaps even allow that they are *generally* sound, but then show that there may be limits, room for exceptions.

IN A NUTSHELL

About Your Argument . . .

Traditional philosophers identify two kinds of reasoning:

*   *Inductive* reasoning from specifics to a general conclusion about all of them: *Many samples of ocean water are salty, so ocean water must be salty (but there could be exceptions).*

*   *Deductive* reasoning from a general warrant and reason to a specific claim: *Ocean water is always salty; this water is from the ocean, so it must be salty.*

But the more common kind of reasoning is *abductive*—reasoning that begins with a hypothesis that might explain the data in question. We then test that hypothesis using whatever reasoning seems appropriate. Abductive reasoning is problem-driven, a kind of reasoning that begins with a hypothesis that is the tentative solution to a problem.

Each kind of reasoning is vulnerable to cognitive biases.

*   When you think inductively, you risk basing a conclusion on too few instances. You avoid that risk by gathering more evidence than you

think you need and by learning something about statistical sampling and analysis.

- When you think deductively, you risk formulaic thinking, applying a rote warrant to every situation.

- When you think abductively, you risk fixating on the first hypothesis that springs to mind. Guard against that by holding your earliest hypotheses delicately, by imagining more than one, and by deliberately seeking out evidence that disconfirms your favorite one.

Chapter 10

Arguments About Meanings

In this chapter, we discuss issues in thinking about the relationship between words and meanings. We show you how to make an argument based on meanings by defining terms in a way that encourages readers to see things as you want them to.

In most arguments, we address issues involving words and their meanings or causes and their effects, and sometimes both, because what we think something is usually influences what we think we should do about it. For example, a few years ago some members of Congress thought they knew what they should do when they learned that the National Endowment for the Arts, had funded an exhibit of photographs by Robert Mapplethorpe, whose images are so sexually explicit that many consider them pornographic. Those critics argued that Congress should abolish the NEA because it promoted pornography.

To support their claim, the critics had to make four arguments. Two were about terms and their meanings:

- What is the meaning of *pornography?*
- What is it about Mapplethorpe's images that earns them that term?

Two more were about causes and their effects:

- How does the NEA contribute to the dissemination of those images?
- How would closing the NEA discourage pornography?

The critics thought that if they could get everyone to label Mapplethorpe's images *pornographic*, they would then have a better chance of gaining support for *doing* something about them—abolishing the NEA.

We base many professional and civic arguments on this relationship between words and deeds:

If civilian militia are *patriots*, ₍definition₎ we should support them as defenders of freedom. ₍pragmatic claim₎

175

If competitive ballroom dancing is a *sport,* _{definition} we should make it an Olympic event. _{pragmatic claim}

In the academic world, on the other hand, researchers usually make arguments about definitions not to get us to *do* anything, but to help us *understand* something better:

> The term *language* is used loosely to mean communicating information through behavior or signs. So it is said that bees use a "language of dancing" to communicate information about the direction of flowers. But human language is more than that. It communicates not just predictable and narrowly defined bits of information, but desires, feelings, and ideas unique to the moment. _{definition} Many think such uses of language make us unique in the animal kingdom. But chimpanzees can be taught to do something like it in sign language or by touching symbols on a computer screen. As rudimentary as their communication is, they demonstrate an ability to use language in ways that resemble what we humans do. _{application of definition} Their ability demonstrates intellectual powers so much greater than we have suspected _{reason} that we can no longer think of ourselves as cognitively unique in the animal kingdom. _{conceptual claim}

If we accept that definition of *language* and agree that what chimps do exemplifies it, then we have reason to accept the conceptual claim that we can no longer think of ourselves as unique in the animal kingdom. Those making that argument might also want us to *act* differently—for instance, stop using chimps in medical experiments. But their basic aim is to convince us to *think* differently about our place in the world.

In this chapter, we discuss arguments that focus on words, their meanings, and the consequences of choosing one term over another. But first we have to explain some terms of our own.

Some Terminology

To explain how to make arguments about meaning, we use six words that you know—*category, term, feature, meaning, criteria,* and *definition*—but we'll start with one that you may not—*referent:*

- We usually use words or phrases to talk about something—a person, object, event, concept, idea, and so on. It can be either out in the world (the Eiffel Tower) or in our minds (the square root of 5). We'll call the thing we refer to when we use a term the **referent** of that term.

It is easiest to grasp the idea of a referent when we talk about particular things. If someone asked, *When you mentioned* Sue's cat, *what were you referring to?* You could pick it up or point to it. You would have a harder time pointing to the referent you had in mind if someone asked, *When you talked about* pet cats, *what were you referring to?* You could only point to lots of individual examples of pet cats. And you would have a harder time yet explaining the referent of *cat* in a sentence like *The cat is a mysterious creature,* because there *cat* refers to the abstract category of cats. So a referent can be an individual thing in the world, a concept that categorizes many things in the world, or an abstract concept.

- When we think of sets of things as alike, we group them into mental **categories**. We create categories ranging from very large to very small: *things, creatures, animals, mammals, felines, cats, Persians, Sue's Persian cat.*

We create some categories to match what seem to be natural categories in the world: *tree, dog, water, dinosaur;* other categories we create and then impose on the world: *duty, spice, animals bigger than a breadbox,* even the term *category* itself. (It is a puzzling question whether categories such as "natural kinds" really exist in nature or whether all categories are human impositions.)

- When we talk about categories, we usually name them by **terms**. (We use *term* rather than *word,* because some terms are not single words but phrases.) The terms *animal, mammal, feline, cat,* and *Persian* all name both categories and individual referents in them. We gain and lose terms all the time: *DVD* is a new one; *gramophone* is almost gone. And we invent phrases to name categories for which we have no single word: *creatures that fly.*

- When we distinguish referents in one category from those in another, we talk about their shared and distinguishing **features**. The distinguishing features of Persian cats are that they are fluffy, have pug noses, and meow; Siamese cats are smooth, have pointed noses, and yowl. The problem with distinguishing features is that there may be no one feature that all members of a category share. Some people think that categories are like rigid containers, with referents being either in or out. As we'll see in a moment, that's a mistake.

- We assign **meaning** to a category based on the features that distinguish it from others, but also on the associations, values, and other ideas we have about it. We then attach some of that meaning to the term that names the category. So when we think about the meaning of *cat,* we call up a mixture of images, concepts, feelings, and so on. Like categories, meanings do not have sharp boundaries.

- Psychologists argue convincingly that we experience "meaning" more as a holistic entity than as the sum of individual parts. But when we *talk* about a meaning, we have to break it into elements that we'll call **criteria** of meaning. For example, when someone asks us what the word *friable* means, we say, *It means sort of dry and crumbly and easily broken into little pieces.* Among the criteria for the meaning of *friable* are "dry," "crumbly," "easily breaks into little pieces."

- We create a **definition** when we state in words some criteria of meaning of a term that we attach to a category. Most definitions consist of a word that names a general category, which we then modify with more words that narrow its meaning.

To understand arguments about meaning, keep three things in mind:

- We make up definitions, but meaning is imposed on us by the way we and others use words.
- The meaning of a term is infinitely more complex than its definition.
- Most importantly, we can't use the definition of a term to settle whether we should apply it to some specific referent.

When we decide what to call something, not only do we focus on different features of the referent, depending on the situation, but we also focus on many other things as well, including the problem we want to solve by naming it. We define *water* as the chemical compound consisting of two parts hydrogen and one part oxygen. But the meaning of *water* includes many facts about it, including that it covers the earth, is necessary for life, and washes away dirt. We don't call H_2O *water* if it is ice or steam because we use them so differently: We don't want ice or steam when the problem is to wash our hands.

We invent new terms when we want to group things into a new category. For example, a few years ago people noticed that some drivers _{referents} were displaying hostile behavior. _{common feature} They drove aggressively and used nasty language or made angry gestures toward other drivers, and so on. _{common features} When people saw this behavior pattern, they created a category that had no settled term attached to it. At first, they referred to the category with various terms: *aggressive driving, hostility behind the wheel,* and so on. Eventually one term with a memorable sound stuck to the category, *road rage.* Now when a driver cuts us off, yelling and shaking his fist, we can say, *There's another case of road rage.* If someone asks what we mean, we can point to a specific example, describe a typical case, or give a definition: *driving* (general category) *in ways that seem aggressive, angry, and hostile* (narrowing terms).

If definitions were as clear-cut as that example seems, we wouldn't have to make arguments about terms or their meanings. But within general limits, we all use words and define their meanings in different ways at different times for different purposes to solve different problems. As a consequence, we do not all agree all the time about what words mean or how we should use them.

For example, suppose you tell your host at a dinner party that a dish you thought was awful tasted great. You have knowingly told an untruth. But would you call that untruth an *out and out lie?* If you told it to be kind to your host, you might call it a *white lie* or maybe a *fib.* Most of us, however, would be reluctant to call it an *outright lie* even though it might "technically" be one. In other words, we choose one term rather than another in order to solve a social problem: we do not want to be guilty of lying, so we call our untruth a *fib.*

On the other hand, suppose you said the dish was good, hoping that your host would prepare it again for his (and your) boss, get fired, and you'd get his job. You said the same words (*Great dinner!*) referring to the same referent (an awful dinner), but with a different intention. Now do we call that same untrue statement *a fib, a white lie,* or a *real lie?* Probably the last.

Meaning is, to mix metaphors, slippery and fuzzy at the same time.

Meanings and Problems

What Problem Does Your Definition Solve?

As with any argument, you plan one about meaning by first asking what problem motivates you to make it and whether it is conceptual or pragmatic:

- In a conceptual argument, you create a definition to help readers understand something important about a larger issue or question.
- In a pragmatic argument, you discuss meaning so that readers will see why an action is necessary.

For example, in Part 1 we defined *argument* in a way that we thought would help you write good arguments. We focused on a practical outcome and ways to reach it. If that definition worked for you, then together we solved a pragmatic problem. If, however, we had been writing a scholarly analysis of argument, we would have defined that term differently, because our aim would have been not to help you *do* something about argument (write better ones), but to help you *understand* how the meaning of that term has changed and what it tells us about the social history of reasoning and communication.

So before anything else, you have to understand what specific problem occasions your argument and whether you want readers only to *understand* something or to *do* something.

Is the Issue of Meaning a Surrogate for a Larger Problem?

Sometimes we aren't clear about the kind of problem we want to solve because we unknowingly get bogged down in a *surrogate argument.* A surrogate argument is one that stands in for another, usually one we want to avoid because its problem is too large or too contentious for us to solve directly. Surrogate arguments about meaning typically lead us astray in one of two ways: an apparently conceptual problem about definitions masks an underlying pragmatic problem, or a question about meaning masks a conflict over values and feelings.

Don't Confuse Words and Deeds

When you and your readers disagree about terms, don't assume that you will get anywhere by arguing about definitions. If the terms affect a larger pragmatic problem, the pragmatic problem may be what's really at issue.

Here is an example. Thelma and Louise are debating whether two people of the same sex can have a ceremony we call a *wedding:*

Thelma: I had an interesting weekend. I went to the wedding of two women friends of my aunt.

Louise: Well, maybe it was a ceremony, but it wasn't a wedding because *wedding* means joining a man and woman in marriage. Two women can't marry, so they can't have a wedding.

Thelma: Who says you can't have a marriage between any two people when they publicly commit themselves to each other? Who says they can't be the same sex?

Louise: Look at how the word's been used for thousands of years. A wedding has always meant creating a marriage bond between a man and a woman.

Thelma: Words change their meaning to suit new realities.

Louise: Maybe some do, but you can't invent new meanings just to suit your purpose. For most people, *wedding* still means a ceremony between a man and woman. That's just what it means.

Thelma and Louise risk endlessly debating the meaning of *wedding* and *marriage* until they agree on the kind of problem they want the definition to solve. They could be debating a conceptual problem of linguistic change: *Can individuals change the meaning of terms when it suits their purposes?* More likely they are really concerned about a pragmatic problem that can be solved if society uses the terms *wedding* and *marriage* in particular ways:

- Thelma may think that using the term *wedding* for same-sex ceremonies *solves* a pragmatic problem: Same-sex couples are deprived of social, personal, and economic benefits associated with traditional marriage partnerships. It is for her a problem of social injustice. To solve it, she wants to put same-sex couples in the same category as different-sex couples, an aim she could further by getting Louise to call their ceremony a *wedding* and their relationship a *marriage*.

- Louise may think that using the term *wedding* for same-sex ceremonies *creates* a different pragmatic problem: She believes that if society condones same-sex relationships by calling them *marriages*, it implicitly condones what she believes is immoral behavior. It is for her a problem of morality. To avoid that moral problem, she wants to keep same-sex couples in a different category from different-sex couples, an aim furthered by not calling their ceremony a *wedding* and their relationship a *marriage*.

If those underlying pragmatic problems are what really motivate Thelma and Louise to debate the meaning of *wedding* and *marriage*, they are stuck in an unproductive surrogate argument. They are defending their positions not (just) because of what they think the term *wedding* "really" means, but because of how they think society should treat same-sex couples. They are unlikely to agree about anything, so long as they fail to recognize that what's at stake is more than competing definitions and meanings of terms.

Here's what to watch for: If you think you have to make a conceptual argument that turns on the meaning and definition of a key term, ask yourself whether your seemingly conceptual argument might be a surrogate for a pragmatic one. If you find yourself going round and round about the "real" meaning of a term, step back and look for a pragmatic problem that occasioned the need to define the term in the first place. Ask what *consequences* flow from using one term or another to describe its referents.

If you decide your argument might be a surrogate for a larger problem, try to define that problem and confront it directly. If the real problem is too big or too sensitive to address directly, try addressing the question of meaning not as an unacknowledged surrogate but as an aspect of the larger problem. Otherwise, you risk trapping yourself and your readers in an aimless debate that misses the point.

Don't Confuse Definitions and Values

You can also create a surrogate argument if you fail to recognize that what you really want is for your readers to evaluate something as you do, and thereby to feel about it as you do. Consider this exchange:

Maude: I think *Titanic* is a masterpiece of film art ~claim~ that movingly dramatizes the tragedy of an epic event from an intimately human point of view, celebrating human courage and self-sacrifice for another. ~reasons~

Harold: I think it's commercial exploitation ~claim~ that crassly appeals to our emotions by cynically denigrating the rich as selfish and cowardly and shamelessly flattering the lower classes as selfless and brave, thereby pandering to class resentments for a bigger box office. ~reasons~

Maude and Harold seem to be concerned with a problem of categorizing *Titanic* and finding terms to name it: Does *Titanic* fit into the category called *masterpiece of film art* or the one called *commercial exploitation*? They could try to find criteria for each category, match them to the features of the movie, and agree which it is—perhaps that it's a bit of both. But their value-laden language suggests that something is at stake beyond mere categorization. They use strong words that invoke strong values and strong feelings: *movingly, tragedy, epic, celebrating* vs. *crassly, cynically, shamelessly, pandering*.

If Harold and Maude are talking about *Titanic* to express their values or vent their feelings (two sides of the same coin), then they are arguing not about what *Titanic* "really" is, but about how they feel about it and how each wants the other to. If so, neither is likely to change how the other feels by arguing over definitions. Suppose Harold carefully matched features of the film to criteria for the category *commercial exploitation,* but Maude still responded, *Of course it's commercial exploitation, but so what? It's still a great movie. I love it.* Harold would have won an empty victory in a debate he was finally bound to lose.

Here's what to watch for: Don't debate definitions when you want others to like or dislike, approve or disapprove of something. You won't persuade them by defining terms that someone is *thrifty* rather than *stingy* or *plain speaking* rather than *opinionated.* When a term implies approval or disapproval, we attach to its meaning evaluations and feelings *we already have.* We use evaluative terms *after* we approve or disapprove. What's at issue is not finding the right word but expressing the right feeling.

When you find yourself in an argument that seems to go round and round over definitions, step back and ask whether you are having a surrogate argument that you cannot settle until you settle another one. If so, you have the uphill task of matching features to criteria, hoping to overwhelm the other person with detail. (On a personal note, GGC and JMW can testify that it has never worked with their wives or children, or with each other.)

How to Argue About Meanings

When you make an argument about meaning, you usually have a relatively straightforward aim: You want readers to think of a referent in a certain way, so you give them reasons to call it by a certain term. If they do call it by that term, they put it in the category named by the term, and that leads them to think of the referent as you want them to. Let's say you want to argue that Mapplethorpe's photographs _{referents} are not *pornography* _{term 1} but are instead *erotic art.* _{term 2} You therefore have to build an argument in which you do two things:

- You have to give readers reason to accept certain criteria of meaning for your key terms. So you first have to get them to agree with your definitions of *pornography* and *erotic art.*
- You also have to give them reason to see that features of the referents, the photos, don't match the criteria of *pornography* but do match the criteria of *erotic art.*

You may have a hard time doing that, because meanings are not as fixed as many think, or wish. Some philosophers treat a category as a rigid container filled with meaning defined by an "essence" that distinguishes that meaning and that category from all others. They claim we can always know whether a particular referent is in or out of a category, because if we just think hard enough, we can discover the fixed, essential criteria that define the category and decide whether a referent has the essential features that match them.

But as much as philosophers might wish we would use words and meanings in fixed and predictable ways, that's not how we do it in real life, especially in arguments. Categories are not prefabricated containers, and referents are not predetermined to fit into them, the way a round peg fits a round hole. In real-life arguments, we shave pegs and stretch holes to fit each other.

Do Readers Expect Common or Authorized Meanings?

To determine how much freedom you have to stretch a meaning, you have to decide what kind of meaning readers expect you to use, *common* or *authorized*.

- A *common meaning* is our everyday, nontechnical understanding of a term, like our ordinary meaning of *dog*. In casual conversation, most of us think a coyote is a "kind of" dog, and for most of us urban dwellers, so is a wolf. When we see hyenas on TV, a lot of us think of them as really ugly dogs (even though they are more closely related to cats and most closely to the mongoose).

- An *authorized meaning*, on the other hand, is a technical "officially" defined meaning, such as the meaning a biologist would associate with *dog* when writing a scientific article about the evolutionary relationships among dogs, wolves, and coyotes. For a biologist, a hyena is no more a dog than a cat is.

If your readers expect you to use a word according to its common meaning, you are free, within limits, to shape your definition to achieve your aim. If you are offended by a sexually explicit image, you can call it *pornographic* and we will all know what you mean. If, however, readers expect you to use a term with its authorized legal meaning, they will hold you within its four corners. The Supreme Court, for example, has stipulated that for a referent to be "technically" (that is, legally) pornographic, its features must match three criteria of authorized legal meaning. They are in *Black's Law Dictionary*:

> Material is pornographic or obscene [1] if the average person, applying contemporary community standards, would find that the work taken as a whole appeals to the prurient interest and [2] if it depicts in a patently offensive way sexual conduct and [3] if the work taken as a whole lacks serious literary, artistic, political, or scientific value (*Miller v. California*, 413 U.S. 15, 24-25, 93 S.Ct. 2607, 2615, 37 L. Ed. 2d 419).

In court, critics of the National Endowment for the Arts would have to work inside the boundaries of that authorized definition of *pornography* to argue that Mapplethorpe's photos are legally pornographic. But in a speech to the PTA back home, they could rely on common meanings to create their own "loose" definition: *Mapplethorpe's images are pornographic because they degrade human dignity by reducing sex to animal behavior.*

When you write for readers in a particular field, especially teachers, remember that the key terms they work with probably have authorized definitions, some of which have been debated for centuries. So you should anticipate that they will expect you to use those terms with their agreed on, authorized meaning, or if their meanings are disputed, to acknowledge the debate. If, for example, you use the term *social class* in a sociology paper, *tragedy* in a drama class, or *inertia* in a physics lab, your readers will expect you to use those terms as authorized by the fields of sociology, literary criticism, and physics.

The problem is that a term with an authorized definition in one field can be used with its common meaning in another: *tragedy* is a technical term in literary criticism, but is used with its common meaning in sociology: *the tragedy of teenage suicide.*

Just a Theory?

No word causes more misunderstanding between science and the public than the word *theory.* Scientists use the word in its well-defined authorized sense to mean a clearly stated, well-supported explanation of a phenomenon. So when a scientist talks about quantum *theory* or the *theory* of relativity, she doesn't mean speculation or unsupported belief about electrons or the speed of light, but an explanation that enjoys wide acceptance in the community of scientists. Among a large part of the general public, however, *theory* has a common meaning that is almost the opposite: mere speculation, a hunch or guess And so when some attack Darwin's theory of evolution specifically because it is called a *theory,* they give the word its common meaning, which is at odds with the biologist's authorized meaning. There may be reason to argue about evolution, but the fact that it is called a *theory* is not one of them.

Strategies for Using Common Meanings

Even though you have some freedom to stretch a meaning and shape a referent to fit it, you have to stay within common sense limits. The more readers use a term and the more they know about a referent, the more likely they will accept only definitions and descriptions that match their sense of things. You could call Timothy McVeigh a true patriot, but most of us have a definition of *patriot* that won't stretch that far. But however fuzzily bounded a meaning is, you have to give readers good reason to apply it to a particular referent. Here are three strategies for doing that.

Strategy 1: Shape Criteria of Meaning and Features of Referents to Match Each Other

If you are not bound to an authorized meaning but can work with a common one, you can shape a referent to fit the meaning *at the same time* you shape the meaning to fit the referent. It's like shaving a peg to fit a hole at the same time you shave the hole to accept the peg.

For example, imagine someone wants us to reject a Constitutional amendment that criminalizes burning the American flag. To do so, she decides to use the term *patriotic* to describe those who burn the flag to protest immoral actions by our government. She reasons that if she can get people to think of flag-burners as patriots, then they may agree that the Constitution should not ban flag-burning but protect it. Since there are no authorized criteria for *patriotic*, she has room to develop its common meaning in ways that help her achieve her aim:

> Those who support a Constitutional amendment criminalizing flag-burning appeal first to our patriotism. Many of them define *patriotism* as honoring the flag: waving it, saluting it, standing at attention as it passes by. They see the flag as synonymous with our country itself: damage it, and you damage America. _{acknowledgment of alternative definition} But for those who see more deeply, real patriotism is loyalty not to symbols, but to the principles those symbols represent, including the idea that when a government violates them, truly patriotic citizens must protest. Real patriotism calls attention to such wrongs, even if it takes burning the flag to do it. _{criteria for the meaning of patriot} If such symbolic expression is made a crime, _{destabilizing condition of problem} we will threaten our values more than any flag-burner could. _{cost of problem} Congress should reject such an amendment. _{solution/claim}

This writer picks out features of flag-burners that she thinks make them admirable, but *at the same time,* she crafts criteria for the meaning of *patriot* to match their features: *A true patriot is someone with the courage to enrage others in order to preserve the highest values of our nation. Flag-burners have that courage.*

She is, of course, constrained by how much our beliefs limit the common sense criteria we will accept for the meaning of *patriot*. She cannot succeed if we think all civil protest is wrong, even in defense of "the principles this country stands for." So your freedom to shape features and criteria is ultimately limited by your readers' ideas of both the term and the referent.

Strategy 2: Match the Referent to a Model

We commonly talk about meaning in terms of discrete criteria, but psychologists have shown that we probably think about most meanings and categories differently: When we apply a term to a referent we don't test the referent against a check-list of criteria of meaning. We compare it holistically to what we think of as the best or most typical instance of the category (what psychologists call a *prototype* but we call a *model*). It's a bit like showing readers that your peg is so much like a model peg that it obviously fits the hole.

For example, the following passage describes a familiar instance of a patriot, the Minutemen of 1775. If the reader accepts it as typical, the writer can show that a civilian militia member of today matches that historical model:

> Critics of citizen militias forget that it was civilians with their own guns who won our freedoms 200 years ago. The Minutemen of 1775 were patriots who defended their homes and families by grabbing their rifles from over their fireplaces and joining others in common defense against a tyrannical government, _{model} just as the freedom lover who joins a militia today leaves his home to prepare to defend our freedoms. _{referent} As we honor those patriots who won our freedom then, so should we respect those who defend it now.

Readers will accept a meaning based on a model when they accept the model as typical of the category *and* they think a referent closely resembles it.

The more vividly you portray the model and the referent, the more persuasive your argument. Of course, you still have to use terms to describe the model, and they all have criteria of meaning. So in a sense, even when you create a model and match your referent to it, you are still matching features to criteria, but less as a checklist than as a word picture.

Strategy 3: Combine Matching and Modeling

You can always combine feature matching with modeling:

> Those who condemn citizen militias as paranoid gun nuts ignore their deep love for the principles that this country was founded on. _{criterion 1} Civilian militias are ready to join with others to rise up against unjust tyranny, relying on force, if necessary; _{criterion 2} and they are ready to lay down their lives to preserve their freedom and yours. _{criterion 3} They are the true patriots of our time, no different from the Minutemen of 1775, who defended their homes and families by grabbing their rifles from over their fireplaces and joining others in common defense against a tyrannical government. _{model} In the same way, civilian militia keep their guns ready to resist a tyranny that wants to deprive us of our freedom to use them. _{referent} If we honor the patriots of 1775, so should we respect those of today. _{claim}

Our language imposes limits on meanings that we violate at our peril. But within those limits, we are free to craft descriptions of referents, criteria of meaning, and models in ways that solve our problem.

Strategies for Using Authorized Meanings

When readers expect you to use an authorized meaning, you have less freedom. You usually have to accept the stipulated criteria and describe the features of the referent in a way that matches them. For example, the diagnostic manual of the American Psychiatric Association breaks the common term *alcoholism* into several specific conditions and stipulates criteria for each. The most serious condition is *alcohol dependence*. A person is alcohol dependent if he or she meets at least two of four criteria:

1. *Tolerance:* The body's cells adapt to high levels of alcohol so that it has less effect on them.

2. *Dyscontrol* (psychological dependence): The person drinks to relieve bodily or emotional pain, but does not control when, where, or how he or she drinks.

3. *Medical complications:* The person suffers physical damage from alcohol.

4. *Withdrawal:* When the person abstains from drinking, he or she suffers convulsions, hallucinations, or delirium.

A clinical psychologist arguing in a professional setting must observe that definition, because it is enforced by canons of professional ethics and peer pressure. So if she makes a case that someone is alcohol dependent, she will describe the features of that person to fit the criteria:

> Mr. Jones shows a high tolerance with no visible effects until his blood alcohol level reaches 0.2, twice what should make a man his size intoxicated. Although he has no medical complications, he does exhibit psychological dependence. He begins drinking every morning, usually alone, and cannot stop. Since Mr. Jones drinks every day, we cannot say whether he suffers withdrawal, but it is likely he would if he stopped drinking.

When an authority and its backing institution set out criteria of meaning, you have to match the features of the referent to them. It's a one-way fit, like fitting a wooden peg into a rigid hole: though you can't change the hole, you can shape the peg to fit, within limits.

When to Rely on Authorized Definitions

When readers in a field read its professional prose, they expect writers to use terms in their authorized sense. For example, the terms *tragedy* and *comedy* have common meanings that we use in everyday conversation. But over the last 2,500 years or so, literary critics have given them technical definitions. So students in a drama class seem more authoritative when they use those terms in their technical sense. In fact, when aspiring professionals use the common meanings of terms that have technical definitions, they seem ignorant.

On the other hand, if your readers understand only the common meaning of a term but you use an authorized one, you risk confusing them and damaging your ethos. Don't try to override their understanding with an authorized, technical meaning: they will only resist.

For example, medical and environmental scientists have long failed to educate the public about the "true" risks of nuclear waste and toxic dumps. Only recently have they realized why: We define *risk* differently from the way they do. Experts use an authorized, statistical definition of risk roughly like this:

Risk = Probability of occurrence × Cost

Risk is the probability that something will happen (over a certain period of time and level of exposure) multiplied by its cost (death, injury, or illness). So a scientist might say that if you lived for 30 years within two miles of an atomic power plant, your increased risk of cancer from that plant would be .0001, a risk lower than stepping into your bathtub. But for years, risk communication experts could not understand why ordinary folks wouldn't buy their assurances.

It took a long time for social psychologists to figure it out, but now they understand that most of us ordinary folks do not define risk statistically (even when we understand the math), but psychologically, in terms of our own common definition. We judge risk by summing at least these four factors:

1. *Magnitude of the cost*: If the worst happens, will a lot of people be hurt?
2. *Immediacy of the cost*: If the worst happens, will people be harmed all at once or over a long period of time?

3. *Control over the risk*: Does our risk depend on what we do or on what someone else does?

4. *Choice of the risk*: Is the risk one that we choose to run?

There are a few other criteria we use to define risk, but those are the important ones:

RISK = Magnitude + Immediacy + Lack of control + Lack of choice

So long as risk experts talked to us only in terms of their authorized, statistical definition, they had no chance of persuading the rest of us that trucking atomic waste through town posed an "insignificant" risk. But now that they know how to explain risk using our common definition, they are better able to help us make sound judgments.

Here are two things to watch for:

- When you use a term that might have a specialized meaning for your readers, look it up in a specialized reference work. You would seem foolish writing to experts in risk communication if you did not acknowledge their authorized definition.

- But when you write for ordinary readers, do not expect to override their common definitions with your authorized ones. You may think that your technical terms carry an authority that *should* persuade readers, but they rarely do. You have to adapt your terms to their understanding.

Why Dictionaries Cannot Settle Arguments Over Meaning

When we said that no authority stipulates the criteria for the meaning of ordinary words like *patriotism* and *athlete,* some of you surely thought of dictionaries. Even the Supreme Court relies on them to settle disputes over the meaning of a term as simple as *carry.* (If you have a gun locked up in the trunk of your car as you commit a crime, are you "carrying" a weapon while committing that crime? The court said yes.) But as prestigious as dictionaries are, they cannot capture the full complexity of any meaning, and few readers let a dictionary definition outweigh their sense of what a term "really" means.

The Role of Criteria in Dictionary Definitions

Consider this conversation between Erin and her friend Ethan:

Erin: If ice dancing is an Olympic sport, and ice dancers are athletes, why shouldn't competitive ballroom dancing also be a sporting event and competitive dancers be considered athletes?

Ethan: I can't buy that. Dancing is entertainment, like the ballet.

Erin: So what? The Olympics are entertainment, and rhythmic gymnastics is like ballet, and so is synchronized swimming, but both are still considered sports.

Ethan: You just don't get the real meaning of *sport* and *athlete*. Let's look them up in Webster's.

Ethan would find that those dictionary definitions have two parts:

1. A word or phrase that names a general category (some call it the *genus*).

2. More words or phrases that narrow the general category to a specific one (some call them the terms that define the *species*).

athlete: A person _{general category} who competes in contests requiring strength, stamina, or physical agility. _{specific criteria}

sport: An athletic activity _{general category} requiring skill or physical prowess. _{specific criteria}

A dictionary definition succeeds if it helps us distinguish the meaning of that word from every other. Some might think we can then know whether the word correctly names any referent. But if Ethan believes that, he is led to a conclusion as unwelcome as it is logical:

Ethan: Well, it says here that athletes are "persons," and they "compete in contests requiring strength, stamina, or physical agility," so I guess ballroom dancers fit the criteria for athletes. And then it says that a sport is an "activity" that is "athletic," and "requires skill or physical prowess," and competitive dancing does that. So I guess you're right: The tango should be an Olympic event.

He has come to a logical conclusion, but one few readers would accept.

The Limitations of Dictionary Criteria for Common Meanings

Here are two facts about dictionary definitions:

- Dictionary definitions list just enough criteria to distinguish a word from every other word, *but no more.*

Meanings are infinitely more complex than definitions. A dictionary definition is to meaning as a hand-drawn map is to the place it describes. A lot gets lost.

- The dictionary definition of a term cannot tell you whether a particular referent does or does not belong in the particular category the term names.

When we decide what to call a referent, we use many features of the referent that do not appear in dictionaries as criteria of meaning.

For example, when we decide whether to call an activity a sport, one relevant feature is its history—something no dictionary definition cites. Ice dancing became an Olympic event in 1976, partly because it was related to figure skating (already an Olympic sport), which was linked to speed skating (a model sport). Speakers widened the category named by *sport* by dropping out particular criteria of meaning: Now, if you do anything on skates that takes skill and strength, it's a sport.

Ethan could have seen the limits of dictionaries by testing their sparse criteria for *athlete* and *sport* on borderline referents. If an athlete is *anyone* who competes in a contest requiring strength, stamina, *or* physical agility, then Miss America contestants are athletes, along with violin players, lumberjacks, even cooks. But that contradicts our common sense *use* of the term *athlete,* which is based more on our mental model of a "real" athlete than on criteria listed in a dictionary.

The Limitations of Dictionary Criteria for Authorized Meanings

You might think that officially sanctioned dictionaries that include only authorized definitions escape the limits of standard dictionaries, but their authorized criteria ultimately suffer from the same problem that common ones do.

For example, those critics who wanted to shut down the NEA because it supported pornography might have used the authorized criteria for the legal definition of *pornography* as listed in *Black's Law Dictionary:*

- The average person, applying contemporary community standards, would find that the work appeals to the prurient interest.
- It depicts sexual conduct in a patently offensive way.
- It lacks serious literary, artistic, political, or scientific value.

Relying on those criteria, those critics could have made a criteria-matching argument claiming that Mapplethorpe's photographs are pornographic.

But that is deceptively simple, because they might have been challenged to define the terms naming the criteria. What criteria define the criterion named *prurient?* We could look in *Black's Dictionary* for its authorized definition:

prurient: A shameful or morbid interest in nudity, sex, or excretion . . . having lustful ideas or desires . . . an obsessive interest in immoral and lascivious matters.

But what criteria define the criteria named *shameful, morbid, immoral,* and *lascivious?* Here's *Black's* authorized definition of *lascivious:*

lascivious: Tending to excite lust; lewd; indecent; obscene; sexual impurity; tending to deprave the morals in respect to sexual relations; licentious. [cites]. . . . See *lewd; obscene.*

But now what does that criterion *lewd* mean? Here's part of its definition:

lewd: Obscene, lustful, indecent, lascivious, lecherous.

We have a problem: The criteria for *lascivious* told us to see *lewd,* but the criteria for *lewd* direct us back to *lascivious.*

That's why, ultimately, we cannot mechanically depend on criteria-based arguments of any kind. Legislators and scientists can stipulate criteria for the meaning of *pornography* or *planet,* but that just shifts the question one step down: What terms name the criteria, and what criteria define those terms? And what criteria define *those* terms, and then . . . You get the idea. And at some point, the criteria loop back on themselves: *lascivious* means *lewd,* but *lewd* means *lascivious*. Ultimately, all these criteria depend on our agreeing to some meanings *without* criteria or arguments to support them.

Definitions ultimately rest only on our agreement. But that's not a problem; it's an opportunity. It frees you from the rigidity of *all* dictionary definitions (well, at least it gives you some wiggle-room). By defining criteria, you can, within limits, develop your own meanings. Even the court-authorized legal definition of *pornography* ultimately depends on the criteria for terms like *average person, community,* and *serious artistic value*, all terms that depend on common meanings.

The Pluto Problem

Not much seems at stake in whether we call Pluto a planet or a big blob of ice, which it resembles more than it does other planets. So it's a purely conceptual question (though see Inquiry 3 on p. 196). Yet astronomers debate what to call it. Pluto is so different from the other planets that if it were kept in the category of planets, astronomers could not generalize about their origin, age, physical features, even how they rotate. Alternatively, astronomers might argue that even though Pluto differs from other planets, it is not so different that excluding it is worth the small saving in conceptual consistency. What they decide to call Pluto—a planet or an ice blob—depends on what else they want to say not just about it but about the other planets as well. In other words, they pick the definition that is most consistent with everything else they believe about planets and blobs of ice.

If you are not yet immersed in an advanced field of study, this issue of intellectual consistency may seem remote, even hairsplitting. But once you are in a specialized field, you'll find that your conceptual arguments will be tested not just by whether a definition you propose solves your local conceptual problem, but by whether it is consistent with the whole body of knowledge, principles, facts, and beliefs that constitute your field.

EXAMPLE

A Definition that Challenged Beliefs

When we define terms in a conceptual argument, we normally observe the rule of consistency. Some writers, however, offer definitions so new but so compelling that they change widely accepted beliefs. We call them geniuses. Isaac Newton was one: he redefined the term gravity *in ways that revolutionized not only physics but common sense, until Einstein redefined it again. Another was Charles Darwin, whose term* natural selection *challenged common beliefs about science, history, religion, and society—challenges we still debate today. Here Darwin reflects on the difficulties his term caused. As revolutionary as that term was, he works hard to make his definition fit rather than contradict the common meaning of* natural *and* selection. *Note how he tries to "naturalize"* natural selection *by finding familiar analogies that match his criteria. (Note as well his deft use of acknowledgment and response.)*

Several writers have misapprehended or objected to the term *Natural Selection*. Some have even imagined that natural selection induces variability, whereas it implies only the preservation of such variations as arise and are beneficial to the being under its conditions of life. No one objects to agriculturists speaking of the potent effects of man's selection; and in this case the individual differences given by nature, which man for some object selects, must of necessity first occur. Others have objected that the term *selection* implies conscious choice in the animals, which become modified; and it had even been urged that, as plants have no volition, natural selection is not applicable to them! In the literal sense of the word, no doubt, *natural selection* is a false term; but who ever objected to chemists speaking of the elective affinities of the various elements?—and yet an acid cannot strictly be said to elect the base with which it in preference combines. It has been said that I speak of natural selection as an active power of Deity, but who objects to an author speaking of the attraction of gravity as ruling the movements of the planets? Everyone knows what is meant and is implied by such metaphorical expressions; and they are almost necessary for brevity. So again it is difficult to avoid personifying the word Nature; but I mean by Nature, only the aggregate action and product of many natural laws, and by laws the sequence of events as ascertained by us. With a little familiarity such superficial objections will be forgotten.

Source: Charles Darwin, *Origin of Species,* Chapter 4.

WRITING PROCESS
Arguments About Meanings

PREPARING AND PLANNING

Anticipate Questions About Meaning

No question about a contestable claim is more common than *But doesn't it depend on what you mean by . . . ?* Anticipate that question by identifying your key terms, then imagine readers asking *But what do you mean by . . . ?* If your argument in fact depends on a meaning that may be in doubt, you have to define and illustrate it. *A patriot is someone who . . . , such as . . .*

Pick a Strategy for Matching Referents and Meanings

When you make an argument about meaning, you can create a model as a benchmark for your referent, match features to criteria (and vice versa), or both.

Develop Models

To build a model of a category, close your dictionary and crank up your imagination. Imagine a "real" example of, say, a *patriot,* and then bring that image to life in a way that matches your referent. The problem is that we all have somewhat different images, both of a model instance of the category and of the referent you want to apply it to. So to base an argument on a model, you have to determine how closely you can make your model and your image of the referent resemble those of your readers.

For example, to argue that militia members are (or are not) patriots, you'd start by comparing your model of a patriot with that of your readers:

- What image first comes to mind when *you* think of an example of *patriotic?* Is it an action, like waving the flag and singing the national anthem, or sacrifice, or protesting laws? Or is it an attitude, a feeling?
- What image do you think first comes to your readers' minds when they think of a prototypical example of patriotism? If you don't know, find out.

Now compare your image of your referent with that of your readers:

- What is your image of a militia member? Is it a potbellied middle-aged gun nut in a camouflage costume running around playing soldier? Or is it a survivalist able to live in the wild while resisting unjust government?
- What do your *readers* think of as a prototypical militia member? If you don't know, find out.

If your images of a patriot and a militia member match theirs, good; if not, you've got a problem. Acknowledge the difference, and try to bring your models in line with those of your readers. If that won't work, find a way to make your argument without relying on models.

Find Analogies

Analogies give you more leeway than models, because you don't need a prototypical instance of the category, just an unambiguous one.

Analogies appeal to intellectual consistency:

1. Referent $_1$ is like referent $_2$.
2. We say referent $_2$ belongs in category C, so we call it by term T.
3. Therefore, logical consistency allows us to call referent $_1$ by term T as well.

For example, those debating whether alcoholism is a disabling illness or a character flaw analogize it to other mental illnesses or to other character flaws:

Alcoholism $_{referent\ 1}$ is a weakness of character, $_{term\ T}$ like sloth or self-indulgence, $_{referent\ 2}$ because if alcoholics wanted to recover, they could, just as lazy people can get up and go to work if they want to. $_{distinctive\ feature}$ Do we start supporting lazy people? $_{appeal\ to\ intellectual\ consistency}$

> Alcoholism ~referent 1~ is an *illness* ~term T~ like depression, ~referent 2~ because it is as difficult to overcome as depression and just as debilitating. ~distinctive feature~ If we do not help alcoholics overcome their condition, then do we stop supporting all mental illnesses such as schizophrenia and depression? ~appeal to intellectual consistency~

For an analogy to work, you have to persuade readers to accept two claims:

- The referents are alike in relevant ways.
- They should apply the principle of logical consistency.

The problem is, as these examples show, we can find analogies on both sides of most questions.

Appeal to History

You can also appeal to intellectual consistency by arguing that readers should use a term as others have in the past, the argument Thelma made about *wedding.* There is, for example, a debate about the term *holocaust.* Some Jewish historians want to restrict it to what Nazis did to Jews. But some African-Americans want to use it to refer to the forced ocean trip from Africa to the Americas that killed countless slaves; and some Cambodians want to use it to refer to the killing by the Khmer Rouge of millions of their own people. To argue their cases, African-Americans and Cambodians can point out that *holocaust* was used as early as 1671 to refer to an immense loss of life from fire, and thereafter to any immense loss of life. But that wouldn't settle the issue, because a debate about the use of the term *holocaust* is almost certainly a surrogate argument.

Duck the Definition Entirely

Do this when you think that readers may never accept your definition, model, analogy, or historical appeal. Focus instead on what's at stake in the problem and what will solve it. For example, a conceptual argument about what alcoholism *is* may be a surrogate for the larger pragmatic problem of what we should *do* about it:

- Many see alcoholism as a character flaw because they believe that if we call it an illness, we undermine personal responsibility and encourage alcoholics to see themselves as helpless victims.
- Many see alcoholism as an illness because they believe that if we call it a character flaw, we encourage people to ignore their human duty to care for those unable to overcome disabling afflictions.

Those on either side of the issue can endlessly debate criteria for *character flaw* and *illness,* but the more productive strategy might be to ignore definitions and focus instead on what good and bad will actually happen, what costs and benefits will actually follow, depending on what we *do* about alcoholics.

DRAFTING

Creating Room to Redefine Terms

There are words and phrases that give you room to define terms and build models to suit your purpose. For example, the writer who wanted to call flag-burners *patriots* gave herself some leeway by starting with a standard definition of *patriotism,* waving the flag and so on; she then contrasted it with what she called *real* patriotism. When you need to argue against a standard definition, characterize your definition of a word as defining the *real, true,* or *genuine* thing. When you want to reject someone else's definition, describe theirs with terms like *broadly, loosely, technically,* or *strictly speaking.*

> *Broadly speaking,* anyone devoted to his country is a patriot, but a true patriot is . . .

> *Technically*, risk is a mathematical probability, but it is *actually* a feeling that . . .

Introducing Dictionary Definitions

Since dictionary definitions settle few issues, you should generally avoid using them. Any term whose common meaning is important enough to define is too complex for a dictionary definition. But if you feel you need help from a dictionary, don't simply quote it:

> According to *Webster*, a *patriot* is "a person who loves his country, zealously supporting it and its interests."

That is amateurish at best. Instead, paraphrase the definition and introduce it as a common meaning:

> Most of us think of a patriot as someone who loves his country and zealously acts to support and defend it.

If you want to invoke the authority of a dictionary, cite it in a footnote.

When you need to introduce an authorized meaning in a formal way, paraphrase; don't quote the definition or mention a dictionary in your main text. Mention instead the authority that stands behind it:

> Most experts in risk communication define *risk* as . . .

> The legal meaning of *pornography* depends on three features that the Supreme Court stipulated . . .

> According to the APA, alcoholism is . . .

Document the definition in a citation.

INQUIRIES

1. For a long time, the diagnostic manual of the American Psychiatric Association categorized homosexuality as a mental illness. Then in 1980, psychiatrists voted to remove it from the list. Were they mistaken before about homosexuality being an illness? Lay out the considerations that a search for an answer would involve. Start, as always, by thinking about the problem. Is the debate really about whether homosexuality is an illness, a choice, or an inherited disposition, or is that just a surrogate argument?

2. What might be at stake in deciding whether something should be called by the following:

   art vs. craft   pet vs. livestock   athlete vs. competitor
   sport vs. game   addiction vs. habit   housewife vs. homemaker
   eccentric vs. mentally ill   hate speech vs. free speech
   economic stagnation vs. slump vs. recession vs. depression

3. Search the Internet to find Web sites that concern addiction. How many different conditions do people include in the category *addiction?* List five that seem to you either not "real" addictions or borderline cases. What disqualifies or makes them borderline? What does that tell you about how you understand the term? Why do the writers of the sites want to call them addictions?

4. In recent years, our society has renamed many things. When the two of us were young, someone in a wheelchair would be called a cripple; later, *cripple* was replaced by *handicapped,* which has been replaced by *disabled, differently abled,* or *physically challenged.* Although some people complain that we have gone too far and bristle at terms ending in *-chal-lenged* (one of your authors is vertically challenged, the other horizon-tally), there are often good reasons for proposing such changes. Think of a pair of terms, one that was once common but would now be judged offensive and one that is a politically correct alternative: *crippled–disabled, drunk–alcoholic, retarded–mentally challenged, old –elderly;* etc. For each term (1) list your criteria of meaning and (2) sketch a verbal portrait of a model instance of each category. Do your criteria change when the word changes? Does your model? What does this say about the value of changing terms for sensitive categories?

IN A NUTSHELL

About Your Argument . . .

We typically make arguments about meaning when we want readers to under-stand what something *is*—in pragmatic arguments, because we believe that what it *is* justifies *doing* something about it; in conceptual ones, because we believe that understanding what it *is* helps us understand a larger issue.

An argument about meaning almost always addresses two issues:

- What criteria of meaning define the term in question?
- What features of the referent qualify it to be named by that word?

Your problem is to match the features to the criteria, in one of three ways:

- When you work with an *authorized meaning* whose criteria are stipulated by some authority, you have to accept those criteria and describe the referent so that its features match them. For example, the criteria for *U.S. citizen* are relatively fixed; so you have little latitude to modify them, only to adapt the features of a referent to match them.
- When you work with a *common meaning,* you can shape both its criteria and the features of the referent, so long as you remain within your readers' common sense understanding of the term and referent. The common meaning of *good American* is flexible enough to let you shape it to fit very different referents.
- When you work with a *model of a common meaning*, you are free to portray any model that your readers will accept as within the common sense meaning of the term and to describe your referent to fit the model. Readers know many model Americans, and you can choose whichever ones suit your referent and your purposes.

In a pragmatic argument, readers focus on the pragmatic consequences of using one term or another to refer to a referent. People called the Branch Davidians who died at Waco either a *religious sect* or *cult*, depending on how people thought the government should deal with them. In a conceptual argument, readers expect your definitions to be consistent with everything else they know. Whether Pluto is a planet or an especially large chunk of space rubble depends less on Pluto than on our whole system of understanding and belief about planets and space rubble.

You can go astray in arguments based on meaning in two ways:

- You unknowingly use an argument about meaning as a surrogate for other issues, either a pragmatic problem or a question of feelings and values.

You are most likely to fall into a surrogate argument when the larger problem behind the question of meaning involves values and has consequences that you would rather not deal with directly.

- You use dictionary definitions as though they carried more authority than they do. A dictionary alone will never settle a question of meaning.

Anticipate the kind of definition your readers expect you to use. If they are experts, use their terms according to the criteria authorized by their field. If, however, you are the expert and writing to those who are not, you cannot assume that your readers will accept your authorized definition, no matter how much academic or technical weight it carries.

. . . and About Writing It

As you plan your argument, list every key word that you think you will use. If you are confident that your readers understand those words as you do, don't define them, especially not from a standard desk dictionary: You'll make yourself seem uncertain. If your readers might not understand those words as you do but won't question your meaning, define them in passing, as in this definition of *themes:*

> No question about an argument is more common than *But what do you mean by* _____?, especially about your key themes, those terms that you will mention in your main claim and repeat often in the body. If you expect readers to disagree about their meaning, define them explicitly.

When you make an argument about meaning, state the meaning, describe the referent, and show how they match so that readers accept all three.

- When you argue about an authorized meaning, do this:

  state your criteria so readers recognize them as authoritative, stipulated ones (cite a technical reference work if you want to be sure that they do);

  describe your referent one feature at a time, so that readers see how each feature fits the stipulated criteria;

  if the fit is not obvious, make a small argument to support it—thus thickening your larger argument.

- When you argue about common meaning using criteria, do this:

  state your criteria to match features of the referent, but remain within the bounds of readers' common sense understanding;

  describe your referent one feature at a time, so that readers see how each feature fits your criteria;

  if readers might question your criteria or the fit, you can make a small argument to support them.

- When you argue about common meaning using a model, do this:

  describe the model so that readers recognize it as typical of their common sense understanding of the term;

  describe your referent so that it is as close to the model as is consistent with your readers' common sense understanding of it;

  if readers might question the match, make an argument supporting it; but if your readers reject your model, do not try to make an argument that they should accept it: that's not how models work. Models are so deeply entrenched in our social and cultural understanding that they are the equivalent of visual warrants.

Chapter 11

Arguments About Causes

In this chapter, we discuss arguments claiming that one event or condition causes or will cause another. We discuss the nature of causation, how we decide what causes to focus on, and why we so often think about causation less carefully than we should. Then we show you how to design arguments about causation.

We spend a good part of our lives figuring out why things happen as they do or how to make them happen as we want. We tackle problems ranging from the trivial—why the car won't start—to ones that require complex written arguments: Why do teenagers kill and how do we keep them from doing it? To understand an issue that complex, readers expect more than a narrative of one event after another; they want reasons to believe that one event in fact causes the next. Then if we're addressing a pragmatic problem, they also want reason to believe that our solution will change things as we say it will. Our desire to understand and control causes is a uniquely human trait.

The Impossible Vastness of Causes

Causation itself seems simple enough. The classic example is a cue stick hitting a billiard ball, causing it to move and hit another. To explain the causes of a more complex event like binge drinking, it might seem that we just have to track more balls on a bigger table. But philosophers have shown how little we actually understand causation and how often we explain it badly.

First, causation is not something we see. We say that the cue hitting a ball "causes" it to move, but that is only shorthand for saying that when the stick touches the ball, the ball moves, as we expect it to. What we call *causation* is only a predictable relationship between two or more events or conditions.

Moreover, we cannot, even in principle, account for more than a fraction of all the events and conditions that cause the cue to move the ball:

- *Every cause is part of an endless chain.* The immediate cause of the ball's moving is the cue's hitting it, but the cue is caused to move by an arm, which is caused to move by muscles, which are caused to contract by a thought, which . . . How far back must we trace the chain of causes? To an earlier thought? To the beginning of time? We cannot describe them all, so how do we decide where to begin?

- *Every "link" in a chain of causes consists of countless smaller ones.* A contracting muscle moves the arm, but that contraction consists of countless muscle cells, each involving countless electrochemical events, each of which . . . You get the idea. We cannot describe them all, so how do we decide how finely to describe the links in the chain?

- *A cause has an effect only when enabled by countless conditions.* The arm has to be strong enough to move the cue, the cue straight enough to hit the ball, the ball light enough to roll. We cannot describe every condition, so how do we decide which ones to ignore?

- *Every cause depends on the absence of disabling conditions.* The arm can move only because it was *not* paralyzed a moment before. And what about a plane that did *not* crash into the building, because a part did *not* fail, because . . . ? Events and conditions that do *not* happen are effectively infinite, so how do we decide which ones to select as relevant?

Finding Relevant Causes

The causes and conditions that contribute to any effect are so vast that we can never name them all. So when we argue about causes, we must select only relevant ones. We do that in two ways. The first is our unreflective, everyday way of thinking about causes; it is easy, and as a consequence, typically superficial and simplistic, often misleading. The other way forces us to be more focused, more self-conscious, but in the long run, it is more reliable and productive. Since the first kind of thinking is so pervasive, however, it's useful to understand why it is so unreliable, because an argument we make about causes is only as strong as the thinking that we put into it.

Everyday Thinking About Causation

We systematically tend to mislead ourselves when we think about causes, because, as hundreds of studies show, our minds are tuned to focus on certain causes and to ignore others. For example, binge drinking is becoming more common among college students, causing increasing numbers of injuries and even deaths. To solve that problem, we have to change something, but before we can know what, we first have to understand why some students binge and others don't. Two possibilities leap to mind, usually in this order:

- Bingeing is caused by something in a binger's personality: immaturity, insecurity, recklessness.

- It is caused by something in a binger's circumstances: bad friends, peer pressure, easy availability of alcohol.

If we knew which was the "real" cause (maybe both are), we could do something about it. But there are many other possible causes that don't occur to most of us, at least not at first. Here are two:

- Most students don't know the risks of drinking lots of alcohol in a short time.
- Schools fail to educate first-year students about those risks.

Most of us overlook those causes, because we tend to focus on causes that are present and visible. It's not that we're stupid or careless; it's just how we humans tend to think. So before you plan an argument about causes, you should be aware of the tendencies that predictably undermine sound thinking about them, tendencies that are called *cognitive biases*. There are five common ones, and they all lead to the same problem: a causal explanation that is too simple to explain a complex effect convincingly.

1. **We tend to assign causality to the event immediately before an effect.** We call such causes "proximate" or "immediate." For example, when someone sinks a two-point basket at the buzzer, winning the game by one point, we are more likely to think that shot won the game than a three-pointer a minute earlier, even though but for the three pointer, the two pointer at the buzzer would have made no difference. In the same way, when we think about binge drinking, we think first of its immediate causes: *It's Friday night, finals just ended, there's a party, . . .* We are less inclined to think of a remote cause, such as the person was not told a year *earlier* about the risks of bingeing. So when you think about causes, consider immediate ones, but systematically look for more remote ones as well.

2. **We tend to assign causality to events that occur rather than events that do not.** Imagine you are driving along and your passenger asks you to slow down, causing you to catch a red light. You stop, and get rear-ended. You might think, *If he hadn't asked me to slow down, I wouldn't have been stopped at that moment.* You are less likely to think, *I stopped at that light at that moment because my friend did* not *ask me to slow down five minutes ago.* We are more likely to see what did happen as a relevant cause than what did not, even though both contributed to an outcome. As for why a student binges dangerously, we are not inclined to think first about what does not happen, like a friend *not* intervening, much less that remote negative cause—the lack of education a year earlier. When you think about causes, consider what did happen just before an effect, but think as well about what did not and thereby contributed to that effect by its absence.

3. **We tend to assign causality to surprising events, not routine ones.** Imagine your teacher always announces a test before he gives it. Then he pops a quiz and you get a zero. You are more likely to think that you got the zero because your teacher *unpredictably* didn't announce the quiz than because you *routinely* didn't prepare until warned. Similarly, bartenders predictably serve drinks, so we don't identify that ordinary action as a cause of someone's dying from bingeing. But imagine that the bartender offers a "lucky fan" all the free drinks she can down in five minutes, someone takes the offer and dies. That offer is unusual, so we'd focus on it as a relevant cause, not on the fact that the bar exists. When you think about causes, note unpredictable, unexpected ones, but think as well about those that are so routine that they escape notice.

4. **We tend to find causes that confirm our assumptions.** Some claim that childhood violence results from the erosion of family values, a cause that they think explains most ills of American life—crime, divorce, drugs, and so on. So when a child shoots a classmate, they offer their standard explanation: *No family values.* We all tend to fit facts to our beliefs rather than change our beliefs to fit the facts. In regard to bingeing, many of us hold assumptions that we can state as one of these two common warrants:

> Those who behave self-destructively have a weak character.

> Those who behave self-destructively are victims of bad influences.

When you think about causes, don't jump to a favorite account. Explore other possibilities, such as that self-destructive behavior is caused by complex, unpredictable interactions of many factors, including chance.

5. **We look for causes whose magnitude is proportional to their effect.** When a few years ago TWA flight 800 exploded over Long Island, many looked for a cause that would balance the enormity of the disaster. So they blamed terrorists or the U.S. military, because only a massively evil cause could balance so massive a tragedy. When you explore an effect as emotionally "big" as a student drinking herself to death, look for causes large enough to bear the blame, like recklessness or the irresponsible encouragement of friends, but think as well about the little causes that otherwise escape your attention.

The Aesthetics of Causation

The historian William Manchester explains why people still can't accept that Lee Harvey Oswald acted alone when he shot President John F. Kennedy:

> In the wake of that dreadful Oliver Stone movie [about the assassination], I read that some 70 percent of the American people believed that Kennedy was the victim of a conspiracy. I

think I understand why they feel that way. And I think, in a curious way, there is an esthetic principle involved. If you take the murder of six million Jews in Europe and you put that at one end of a scale, at the other end you can put the Nazis, the greatest gang of criminals ever to seize control of a modern government. So there is a rough balance. Greatest crime, greatest criminals.

But if you put the murder of the President of the United States at one end of the scale, and you put Oswald on the other end, it just doesn't balance. And you want to put something on Oswald's side to make it balance. A conspiracy would do that beautifully.

Source: Bob Herbert, "In America: A Historian's View," *New York Times,* June 4, 1997.

The sum of these biases is typically the One True Cause story and the Silver Bullet Solution: *If we could just get parents to spend more time with their children, . . .* As you develop your argument, consciously monitor your own thinking. Remind yourself that no one cause is responsible for any complex problem and no one action is likely to solve it. But as you draft, keep in mind that your readers will be just as attracted to One True Cause and a Silver Bullet Solution—more attracted to them if they are less familiar with the problem than you. You may have to acknowledge what seems the most obvious cause and then show what led you to move beyond it.

Thoughtful Thinking About Causation

Other ways of finding relevant causes are harder, but more reliable. The first step is to decide which causes might be relevant to solving your problem. For example, to choose from among the infinity of causes that contribute to the cue stick's moving the billiard ball, we'd first have to know why we want to talk about the movement of the cue ball at all: what problem does explaining its movement solve? If we want to improve someone's game, we'll look at certain causes; if we want to explain the ballistics of round objects, we'll look at others; and if we want to explain free will, we'll look at others yet.

Of course, we define relevance differently for pragmatic and conceptual problems.

Causation in Pragmatic Problems

In solving a pragmatic problem, we look for causes that we can change or remove to eliminate the costs that make it a problem. We'll call such causes *pragmatically relevant.* For example, when your car won't start, you might hypothesize that the pragmatically relevant cause is a dead battery, because that's a cause you can do something about. You might suspect it's dead because someone left the lights on all night, but while that remote cause might be *conceptually* relevant in helping you understand why the battery is dead, it is not *pragmatically* relevant to solving the immediate problem of starting the car (though it might be pragmatically relevant to making sure it doesn't happen again). Use your problem to focus your thinking on the point in the chain of causes and effects where you—or someone—can intervene to eliminate its costs and thereby solve the problem.

Causation in Conceptual Problems

It's harder to define relevant causes in conceptual problems, because every cause of an event, no matter how small, is potentially relevant to understanding it. For example, those trying to end the troubles in Northern Ireland have a pragmatic problem: Where do they intervene in the chain of causes and effects that lead Catholics and Protestants, Irish and English to attack each other? But a historian trying to solve the conceptual problem of explaining those causes would in theory have to consider every single cause that has ever contributed to the current troubles, including centuries of conflict over religion, politics, economics, ethnicity, and social class. And there is no limit to how finely he could decompose those causes into constituent ones. Even a fleeting thought a century ago could be relevant to explaining an event today.

So where do we start? That decision is usually made for us by our personal background, academic training, and other interests that point us toward some issues and away from others. A historian trained as an economist, for example, is more likely to study how religion affects income than how it affects attitudes toward violence, because she is trained to look at economic causes.

That explains why those new to an academic field often struggle to find conceptual problems to write about. They typically do not yet have special academic interests that focus their attention on specific issues, and so they feel overwhelmed by the possibilities. It is a problem only experience can solve.

Analyzing Causation Systematically

Once you identify causes that might be relevant to your problem, you must evaluate them to be sure they are in fact causes. When you do advanced work, you will learn how to analyze causes in the specific ways appropriate to your field. In basic courses, you evaluate causes more informally, but that doesn't mean superficially. To be sure you have analyzed causation thoughtfully, you can use two principles formulated by a nineteenth-century philosopher, John Stuart Mill: the principle of similarity and difference and the principle of covariation. These principles will not help you discover causes to test, but they will help you demonstrate that those you propose are worth consideration.

The Principle of Similarity and Difference

When researchers try to decide whether something is a plausible candidate for a cause, they try to determine how regularly it "correlates" with its alleged effect: Does the effect occur more often when the proposed cause is present than when it is absent?

For example, when researchers study why some first-year students get better grades than others in writing classes, they try to discover factors shared by students who do well (their similarity) that are not shared by those who do worse (their difference). Researchers might argue that those who get better grades write on computers (the similarity). But they would also have to show that those who do less well do *not* write on computers (the difference).

To use this principle of similarity and difference systematically, some researchers use a 2 × 2 grid that forces them to consider all combinations of cause and effect, both present and absent. It looks like this:

	Effect occurs	Effect does not occur
Cause present	__%	__%
Cause absent	__%	__%

Down the left, list a proposed cause as present and absent; across the top, list whether a proposed effect does or does not occur. In the boxes, put the *percentages* (not raw numbers) of the correlations between the presence or absence of a cause and the presence or absence of an effect. (The percentages in the horizontal rows must add up to 100). Social scientists call this an *analysis of variance,* or *ANOVA,* for short.

Here's a simple case: An astronomer wants to prove that massive objects bend light. He assembles his data and finds this:

	Light bends	Light does not bend
+ Massive object	100%	0%
− Massive object	0%	100%

According to these data, light bends always when an object is present, never when an object is absent. The researcher can therefore tentatively argue that massive objects cause light to bend (unless bent light causes the presence of an object or a third cause both bends light and causes the object's presence).

Natural scientists hope for such unambiguous all-or-nothing results, but social scientists can't. They have to settle for "more or less." For example, those looking at writing by first-year students might find these numbers:

	Upper half of class	Lower half of class
Always use computers	72.1%	27.9%
Never use computers	34.5%	65.5%

The correlation is not perfect, but students who always compose on computers are more likely to be in the upper half of their group than those who never do.

The more the numbers differ vertically, the more likely you can convince readers that you've found a possible causal relationship. But if the numbers are close vertically, as in the next table, you can claim a causal relationship (and only a slight one) only if you have counted very large numbers of students.

	Upper half of class	Lower half of class
Always use computers	72.1%	27.9%
Never use computers	65.5%	34.5%

To know how much difference you need in order to claim that it is a significant one, you have to make complex statistical computations that everyone who expects to make a living in the twenty-first century ought to learn.

Be aware that, if the percentages are less than 100 percent, as they almost always are outside the physical sciences, you can support a claim of only partial, *contributory* causation. In that example about computers and writing, for example, some students who *do* use computers are in the *lower* half of their class and some who do *not* use computers are in the *upper* half. We must therefore assume that causes in addition to computers influence who ends up where. We *can* claim that the cause we have tested is a *relevant* one, perhaps even the one that points to the best solution. But we *cannot* claim that it is a *sufficient* cause, able to bring about the effect in question by itself. As we said before, complex events never have a single cause. (You also have to check whether your analysis has reversed cause and effect: Maybe students who write better choose to write on computers.)

The Principle of Covariation

Researchers are most confident about causes when the magnitude of a possible cause varies with the magnitude of a proposed effect. For example, *Do students who have composed on computers for many years write better than those who have written on computers for fewer years?* If so, then the use of computers is a plausible cause of better writing. To test for covariation, we add additional cells for different magnitudes:

Computer use	Upper third	Middle third	Bottom third
6 years	62.2%	21.9%	15.9%
4 years	41.3%	39.0%	19.7%
2 years	32.5%	45.6%	21.9%
0 years	25.3%	32.8%	41.9%

Results are rarely so neat, but it's what researchers hope for.

ANOVA as Exploration

You don't need a lot of data to use an ANOVA table if you are using it simply as a device to force yourself to think more systematically than you might have otherwise. For example, some have claimed that students binge because they are attracted to risk. We might imagine this table:

	+ Binge	− Binge
Attracted to risk	?%	?%
Not attracted to risk	?%	?%

Simply by imagining this table, you force yourself to speculate about four correlations:

1. How many students attracted to risk *do* binge?
2. How many students attracted to risk *do not* binge?
3. How many students *not* attracted to risk *do* binge?
4. How many students *not* attracted to risk *do not* binge?

If you cannot imagine a 100 percent correlation between bingeing and risk taking, then you know bingeing is too complicated for a One True Cause explanation.

The Dog that Didn't Bark

Of course, sometimes there is one cause. In one case, Sherlock Holmes noticed that a dog did not bark when the person who committed a crime must have walked by it. What Holmes found significant was the *not* barking. In effect, he created a mental ANOVA table like this:

	+ Bark	− Bark
Stranger walks by	100%	0%
Master walks by	0%	100%

Holmes concluded that since the dog did not bark, his master must have committed the crime.

Four Cautions About Using the Principles

1. **Imagine and test as many causes as you can.** These principles help you test causes but do not help you find ones to test. If all your hypotheses are wrong, these tests show you only that—a useful result, though not always one to celebrate. Years ago, for example, malaria was a mystery until someone thought to investigate mosquitoes. Today researchers face the same problem with Alzheimer's. They have tested every cause they can think of, but all have failed the tests.

2. **Create contrasting groups.** Once you hypothesize a cause, you have to create contrasting groups, one exposed to a possible cause, the other not. Some researchers can directly create those groups, as when a biologist plants two fields of corn and treats only one with a new fertilizer. Often, though, researchers have to assemble contrasting groups by retrospective sampling. That's how smoking was discovered as a cause of cancer. The problem is that retrospectively created groups can always differ in some unexpected way that turns out to be crucial. In fact, cigarette manufacturers once argued that the urge to smoke and cancer might both be caused by some third thing.

3. **Be wary of oversimplification.** When we find that an effect covaries with a suspected cause, we tend to think *Aha, I've figured it out. We can get students to write better if we make them write on computers.* But complex effects have complex causes. Maybe students who compose on computers come from wealthy neighborhoods with better schools. And be aware that you may be reversing cause and effect. Maybe those who write better choose to write on computers because they can write faster.

4. **Don't ignore interactions.** Even when you think you have found a cause, consider the complex ways that causes and effects may interact:

   - *Shared cause*: Sometimes two *effects* correlate not because one causes the other, but because both are caused by a third thing: Chronic unemployment and crime correlate, but both may be effects caused by long-term poverty.

   - *Mutual cause*: Some causes and effects influence each other. Poverty correlates with poor education, poor education with crime, and crime with poverty, and they probably all cause one another.

   - *Compounded effects*: A recent study reported that the mentally ill are no more likely to commit a crime than well people, while drug addicts are four times as likely. But when the mentally ill are on drugs, they are seven times more likely to commit a crime. The effect of combined causes may be more than the sum of their individual effects.

A last caution: we can't easily use this kind of analysis to account for the cause of a unique event, such as the Civil War or the explosion of TWA 800.

For singular events, we have to reason by analogy from a set of similar cases or closely trace the specific chain of events that resulted in the event we are explaining (see pp. 216–220).

Causation and Personal Responsibility

Sometimes we face problems that we can solve only by convincing readers to hold a person or institution responsible for specific consequences of their actions. In those cases, we have to think about causation differently from the way we do when we conduct scholarly, objective research. It's important to evaluate cause and effect as objectively as we can, but we can't avoid some subjectivity when faced with a problem of assigning personal responsibility, especially for purposes of meting out praise or blame.

Who's Responsible?

A few years ago, some preschool children on an outing at a riverfront park let go of a hand line used to keep them together, and they fell in the water. They were saved when a bystander jumped in after them. Everyone agreed on the facts, but made different claims about who was responsible for the accident:

- The media blamed the teachers, because they didn't watch the kids as they should have.
- The children's lawyers blamed the teachers, but also the Park Department, because it hadn't built a protective railing along the river.

They also differed on who was responsible for saving the children:

- The mayor and the media praised the rescuer for his heroism.
- The Red Cross praised its life-saving course, which the rescuer had taken.
- A psychologist said that the rescuer's actions were caused by an instinct to aid the helpless, reinforced by cultural training from TV and movies.

We can explain two of the claims about responsibility easily enough:

- The teachers were a responsible cause of the accident, because they were there and did not do what they were expected to do: They did not watch the children.
- The person who jumped in to save them was a responsible cause of their surviving, because they would have drowned but for his action.

Even though the next two explanations seem a bit of a stretch, they solved the problems of those who proposed them:

- The lawyers for the children had the problem of finding someone to sue who had more money than the teachers. Those missing railings pointed to a solution: The lawyers said the city was a responsible cause because it failed to build railings along the wharf.

- The Red Cross solved its problem of publicizing its programs by saying it was a responsible cause of the rescue, remote to be sure, but nevertheless relevant because but for its course, the rescuer might not have jumped in.

But why didn't anyone focus on other obvious causes?

- No one held the children or their parents responsible, even though the children let go of the ropes and their parents sent them to that school.
- Nor did anyone give credit for the rescue to a bystander who threw a rope in the water and pulled the rescuer ashore.
- Nor did anyone name gravity as a cause, even though but for it, no one falls into anything.

None of these factors met our criteria for responsible causes, and (except for the psychologist) the parties involved could solve their respective problems only by identifying someone to hold responsible.

Five Criteria for Assigning Personal Responsibility

When we can solve a problem only by making a person a *responsible* cause, we have to address more questions than for a problem involving "pure" causation. After we determine what events and actions actually caused an outcome, we have to answer two more questions: *What was the state of mind of the persons involved?* and *How did external circumstances affect their actions?*

To infer a person's state of mind, we ask three questions:

1. Did the person *choose* to perform the action that led to the effect in question? Or did someone or something force that person to act?
2. Could the person have *foreseen* the consequences of the action, both its benefits and its risks?
3. Were the person's *motives* appropriate or questionable?

Then we ask two more questions about circumstances:

4. How commonly do people in similar circumstances act in that way?
5. Did circumstances create an obstacle to the action or enable it?

Those criteria suggest why people assigned responsibility for the riverfront accident as they did:

- Though the children were the immediate cause of their accident, no one blamed them because they could not foresee what would happen if they let go of the rope.

- Nor did anyone hold the parents responsible, because parents commonly send children to day care and they could not have foreseen that the teachers would be inattentive.

- Everyone held the teachers responsible because they should have foreseen the consequences of not paying attention to the children and nothing kept them from doing so.

- The lawyers held the city responsible because it should have foreseen the risks of not having railings along the river and nothing prevented them from building railings.

- The media praised the rescuer because he seemed to perform his action freely, foreseeing the benefit to the children and the risk to himself, and because few people would have done the same.

- The Red Cross made itself responsible, because it did something with foreseeable benefits that few other agencies do—train people in life saving.

But the psychologist didn't seem to make the rescuer "responsible" at all. He seemed to say that the rescuer acted impulsively, without conscious choice. And that's why his explanation is so different from the others. Instead of framing the problem as one of assigning responsibility, as others did, he framed it as a problem in the social sciences, as a purely conceptual problem of objective causation: What causes people to act impulsively?

So when you make an argument that someone is responsible for an outcome, be clear why you do so: Do you want only to explain the outcome? Or do you want readers to praise or blame the person who brought it about?

Explain or Judge?

In a 1999 interview, Hillary Clinton suggested that a factor in her husband's infidelity was conflict in his childhood. Critics charged that she was trying to excuse his actions. One commentator saw in this a lesson about how we tend to think:

> [There is a] tendency of modern Americans to either misunderstand or fail to recognize the distinction between *explaining* a person's or group's actions and *justifying* them ....[I]t is the one error committed by both conservatives and liberals, although usually for opposing reasons. Conservative Americans are so committed to the principle of personal responsibility that they either deny or are hostile to any explanation of human action in sociological or psychological terms, fearing—incorrectly—that this implies people are not answerable for their actions. Many liberals fall in the opposite trap: an oversocialized view of people, so sensitive to the social forces conditioning us that they are unable or unwilling to hold those who fail responsible for their actions. What each side misses is that it is possible to both explain a person and hold that person responsible for his or her actions. The failure to make this distinction between explanation and justification bedevils human relationships and public policy.

Source: Orlando Patterson, "The Lost Distinction Between 'Explain' and 'Justify,'" *New York Times*, August 8, 1999.

Attribution Bias

To solve a problem involving personal responsibility, we must infer the thoughts, feelings, and motivations of others. If we apply the five criteria on page 210 thoughtfully, we can limit, though not avoid, the subjective element in making that calculation. But our thinking about responsibility becomes unreliably subjective when we fall into a common cognitive bias that psychologists call *attribution bias.*

When we decide a question of personal responsibility by explaining why someone has taken an action, we typically do not refer to a complex array of causes. Instead, we tend to oversimplify by attributing the cause of the action either to his personal qualities or to his immediate external circumstances, a decision that we seldom make objectively. For example, why did Mark McGuire and Sammy Sosa hit so many home runs in 1999? Was it their personal qualities—talent and hard work—or their circumstances—weaker pitchers and livelier baseballs? If we are disposed to give them credit for their achievements, we emphasize the personal causes; if not, we emphasize circumstantial ones. A more objective observer would have to say that all four were relevant causes, and many others as well.

We might think that we only need to approach the question objectively to find the "right" explanation. But as many studies have shown, we are biased toward thinking that the right explanation is the personal one. In attributing the causes of others' actions, we systematically overvalue the influence of personal qualities, motives, and psychological dispositions and undervalue the force of external circumstances. But how much we succumb to that tendency depends on our own subjective dispositions. So as you develop an argument assigning personal responsibility, be aware of your own disposition to make that assignment subjectively. Here are four variables to watch for: (1) knowledge, (2) personal investment, (3) ideology and politics, and (4) culture.

Knowledge

The less we know about a person and the circumstances of her actions, the more likely we are to attribute the cause of her actions to her character and motives. For example, those who know few gays and lesbians are more likely to attribute their orientation to choice; those who know many are more inclined to attribute the cause of their actions to circumstances—genetic predisposition, for example. It is a consistent (but by no means universal) pattern of causal attribution.

So if you have to argue why someone behaves as she does and you know relatively little about her or her situation, be aware that you are likely to overvalue her motives and character as causes of her action and undervalue her circumstances. But you must think about your readers as well: If they know more than you do, they will be inclined to make the opposite interpretation: they are more likely to assign responsibility to her circumstances than to her personal qualities. (Of course, the situation may be reversed: you may know more than your readers do.) So assess not only your own bias, but whether it matches that of your readers. You don't want to risk unknowingly making an argument that your readers are predisposed to reject. (A harder ethical question is whether you should knowingly appeal to their biases.)

Personal Investment

A second variable concerns how we feel about a person and the results of her actions. For example, when someone we like does something we admire, like winning an award, we tend to attribute her achievement to her intelligence, hard work, and so on: we say she earned her award. But if she loses, we say circumstances conspired against her. On the other hand, if someone we dislike wins, we are more likely to attribute her success to luck or other circumstances; if she fails, we attribute it to personal weakness.

It's familiar behavior. To his supporters, President Clinton was responsible for everything good that happened during his administration, but was a victim of circumstances in regard to the bad. To his detractors, he was not responsible for any of the good but was personally responsible for all the bad. We don't all make decisions along these lines all the time; it's only a tendency. But it is a tendency worth reflecting on when you have to make an argument assigning praise or blame. When you feel personally invested in someone, either positively or negatively, be aware that your judgment about personal responsibility may be biased. And depending on how your readers relate to that same issue, you may be working with or against the grain of their judgmental tendencies.

Ideology and Politics

A third variable is our politics. Stereotypical liberals argue, *Circumstances deprive those on welfare of opportunities to escape poverty;* stereotypical conservatives argue, *They don't want to work.* Liberals justify gun control by arguing, *Our high murder rate is due to the easy availability of guns;* conservatives respond, *Guns don't kill. People do.* Conservatives tend to locate responsibility in individual will; liberals tend to emphasize circumstances. But we can't apply this distinction too broadly: When there was a controversy in Los Angeles over racial profiling by police, liberals who distrusted police attributed it to their racist disposition; conservatives who trusted them attributed it to the dangerous circumstances of urban life.

Culture

The fourth variable, our culture, may have the greatest influence on our thinking about causation. Anthropologists point out that unlike other world cultures, Westerners in general and Americans in particular are inclined to believe that people control their own actions. In contrast, researchers have found that in many Asian cultures people tend to think personal actions are due more to social context than to individual choice. So when you have to make an argument with someone from a culture different from yours, keep in mind that you may judge personal responsibility much differently from the way the other person does.

Those four factors strongly influence how you will think about explaining causation. But when you construct your argument, you must also consider how *your readers* are likely to think about It. If you argue for a circumstantial explanation of someone's actions, think whether your readers might have a personalistic one (or vice versa). If so, you have a tough job ahead of you, because you will then have to do more than offer lots of reasons and evidence in support of your argument. You will also have to overcome a deeply entrenched *way of thinking* about causation.

Blame in Two Cultures

A study comparing Japanese and American newspaper reports of financial scandals found that American writers tended to focus more than twice as often on personal motives while Japanese newspapers tended to focus on circumstances:

> One [*New York Times*] article described Mozer as "Salomon's [a financial firm] errant cowboy": who "attacked his work as aggressively as he hit tennis balls." Another implied Hamanaka's lack of shrewdness in stating that he "was known more for the volume of his trades than his aptness." Whereas the lack of organizational controls was a minor theme of Americans in the *NYT*, it was a major theme of Japanese reporters . . . [They] commented that "somebody in Sumitomo [a financial firm] should have recognized the fictitious trading since documents are checked every day," and that Daiwa [another firm] "is embarrassed that its internal controls and procedures were not sufficient to prevent the case."

Source: Tanya Morris et al., "Culture and the Construal of Agency: Attribution to Individual Versus Group Dispositions." *Journal of Personality and Social Psychology* (1999).

The Fallacy of One True Cause

Above all, think hard before you attribute the cause of an effect *entirely* to someone's motives or *entirely* to his circumstances. Imagine readers asking either of two questions:

Are you saying X was *entirely* responsible for his actions, that circumstances played no role at all?

Are you saying X was *entirely* a victim of circumstances, that he bears no responsibility at all for his actions?

Knowledgable readers are suspicious of explanations that are that simplistic, but especially when they exclude circumstances as a relevant cause.

WRITING PROCESS
Arguments About Causes

PREPARING AND PLANNING

Five Narratives Supporting Solutions to a Pragmatic Problem

As you outline a cause-and-effect argument addressing a pragmatic problem, you have to plan not just one narrative about causes and effects, but at least two and maybe up to five. These five narratives support the solutions to five conceptual problems that you have to solve before you can solve the pragmatic one. We can express those five problems as questions.

- **Problem 1: What causes this problem?** Readers trust a solution only when they know the story of what causes the problem (imagine each step expanded as a claim at the heart of its own argument):

   Administrators don't know about new research in evaluating teaching, $_{\text{cause 1}}$ . . . so they use flawed evaluations. $_{\text{effect 1/cause 2}}$ · · · As a result, they don't know why students don't learn effectively, $_{\text{effect 2/cause 3}}$ · · · and that deprives students of better opportunities to learn. $_{\text{effect 3}}$

- **Problem 2: How will the action you propose solve the problem?** When you propose a solution, you must construct a second narrative about the future, how intervening in the chain of causes and effects will eliminate the cost of the problem (each of these steps could also be fleshed out):

   We can improve teaching through a better evaluation form. $_{\text{cause 1}}$ · · · to help teachers better understand what confuses their students and how to avoid doing so, $_{\text{effect 1/cause 2}}$ · · · giving students better opportunities to learn. $_{\text{effect 2/elimination of cost}}$

   Even if readers accept your account of the problem and solution, you may have to construct three more narratives to respond to objections and reservations. These narratives would be about the future.

- **Problem 3: How will your solution be implemented?** If readers might think your solution is not feasible, you have to respond to that doubt with the answer to another conceptual problem explaining how the solution can be implemented:

   To create a new teaching evaluation, the administration can appoint a student committee to develop it, $_{\text{step 1}}$ · · · and then with the help of consultants $_{\text{step 2}}$ show faculty how to use and learn from it. $_{\text{step 3}}$

- **Problem 4: Will your solution cost more than the problem?** If readers might think that your solution could cost more than the problem, then you have to tell another story to help them understand that it will not:

  A new evaluation may require resources, acknowledgment . . . but the benefits will outweigh the costs. response First, we are likely to attract more students as we become known for good teaching reason 1 . . . Second, . . . narrative of costs and benefits Some fear that teachers might feel coerced into grading more leniently or giving less work. acknowledgment But that risk is slight, because . . . response

- **Problem 5: Why is your solution better than alternatives?** Every problem has more than one solution, so you may have to show that yours is best, or at least can work with others:

  Some have claimed that instead of revising evaluations, we institute seminars for faculty. Such seminars would be a valuable resource, acknowledgment but if we must choose between them and new evaluations, the evaluations would be a better choice. response/claim First, the cost of bringing in consultants will exceed the cost of revising the evaluations reason 1 . . . Second, it will be hard to offer seminars to every faculty member. reason 2 . . . third, seminars are a one-time event; better teaching evaluations will occur every semester reason 3 . . .

  When you compare solutions, avoid an *either-or* argument.

  We can improve teaching in lots of ways, including *both* seminars and better evaluations.

A Default Plan for Pragmatic Arguments

A cause-and-effect argument about a pragmatic problem consists of solutions to as many as five *conceptual* problems that we can express as questions. Those questions also provide a default plan for your argument:

1. What causes this problem?
2. How will the action you propose cause the problem to go away?
3. How will your solution be implemented?
4. How do you know your solution will not cost more than the problem?
5. Why is your solution better than alternatives, or does it at least complement them?

In your final draft, you need to deal with the first two questions, but you might decide to drop one or more from among the last three.

Strategic Decisions in Designing Narratives About Causes

Once you have a plan, answer a few more questions:

- How far back on the chain of causes and effects do you start? Do your readers need to know the most remote causes of bingeing?

- How much detail do they need? Must they understand the minute psychological processes that compel people to binge?

- How much must you "thicken" your narrative by arguing that event A really does cause B? How do you know that in fact people attracted to risk are most likely to binge?

Where Do You Start Narrating the Problem?

We can't give you a rule for where to start in the chain of causes and effects. For pragmatic problems, readers need enough context to understand the causes you finally focus on, so start at least a step or two before the point where you propose intervening with a solution:

> For more than 200 years, college life has been so associated with drinking that getting drunk is now a tradition. $_{remote\ cause}$ Of course, many students began drinking in high school, often with their parents' tacit approval. $_{middle\ cause}$ But they lose even that loose supervision just when they join a community that seems to encourage them to get drunk. $_{near\ cause}$ So when sitting with a case or fifth in a dorm room or frat house, they risk drinking to the point of injury or even death. In those circumstances, the weak constraints colleges put on them are less useful than those they put on themselves. We might avoid the worst effects of drinking by educating students about its risks from the moment they set foot on campus. $_{claim/solution}$

With conceptual problems, however, we usually go a bit deeper into history: Someone studying student drinking not to control it but only to understand it might recount its centuries-long European tradition, Prohibition in the 1920s, and so on. Historical narratives signal scholarly diligence.

How Much Detail Do Readers Need?

Once you decide where to begin the story of your problem, you have to decide how much detail readers need to understand it. We can't give you a pat answer for this either, because it again depends on the nature of your problem and solution. Readers need enough detail to understand your problem and to be confident that you do too. For example, in addressing the problem of helping students avoid anxieties in their first year of college, a writer might offer this as part of an argument for expanding orientation for first-year students:

> Orientation for first-year students should be expanded from one week to two to help them understand better what lies ahead. Too many first-year students become anxious and frustrated during their first semester because they misunderstand what teachers expect. They think that they can succeed in college if they just do what they did in high school. After all, high school is the only model of education we know, and few of our teachers told us what to expect here.

That account is so general that it is hard to grasp the logic of its implied causes and effects. The writer could craft a more detailed chain:

> Orientation for first-year students should be expanded to two weeks to help them understand better what lies ahead. Many first-year students are anxious and frustrated during their first semester, because they misunderstand what teachers expect. For example, most teachers want us to think and write critically about what we've read, but many first-year students think teachers just want them to report it back accurately. So they summarize their readings and their notes, but get poor grades for doing so. This happens most often with students who succeeded in high school by reporting back what they heard in class. After all, that's what many of our high school teachers told us to do, and no one warned us that our task in college would be different.

If readers need more help, that chain can be broken down into smaller stages.

Inexperienced writers tend to be too general rather than too specific, so as a rule of thumb, create a narrative more detailed than you think it has to be.

How Much Explanation Do Readers Need?

If you could offer a narrative that exactly matched your readers knowledge and needs, they would need nothing more. But more likely, they look for reasons to believe that one event does not just follow another, but is caused by it. If so, you have to weave explanations into your narrative that explicitly establish causal relationships. You do that with analogies, warrants, and explicit analysis.

Analogies

Use an analogy when the cause and the effect in question are so much like another case that readers will quickly infer the same cause-effect relationship:

> First-year students should expect to feel anxious at first. Starting college is like moving to a new town or taking a new job. Everything is uncertain, and it takes a while to get comfortable.

Analogies are especially useful in arguments about the future, because the only way we can predict it is by recalling the past. Analogies suggest that a proposed solution is so like another that what worked before will work again.

> We can rid our dormitories of alcohol as effectively as we did drugs with a zero-tolerance policy. Before we instituted our current policy, we did not enforce rules against drugs for fear of violating student privacy. But once we decided to suspend anyone caught using drugs, and some were, drug use virtually disappeared. _{analogy} A zero-tolerance policy can end alcohol use in the same way. _{claim}

The problem is, history is full of counteranalogies:

> We tried national Prohibition in the 1920s, but that just made alcohol more attractive and drove it underground. If we ban alcohol from university property, the same thing will happen again. _{counteranalogy}

EXAMPLE

Analogy and Causation

Movie critic Michael Medved responds to those who deny that violent entertainment causes violent behavior.

Although hundreds of studies demonstrate a link between brutal media imagery and brutal behavior, skeptics argue that this reflects the tastes of violent kids rather than the influence of violent entertainment. Hollywood's most nimble apologists never tire of pointing out that our prisons are full of cold-blooded murderers who never saw *The Basketball Diaries,* whereas the overwhelming majority of children who regularly enjoy brutal movies or video games will never shoot their classmates.

Yet these reassuring arguments amount to very little, for one can say similar things about cigarettes: some people who never smoke get lung cancer, and most people who smoke never get lung cancer. But so what? Smoking still enormously increases your likelihood of getting sick. By the same token, you prove nothing with the undeniable observation that most consumers can view even the most disturbing and irresponsible products of our pop culture without discernible harm.

Consider the logic behind TV advertising: A commercial's failure to sell everybody doesn't mean it fails to sell anybody. If a Lexus ad inspires even one in a thousand viewers to take a test drive, it has dramatically improved the fortunes of the car maker. And if one of a thousand kids who watch intense violence on TV or at the movies were to try out that violence in real life, then it dramatically changes America.

Source: Michael Medved, "Hollywood Murdered Innocence," *Wall Street Journal,* June 16, 1999.

Warrants

Behind every analogy is an implicit warrant. When you articulate a warrant, you make explicit the principle that lets a reader apply a general cause-and-effect relationship to a specific one:

> Everyone feels lost when they enter a new community whose expectations seem baffling. warrant So when you start your first year here, cause you will feel bewildered. effect

You rely on warrants at the risk of making doctrinaire claims. So take a fresh look at cause-and-effect relationships; don't rely on stock warrants.

Analysis

You offer analyses of cause and effect when you run through Mill's questions (pp. 204–209).

• When a cause is present, does the effect occur more often than when the cause is absent?

• When a cause is absent, does the effect occur less often than when the cause is present?

• Does the magnitude of the effect vary with the magnitude of its cause?

> We can see the contrast between students from high schools that emphasize discussion and critical writing as opposed to those from schools that emphasized rote learning. Almost 90 percent of their graduates report that they feel comfortable in our first-year classes, while almost 60 percent of first-year students from schools that emphasize rote learning report anxiety, confusion, and frustration.

Weaving All Three into a Narrative

Here is how you weave these explanations into your narrative:

> Orientation for first-year students should be expanded to two weeks to help them understand better what lies ahead. _{claim} **Everyone feels lost when they enter a new community whose expectations seem baffling.** _{warrant} **It's like moving to a new town or taking a new job. It takes a while to get comfortable.** _{analogy} In the same way, students become anxious and frustrated during their first semester here _{claim/effect} because they don't know what teachers expect. _{cause/effect} For example, most teachers want us to think and write critically about what we've read, but many first-year students think teachers just want them to report it back accurately. _{cause} And so they only summarize readings and their notes. _{effect} This happens most often with students who succeeded in high school by reporting back what they heard in class. _{cause/effect} After all, that's all that many of our high school teachers expected, and too few warned us that our task in college would be different. _{cause} **We can see the contrast in students from high schools that emphasize discussion and critical writing as opposed to rote learning. Almost 90 percent of their graduates report that they feel comfortable in our first-year classes, while almost 60 percent of first-year students from schools that emphasize rote learning report anxiety, confusion, and frustration.** _{analysis}

Planning an Argument
Assigning Personal Responsibility

To argue that someone is responsible for an action, argue as you do in any argument about causation: use narratives, analogies, warrants, and Millsian analyses. But in an argument about personal responsibility, not only must you establish causation, you must also address the criteria for assigning responsibility.

Establish Causation

• Did the person actually cause what you claim she did?

Often, this is not an issue. If you claim that your school has failed to educate students about the risks of bingeing, readers are unlikely to wonder whether you've missed something. On the other hand, this question is crucial in matters such as who committed a crime.

Establish the Need to Assign Responsibility

- Was the intended outcome good (or bad)?

If someone saves a drowning child, the outcome is self-evidently good. But if the person jumps in to save a child's doll, the child might be grateful, but few adults would praise an action for a purpose so trivial. It may seem obvious that an action had a good effect, but do readers judge it as you do?

Address the Five Criteria for Assigning Responsibility

What was the person's state of mind?

1. Did she freely choose to act?
2. Could she foresee the consequences?
3. Were her motives appropriate?

These three questions require detailed answers. To praise a heroic action, you have to show that the person chose to act (she didn't act impulsively or wasn't forced at gunpoint), that she intended to achieve the benefit and knew the risks (she wasn't drunk or too excited to know what she was doing), and that she did what she did for a good purpose (not just to get a reward).

You may also have to answer questions about the circumstances.

4. Was her action unusual? Would most people have chosen *not* to do it?
5. Was her action aided or hindered by the circumstances?

If most of us would not risk our lives to rescue someone, then the few who do deserve our praise—more if they leap unaided into a swift and dangerous river, less if they wade into placid waters with a life preserver. The more extraordinary and difficult the action, the stronger our judgment of the person responsible for it. Conversely, if most of us would wade into a shallow pond to save a child, then the few who don't deserve our blame. The less extraordinary and difficult the action, the stronger our blame of the person who does not do it.

In answering all of these questions, details matter, so make your narrative more specific than you think your readers need.

 INQUIRIES

1. Here is a quotation from the last few pages of Leo Tolstoy's novel *War and Peace,* written about 130 years ago. Tolstoy was trying to explain

free will versus determinism. Does this have any relevance to anything discussed here?

> [T]o imagine the action of a man entirely subject to the law of inevitability without any freedom, you must assume the knowledge of an infinite number of space relations, an infinitely long period of time, and an infinite series of causes. To imagine a man perfectly free and not subject to the law of inevitability, you must imagine him all alone, beyond space, beyond time, and free from dependence on cause.

Tolstoy, of course, knew that neither was possible. Now what?

2. Here are two stories about AIDS. Why does the second continue to circulate widely even though no evidence supports it?

   a. A virus randomly mutated in an African primate that by chance bit someone who happened to be sexually active and traveled widely enough to infect others, who unwittingly went on to infect more, eventually creating the worldwide epidemic of AIDS.

   b. A CIA lab created a virus as a weapon. As the end of the Cold War approached, they decided to use it to wipe out homosexuals and drug users, and eventually African-Americans. They enlisted drug dealers to create an epidemic of addiction to get people to infect themselves. Once this is exposed, the CIA will be revealed for the evil force it is.

3. When Princess Diana was killed in that automobile accident, just about everyone focused on the drunk driver or on the paparazzi chasing her as the cause. A few pointed out she was not wearing a seat belt and that the person in the front seat who was wearing one survived, so it was perhaps her failure to buckle-up that killed her. But after a day or two, most commentators stopped saying that, and focused on the driver and the paparazzi. Why did so few mention her not buckling up as a plausible cause of her death?

4. Imagine this: Every day for a month, you try to start your car; it doesn't start. You look under the hood. Someone has detached the battery wire. Then one day the car starts: the person *didn't* detach the wire. Do you say that the cause of the car starting was that the person did *not* detach the wire? Or try this: A school crossing guard does not show up one morning, and a child is hit by a car. Do you say that one of the causes of the child's being hit was that the guard did not show up? Now suppose there was never a guard at that crossing. Does that change your account of causation? Why?

5. When you fill in the details of your narrative of a problem or its solution, you do more than help your readers. You also test your own reasoning. Reread the two stories about the origin of AIDS above in Inquiry 2. Make each story more detailed by filling in possible causes for each step in the narrative. Is one story easier to fill in than the other? Does one become less plausible the more you fill it in?

IN A NUTSHELL

About Your Argument . . .

Every event has countless causes. In an argument about causes, you have to decide which ones to single out as most relevant to your solution. A cause is *pragmatically relevant* if, by fixing it, you solve the problem. A cause is *conceptually relevant* if it allows you to understand an event in light of some special interest you and your readers bring to the question.

When you think about causes, you have to guard against cognitive biases we all share:

1. We tend to assign causality to the event just before an effect.
2. We tend to assign causality to events that occur rather than to events that do not.
3. We tend to assign causality to surprising events, not routine ones.
4. We tend to focus on causes that confirm our assumptions.
5. We look for causes whose magnitude is proportional to their effect.

You guard against those biases by systematically and deliberately considering as many causes as you can identify, especially those that most of us tend to miss: what we don't think of because it's absent or too routine to notice.

Use an ANOVA table to help you test your reasoning. Label each row by the presence or absence of a possible cause and each column by an alleged effect or lack of one. You can test covariation by recording the degree of the effect relative to the degree a cause is present. You can claim a plausible cause when you find a significant correlation between the possible cause and the effect, specifically if

- the effect usually occurs when the cause is present, and
- the effect usually does not occur when the cause is absent.

The greater the difference between the percentage of times when the effect is present and when it's absent, the more significant the correlation and the more confidently you can claim to have identified a cause.

. . . and About Writing It

When you plan a cause-and-effect argument about a pragmatic problem, you have to include at least five stories that answer these questions:

1. What causes this problem?
2. How will the action you propose solve the problem?
3. How will your solution be implemented?

4. Will your solution cost more than the problem?

5. Why is your solution better than the alternatives?

When you tell the story of the problem, you have to decide how far back up the chain of causes to begin. For a pragmatic problem, go just far enough back to give readers a sense of the context for your solution; for a conceptual one, go deeper into its history since readers generally want to see more causes when you ask them to understand a question. Decompose your narrative into finer detail than you think you have to, because we all tend to be too general rather than too specific. Flesh out your narrative with explanations that show that a cause in fact produces its effect. Use analogies, warrants, and Millsian analyses.

Part 4

The Languages of Argument

Chapter 12

Clear Language

In this chapter, we discuss how readers judge clarity, how you can recognize when your own writing is unclear, and how you can revise it. We also discuss two other qualities of prose that readers value: concision and vividness, qualities that raise the issue of the role of emotion in rational argument.

Readers will consider your claims if you give them what they need to see in an argument, but if they have to slog through one confusing sentence after another to find it, they may never grasp your argument well enough to judge it fairly. And even if they do, they are unlikely to feel well disposed toward it—or you. Imagine that you had to read forty pages of prose like this:

1a. The Federalists' argument that destabilization of government was the result of popular democracy was based on their belief in the tendency of self-interested groups toward sacrificing the common good in favor of their own narrow objectives.

You would feel friendlier toward the writer if those forty pages were closer to this:

1b. The Federalists argued that popular democracy destabilized government because they believed that self-interested groups tend to sacrifice the common good for their own narrow objectives.

In fact, dense prose like (1a) risks not just your readers' good will, but their willingness to read at all.

So once you draft your argument, you must still be sure it is written as clearly as its substance allows. In making that judgment, however, you face two problems:

- When you read your own prose, you always understand it more easily than your readers do because you remember too well what you meant when you wrote it.

- Even when you recognize what you ought to revise, you might not know how to change it.

We address those two problems in the first part of this chapter. In the second, we discuss how to make your writing concise and vivid. When you achieve clarity, concision, and vividness, your prose both communicates the logical force of your argument and projects an ethos that readers trust. Clarity can't replace sound logic, but it has considerable persuasive power of its own.

Clarity and Your Ethos

Some students think their writing style is merely cosmetic: *What's important are my ideas, not my words.* But that assumes readers are willing to slog through your murky words to find your ideas. In fact, few of us have the time or patience to do that. Worse, many of us believe that the quality of your writing reflects the quality of your mind. So if you write unclearly, many will question how clearly you think. For example, here's what one reviewer said of a book on teaching apes to communicate:

> This is fascinating stuff, but it is amazing how quickly the momentum is lost when the authors begin expounding in science-speak. You're just getting into the mind of the ape . . . when the mind of the cognitive psychologist feels compelled to elaborate: "It was expected that if apes do have language, its presence would be revealed by the animals' innate syntactical competence, a putatively genetically determined ability to order the symbols in multi-word utterances." . . . [T]here are times when the more the authors explain, the less we understand. Apes certainly seem capable of using language to communicate. Whether scientists are remains doubtful.

Source: Douglas Chadwick, *New York Times Book Review,* December 11, 1994.

Some Principles of Clear and Direct Writing

Although we describe passages as clear or unclear, simple or complex, those terms describe only how we feel as we read. We say that *writing* is confusing when *we* feel confused; that *it's* unclear when *we* feel uncertain about what it means; that *it's* convoluted when *we* feel lost in its twists and turns. Terms like that don't tell us what it is in a sentence that makes us feel as we do.

To help you understand why readers respond as they do and how you can identify and revise sentences likely to give your readers trouble, we'll explain six principles of clear writing. To use those principles, you have to know a few common grammatical terms. Three important ones are *subject, verb,* and *noun.* It helps to know a few others: *object, preposition, active, passive, phrase, main clause,* and *subordinate clause.* We also use one technical term you probably don't know, but we'll define it when we need it.

• **Principle 1: Use subjects to name your main characters.**

Readers understand sentences most easily when they see in the simple subjects of VERBS the most important characters you write about. By *character* we mean not just people but whatever you can tell a story about by making it the subject of a lot of sentences. But readers judge sentences to be clearest when the characters are people or concrete objects that you can name in a word or two.

For example, look again at the two examples you read above. We italicize the one-word simple subjects inside the whole subjects (which we underline); we boldface verbs:

1a. <u>The Federalists' *argument* that destabilization of government was the result of popular democracy</u> **was based** on their belief in the tendency of self-interested groups toward sacrificing the common good for their own narrow objectives.

1b. <u>The *Federalists*</u> **argued** that <u>popular *democracy*</u> **destabilized** government, because <u>*they*</u> **believed** that <u>self-interested *groups*</u> **tend** to **sacrifice** the common good for their narrow objectives.

In (1a) the simple subject is *argument*; it is an abstract noun inside a long, abstract phrase constituting the whole subject:

Whole Subject	Verb
The Federalists' *argument* that destabilization of government was the result of popular democracy	was based . . .

Moreover, inside that long abstract subject is another abstract subject:

Whole Subject	Verb
destabilization of government	was . . .

In contrast, look at the whole subjects of (1b):

Whole Subject	Verb
The *Federalists*	argued . . .
popular *democracy*	destabilized . . .
they	believed . . .
self-interested *groups*	tend *to* sacrifice . . .

In (1b), the whole subjects are short and specific. Three name people (*Federalists, they, groups*) and the fourth names a familiar concept (*democracy*). That's why most of us find (1b) easier to read. So the first principle of a clear style is this:

> *Keep your subjects short and concrete, naming your main characters.*

But now we have to qualify that principle: Sometimes, we want to tell stories not about flesh-and-blood characters but about abstractions. Look at the whole subjects of the following sentences (whole subjects are underlined; simple subjects are italicized; main verbs are boldfaced):

> Few *aspects* of human behavior **have been** so difficult to explain as rational thinking. *Rationality* **depends** on a range of short-term behaviors, such as not jumping to a hasty conclusion or action, having the patience to gather evidence, and the ability to bring together evidence and reasons in support of claims. But perhaps the *hallmark* of human rationality **is** the capacity to think about thinking, to reason about reasoning, to reflect on the quality of the thinking that assembles those reasons and claims into an argument.

The subjects of those sentences are abstractions:

Subject	Verb
Few *aspects* of human behavior	have been ...
Rationality	depends ...
the *hallmark* of human rationality	is ...

In that passage we see no human characters, but those abstract characters are so familiar to readers who have thought about the issue of rationality that the terms *aspects of human behavior* and *rationality* seem almost as distinct as the people who behave and think. Moreover, even though those subjects are abstract, the two long ones are only five words.

To decide whether the subjects of your sentences will be clear to your readers, look at them from their point of view. Don't make anything the subject of a sentence if it might seem to readers like an amorphous blob, especially a long one like this:

> The Federalists' argument that destabilization of government was the result of popular democracy . . .

Few readers can easily hold in mind a subject that long and indistinct.

You can usually revise such sentences by recasting their subjects around flesh-and-blood characters. If, for example, you thought readers might find abstractions like *rationality* and *behavior* difficult, you could revise to make flesh-and-blood characters the subjects of verbs.

> Psychologists **have found** it difficult to explain what we **do** when we **behave** rationally. We **think** rationally when, in the short run, we **do not jump** to hasty conclusions, but instead patiently **gather** evidence, and **bring** evidence

and reasons together to support claims. But <u>we</u> **are** perhaps most rational when <u>we</u> **reason** about our reasoning, when <u>we</u> **reflect** on how well <u>we</u> **thought** when <u>we</u> **assembled** our reasons and claims into an argument.

You can't always revise stories about abstractions into stories about flesh-and-blood characters, but to the degree you can, readers will judge your prose to be clearer and more vivid. If you think flesh-and-blood characters make your sentences seem simplistic, especially to specialists, use technical terms as characters in the subjects, so long as your readers are familiar with them.

- **Principle 2: Use verbs, not nouns, to name those characters' actions.**

Once readers get past a short, concise subject, they look for a verb that expresses a specific action. The sooner they find one, the clearer they judge the sentence to be. Compare the verbs (boldfaced) in the two passages about the Federalists:

1a. The Federalists' argument that destabilization of government **was** the result of popular democracy **was based** on their belief in the tendency of self-interested groups toward sacrificing the common good for their narrow objectives.

1b. The Federalists **argued** that popular democracy **destabilized** government, because they **believed** that self-interested groups **tend** to **sacrifice** the common good for their narrow objectives.

In (1a), the only verbs, *was* and *was based,* are empty: they express no real action. In (1b), the verbs do: *argue, destabilize, believe, tend, sacrifice.*

But if the actions in (1a) are not in verbs, where are they? They are in abstract nouns (boldfaced):

1a. The Federalists' **argument** that **destabilization** of government was the result of popular democracy was based on their **belief** in the **tendency** of self-interested groups toward **sacrificing** the common good for their narrow objectives.

We have a technical term for nouns derived from verbs: *nominalization.* (When you nominalize the verb *nominalize,* you get the nominalization *nominalization.*) Writing that feels highly professional and abstract almost always has lots of these abstract nominalizations, especially in subjects. When you use nominalizations as subjects, not only do you use weaker verbs instead of the stronger ones you could have used, but you also have to add prepositions and articles that you don't need when you use stronger verbs:

1a. The Federalists' argument that destabilization **of** government would be **the** result **of** popular democracy was based **on** their belief **in the** tendency **of** self-interested groups **toward** sacrificing the common good **for** their narrow objectives.

So here is the second principle of clear prose:

Use verbs to communicate actions; do not bury actions in abstract nominalizations, especially in subjects.

We can join these two principles: Match key elements in sentences—subjects and verbs—to key elements in your story—characters and actions.

SUBJECT	VERB
CHARACTER	ACTION

Those two principles help to explain why we judge some sentences to be clear and concrete, others unclear and abstract.

- **Principle 3: Get to a verb quickly.**

Contrast the following sentences (whole subjects are underlined; simple subjects are italicized; main verbs are boldfaced):

> 2a. <u>*Parents* who believe that school uniforms would solve most of the discipline problems in our schools</u> **argue** in favor of them, but <u>*many others* who fear that government already intrudes too much into our private lives</u> **object**.

> 2b. <u>Some *parents*</u> **argue** that <u>school uniforms</u> would solve most of the discipline problems in our schools, but <u>many *others*</u> **object** because <u>they</u> fear that <u>government</u> already intrudes too much into our private lives.

In both sentences, the simple subjects are human characters, *parents* and *others,* but is it fair to say that most of us probably prefer (2b)? In the first clause of (2a), we have to read 17 words to get to the verb, *argue,* and in the second clause 16 more to get to the verb *object.* In (2b), we have to read only two words before we get to the main verb in each clause:

> 2b. <u>Some parents</u> **argue** . . . but <u>many others</u> **object** . . .

This principle of quickly getting past a subject to a verb implies three subordinate ones:

- **Principle 3A: Avoid long introductory elements before a subject.**

Compare these sentences (the introductory elements are italicized; whole subjects are underlined; verbs are boldfaced):

> 3a. *In view of recent research on higher education indicating at least one change in their major on the part of most undergraduate students,* <u>first-year students</u> **should be** 100 percent certain about the program of studies they want to pursue before they load up their schedule with requirements for a particular program.

> 3b. *According to recent research on higher education,* <u>most students</u> **change** their majors at least once during their undergraduate careers, so <u>first-year</u>

<u>students</u> **should be** 100 percent certain about the program of studies they want to pursue before they load up their schedule with requirements for a particular program.

3c. <u>Researchers on higher education</u> **have recently claimed** that most students change their majors at least once during their undergraduate careers, so <u>first-year students</u> **should be** 100 percent certain about their program of studies before they load up their schedule with requirements for a particular program.

Most of us find (3a) less clear than (3b) or (3c). In (3a) we must work through a twenty-three-word introductory phrase before we get to the main subject (*first-year students*) and its verb (*should be*). In (3b) we have to work through only a seven-word introductory phrase, and in (3c) we start directly with the subjects of both clauses: *Researchers on higher education have recently claimed . . . first-year-students should be . . .*

- **Principle 3B: Keep whole subjects short.**

This principle connects to our first one, to make subjects distinct characters, because distinct characters usually have short names. Compare these (whole subjects are underlined, verbs are boldfaced):

4a. <u>A social *system* that fails to create a legal environment in which foreign investors can rely on the rule of law and on the strict enforcement of contracts</u> _{subject} **will not thrive.**

4b. If <u>a social *system*</u> **fails** to **create** a legal environment in which foreign investors can rely on the rule of law and on the strict enforcement of contracts, _{subordinate clause} <u>that *system*</u> **will** not **thrive.**

4c. <u>A social *system*</u> **will** not **thrive** if <u>*it*</u> **fails** to **create** an environment in which foreign investors can rely on the rule of law and on the strict enforcement of contracts. _{subordinate clause}

In (4a), we see the whole subject start at the beginning of the sentence; but we can't see at a glance where it stops, because it goes on for 25 more words. In (4b) we quickly identify a shorter subject and its verb in a long subordinate clause. And in (4c) we see a short main subject and verb at the beginning of the sentence: *A social system will not thrive . . .*

- **Principle 3C: Avoid interrupting subjects and verbs with long phrases and clauses.**

Compare:

5a. <u>Some scientists,</u> *because they write in a style that is so impersonal and objective,* **do** not **communicate** with lay people easily.

5b. <u>Some scientists</u> **do** not **communicate** with lay people easily, *because they write in a style that is so impersonal and objective.*

We easily see where the subject of (5a), *some scientists,* starts and stops, but just when we expect a verb, we hit that long interrupting *because*-clause. When we don't see a verb right after a subject, the sentence is probably more difficult than it has to be. Shift an interrupting element to the end or beginning of its sentence, depending on where it fits better.

The sum of these three subprinciples is this:

Help readers quickly get past a short subject to its verb.

- **Principle 4: Begin sentences with information that is familiar to readers.**

This principle has the same effect as the first three. It lets readers build up momentum in a sentence, but it depends less on the grammar of the sentence than on the psychology of its reader: We read more easily when early in a sentence we deal with information that is simple and familiar, before we have to deal with information that is new and complex. Compare:

6a. Particular ideas toward the beginning of sentences define what sentences are "about." The cumulative effect of a series of repeated subjects indicates what a passage is about, so our sense of coherence depends on subjects of sentences. Moving through a paragraph from a consistent point of view occurs when a series of subjects seems to constitute a coherent sequence. A seeming absence of context for sentences is one consequence of making random shifts in subjects. Feelings of dislocation, disorientation, and lack of focus occur when that happens.

6b. As we read, we depend on the subject of a sentence to focus our attention on a particular idea that tells us what that sentence is "about." In a series of sentences, we depend on repeated subjects to cumulatively tell us the topic of a whole passage. If we feel that a series of subjects is coherent, then we feel we are moving through a paragraph from a coherent point of view. But if we feel its subjects shift randomly, then we have to begin each sentence out of context, from no coherent point of view. When that happens, we feel dislocated, disoriented, out of focus.

Most of us have a problem with (6a) that we do not have with (6b). As we start each sentence in (6a), we have to deal not just with long abstract subjects, but with information that *to us* is newer and less familiar than the information at the ends of those sentences:

6a. Particular ideas toward the beginning of sentences . . .

The cumulative effect of a series of subjects . . .

. . . our sense of coherence . . .

Moving through a paragraph from a consistent point of view . . .

A seeming absence of context for sentences . . .

Feelings of dislocation, disorientation, and lack of focus . . .

In (6b), however, we begin each sentence with information that seems familiar and is therefore easier to grasp (subjects are underlined):

6b. As <u>we</u> read, <u>we</u> depend on . . .

In a series of sentences, <u>we</u> depend on . . .

If <u>we</u> feel that <u>a series of subjects</u> . . .

But if <u>we</u> feel <u>its subjects</u> . . .

Then <u>we</u> have to begin . . .

When <u>that</u> happens, <u>we</u> feel . . .

From this principle of how to begin a sentence, we can infer another about how to end it.

- **Principle 5: End a sentence with long and complex units of information.**

And from Principles 4 and 5, we can infer a sixth.

- **Principle 6: Keep your subjects consistent. Avoid beginning several sentences in a row with unrelated subjects.**

In (6a), we sense no consistency in its subjects. When sentences in a series all begin differently, we are likely to judge the passage to be unfocused, disjointed, even disorganized. In (6b), the subjects are more consistent. As a result, we read (6b) more easily. In short:

Don't vary subjects randomly; limit them to just a few different characters.

The Principles in a Nutshell

Here are those six principles again:

1. Name the main characters in your story in the subjects of sentences.
2. Express their actions not as abstract nouns but as verbs.
3. Get to the main verb quickly.
   a. Avoid long introductory elements.
   b. Avoid long abstract subjects.
   c. Avoid interrupting subjects and verbs.
4. Begin sentences with information that is familiar to readers.
5. Push to the end of a sentence information that is newer, more complex, and therefore more difficult to understand.
6. Begin sentences consistently. Focus your subjects on a few familiar characters.

You may have to use difficult language when the substance of your ideas demands it. But you can avoid making readers work harder than they should if you help them build up some momentum at the beginning of a sentence so that they can better deal with newer and more complex information toward the end.

Clear writing is not just a cosmetic feature that makes readers happy. It is itself a force in an argument. Readers are more likely to assent to what they understand and to trust a writer who has taken the trouble to write clearly.

Concision and Vividness

Readers judge sentences to be clear when they see short, specific subjects followed by verbs expressing important actions. But they look for more. Compare the subjects and verbs of these two passages (we underline subjects, boldface verbs):

> The consensus of our national belief **is** the right and freedom to engage in practices reflecting the inheritance of our different cultural and historical backgrounds. Allowing widows to end their lives as sometimes happens in certain parts of the world **must** obviously **be made** illegal and forbidden by law, but there **should be** allowances for things like female head coverings in educational settings. But there **is** a degree of uncertainty and unease in regard to cultural practices and traditions such as the binding force of an arranged future marriage between those not yet old or mature enough to take responsibility for the consequences of their decisions.

> We generally **believe** that Americans **should** freely practice the cultural traditions of their parents. Though we **forbid** a widow from throwing herself onto her husband's funeral pyre, as Indian women **are** sometimes **coerced** into doing, we **allow** Islamic girls to wear head scarves in public school. But about some cases we **are** less certain: **Must** a court **recognize** as binding a contract arranging a future marriage of two eight-year-olds?

The first feels indirect and complex; the second more straightforward, partly because its subjects are shorter, clearer, more familiar, and followed by specific verbs. But the second has another virtue: Its language seems "sharper," helping us better "see" what the words refer to, and if we can vividly see their referents in our mind's eye, we are likely to respond more positively.

You create vivid prose in two ways:

- Express ideas in the fewest words your readers need.
- Use words that make readers "see" what your words refer to.

Do that, and your readers will read your argument faster, understand it better, and remember it longer. Use too many words, especially abstractions, and readers are likely to think that your argument and maybe even you are vague, fuzzy, foggy, muddy—pick your metaphor.

How to Be Concise

It is easy to tell you to be concise, but doing it is hard, because editing for concision is labor-intensive and takes a big vocabulary. But it pays off—first for your readers, because you make their job easier, and then for you, because readers are grateful when you save them effort. If we could, we'd give you rules to make editing easier, but we can't. The best we can do is show you some common kinds of wordiness and ways to eliminate them. No shortcuts here.

Repetition and Clutter

Prose is wordy when it says the same thing twice or uses words with little meaning. For example, this next passage combines both useless repetition and empty words; the revision eliminates both:

> Various improvements in productivity basically depend first and foremost on certain fundamental factors that generally involve psychology more than any kind of particular technology.

> Productivity rises when we improve not just machines but the minds of those who operate them.

Here are some typical examples of clutter that you can usually cut:

certain	various	particular	specific	given	individual
really	basically	generally	virtually	actually	

Here are typical examples of redundant pairs, one of which you can always cut:

full and complete	hope and trust	any and all
true and accurate	each and every	basic and fundamental

Decomposed Meaning

We most commonly befog a concept when we decompose a meaning that we could express in one word and spread it over several. When we read a word in context—*I'd like you to meet my* **brother**—the word *brother* seems to evoke a unified concept. But as we saw in Chapter 10, we can think of the meaning of *brother* as a cluster of criteria (*human, male, descended from the same parents*). So we can express a concept in one word or through several by naming its criteria of meaning. If someone says, *I want you to meet someone who is male and descended from my parents,* we might know what that person means, but judge him to be a bit odd.

That's a silly example, but we read that kind of writing every day:

> You did not read through what you wrote paying close enough attention to finding and correcting errors.

instead of

> You did not edit carefully.

That longer sentence breaks unitary meanings into pieces by naming their separate criteria, smearing the meaning across many words. The shorter sentence uses a single word, which is almost always more vivid:

| read through . . . errors | → | edit |
| paying close attention | → | carefully |

Implied Meaning

Another kind of wordiness states what other words already imply. Compare:

> Imagine someone trying to learn the rules and strategy for playing the game of chess.

> Imagine learning chess.

Learn implies *try, strategy* and *game* both imply *play, chess* implies *game,* and *game* implies *rules and strategy.* So if we cut what readers can infer, we get something more concise and more vivid:

> Imagine learning the rules of chess.

Do not, however, confuse concise with merely short. Compare:

> Write directly.

> Make important characters subjects and make their verbs specific actions.

The first is shorter, but too general, omitting important information.

How to Be Vivid

Once you've squeezed the wordiness from your prose, you still have to be sure that the words left convey not just the meaning you intend, but the nuances of tone and feeling that support it.

Choosing the Right Feel

Words differ along so many scales that it is hard to list them all. Here are some general categories:

- **Slang vs. informal vs. formal** (*wheels* vs. *car* vs. *automobile*):

  > When a fruitcake shows up in an ER too goofy to think straight, the doc has to make the call whether to shoot him up with downers.

  > When someone comes to an emergency room unable to think rationally, the doctor must decide whether to calm him with drugs.

  > When a mentally incompetent individual presents in a trauma center, the attending physician must determine whether to sedate him with tranquilizing medication.

- **Neutral vs. emotional** (*pregnancy termination* vs. *abortion* vs. *infanticide*):

  > Lowering taxes will raise net income.

If we could cut back on what the tax man sucks out of our paychecks every week, we could keep more of the money we sweat for every day.

- **Native vs. borrowed** (*speed* vs. *velocity*):

  You have to show guts when the times call for it.

  It is necessary to demonstrate courage when the occasion demands it.

- **Common vs. scientific** (*belly button* vs. *navel*):

  As you go higher, the air thins out.

  As altitude increases, the atmosphere attenuates.

- **General vs. specific** (*livestock* vs. *pig*):

  A good worker plans carefully in order to do the job right the first time.

  A master carpenter measures twice to cut once.

These criteria often correlate: When a word is formal, like *abdomen,* it is likely to be less common, borrowed from French or Latin, learned in tone, and less vivid, evoking less emotion than informal words from Anglo-Saxon, like *belly* or *gut,* which are informal, more common, more vivid, and more emotionally charged.

These choices affect not just how we read, but how we judge a writer's ethos. Those three ways of describing a patient in an emergency room say something different about the writer and how she relates to readers—intimately, informally, or formally:

When a fruitcake shows up in an ER too goofy to think straight . . .

When someone comes to an emergency room unable to think rationally . . .

When a mentally incompetent individual presents in a trauma center . . .

Our best advice is to choose the middle style most of the time, because that sets a neutral background that magnifies the impact of an occasional, deliberately chosen formal or informal word.

Abstract Versus Concrete

The quality most important to a vivid style is whether a word evokes an image in our mind's eye. The more easily we image the referent of a word, the more vivid the style. Contrast these:

When someone needs emergency care, but acts so irrationally that he cannot legally consent to treatment, only the attending physician can decide whether to give that person medication without his permission before beginning treatment.

When 16-year-old Alex White staggered into the Fairview Hospital emergency room, raving about demons under his shirt and gushing blood where he had slashed his belly with a hunting knife, trauma physician Amanda Lee's first job was to stop the bleeding. But when White grabbed a nurse by her

> hair and threw her to the floor, screaming that she was the Whore of Babylon, Lee had to decide in an instant whether to inject him with the tranquilizer thorazine without asking him to sign her hospital's permission form. Ohio law and hospital rules require physicians to ask for permission before administering drugs, but White could not understand Lee's raving. So as would any physician in that situation, she tranquilized him without his permission.

That second is longer but more vivid, evoking more feeling. (Note that its vividness does not depend on adjectives or adverbs, but on nouns and verbs.) Which is better? That depends on what the writer intends. If the writer wants to evoke feeling, she uses vividly specific nouns and verbs; if she wants to seem cool and objective, she chooses more abstract, general language.

What readers can image, of course, depends on what they know—say *drag racing* to Colomb and up pop lots of vivid images. But to evoke those images in people who don't know the LaPlace Dragway, he would have to be specific: *Sixteen-years-old and burning rubber down a deserted Claiborne Avenue at 3 A.M. on a Sunday morning in a supercharged '57 Bel Aire, hubcap to hubcap with Don Debarbaris' four barrel GTO.*

Most of us usually prefer vivid writing, because we read it faster, understand it better, and remember it longer. So what we might lose in economy measured by number of words, we gain in impact. And of course, a writer can combine the general and specific:

> When someone needs emergency care, but acts so irrationally that he cannot legally consent to treatment, . . . For example, when on the night of May 13, 1998, 16-year-old Alex White staggered into the Fairview Hospital Emergency room raving . . .

The System of Imageable Words

There is, however, more to being vivid than just being more specific, because not all kinds of specificity are equal. In fact, all human languages seem to have devised a systematic way of making some kinds of specificity more imageable than others. For example, what image comes to mind when you read the word *life*? Certainly no image most of us share; nor do we get a distinct image from the more specific word *vegetation*. Now imagine a *pine tree*. For most of us, that term evokes a distinct image with more distinct feeling. But now imagine a *Joshua tree*. Unless you know desert vegetation, this more specific term probably inhibits your imagination, giving you no clear image at all. Words can get so specific that we can't call up an image unless we happen to know the specific referent.

Speakers of every language seem to organize their vocabulary in that systematic way, on a scale from general to specific, but with a break point between words that evoke no distinct image and words that do. In this array, the break point is shaded:

life	thing	stuff	nourishment	utility
creature	object	merchandise	food	transportation
animal	device	household goods	produce	conveyance
livestock	tool	furniture	fruit	vehicle
horse	hammer	table	apple	motorcycle
palomino	ballpean	Federal dropleaf	Fuji	Harley

Words like *horse, hammer, table, apple* and *motorcycle* refer to things at what psychologists call the *basic level of categorization.* Words at this level evoke in us distinct mental images. Above the basic level (*livestock, tool,* etc.), we conjure up random vague images. Below it, we get a more specific image only if we happen to know what a ballpean or Fuji looks like. For the rest of us, a Fuji is just another apple.

Most of us prefer prose that uses words at the basic level because we read, understand, and remember such words most easily. As writers, though, we see images in our prose more distinctly than our readers will, because we know our subject so well (recall Colomb's response to *drag racing*). If you write about a *creature's right to be free from inhumane treatment,* you may see in your own mind a bunny twisting away from chemical drops burning its trusting, black button eyes. But your readers will get that specific image only if you give it to them.

We can even create a gradation of specificity:

There have been recent decreases in weapons crimes.

Recently, crimes involving inexpensive firearms have decreased.

Compared to a few years ago, a person is less likely to be the victim of someone with a cheap handgun.

Compared to 1995, you are half as likely to be robbed by someone shoving a twenty dollar Saturday night special in your face.

What we image more clearly, we respond to more viscerally. If it is visceral response you want from readers, be vivid.

Deliberate Generality

Sometimes, however, you don't want to be specific, especially when you develop general claims in a cool objective style:

We the People of the United States, in Order to form a more perfect Union, establish Justice, insure domestic Tranquillity, provide for the common defense, promote the general Welfare, and secure the Blessings of Liberty to ourselves and our Posterity, do ordain and establish this Constitution for the United States of America.

We do not improve that passage by making it more specific:

> We over-21 property-owning white men signing this document, to create a nation free from the tyranny of King George and the pain and poverty that such tyranny creates, to establish a system whereby white men are treated fairly by the Courts, to insure that people in every town, city, and state do not fight with one another, to provide for soldiers and sailors who will defend our borders, . . .

We need general language to express general warrants stating general concepts. Here's a good example in another of our historical documents:

> . . . whenever any Form of government becomes destructive of these ends, it is the Right of the People to alter or to abolish it, and to institute new Government, laying its foundation on such principles and organizing its powers in such form, as to them shall seem most likely to effect their Safety and Happiness.

That principle of democratic governance still resonates because it covers not just this country two centuries ago, but all countries at all times. The drafters of the Declaration of Independence would have been wrong to write:

> . . . since King George III and his Parliament have taken away our right to be free to do what makes us happy, like acquiring and owning property like farmland and slaves, we have the right to revolt and create a new country . . .

That sentence is too specific to express a universal truth. Later in the Declaration, however, the drafters wrote more vividly and thereby evoked more emotion when they explicitly described King George's crimes against the colonies:

> He has excited domestic insurrections amongst us, and has endeavoured to bring on the inhabitants of our frontiers, the merciless Indian Savages, whose known rule of warfare, is an undistinguished destruction of all ages, sexes and conditions.

This more general version would have served less well:

> He has caused problems by encouraging some native people to act against us.

Some writers, however, use two or more general words specifically to discourage readers from seeing clearly and sharply what they are referring to, an act that can verge on dishonesty. Compare the following:

> To reduce to zero-level the agricultural production of psychotropic substances derived from plants in northern South America, agencies responsible for international covert action should introduce bioactive substances entailing the permanent interruption of growth cycles in ways that avoid calling attention to that project. Such a course of action may have nontemporary deleterious biological effects on collateral agricultural production and on some of those

indigenously associated with it, but the desired results are of sufficient critical importance to warrant such action.

To stop cocaine farming in Colombia and Ecuador, the CIA should kill their cocoa crop by secretly infecting it with disease. Doing this may kill other plants that farmers eat and even poison some farmers, but our goals come first.

When you use two or more words to express what one could, you soften the edges of a concept: *abortion* vs. *termination of pregnancy*; *cancer* vs. *malignant growth*; *crippled* vs. *limited ambulatory capacity*. As always, we aim at the Goldilocks Rule: not too general, not too specific, but just right. What is just right is hard to gauge, but you might hold these two principles in mind:

- When you offer examples, evidence, and illustrations, your readers are likely to prefer language that is concrete, distinct, and vivid.
- When you state general principles, values, and assumptions, readers are likely to sense the power of those statements if you express them in more general language.

Since generalities require less hard thought, we are all are more likely to be too general than too specific. But hard thinking is a quality of all arguments worth making, so thinking hard about the quality of your language is a way to think better about your argument and its effect on your readers.

WRITING PROCESS
Clear Language

REVISING

Revising for Style

Even if you are a slow and careful drafter, don't focus on style until you have completed a draft and revised its organization. Start with passages where you struggled to express yourself or were uncertain about your meaning. At such moments, we all tend to write confusing prose. Then work through the draft sentence-by-sentence, following these steps:

Diagnose

Start by underlining (or skimming) the first seven or eight words in each sentence (ignore short introductory phrases). Consider revising if you find this:

- Subjects are abstractions with lots of phrases attached.

- After seven or eight words, you see no verb, or if you do, it is vague.

- Those first seven or eight words express information that readers would not recognize from previous sentences or have reason to expect.

- Several sentences in a row keep changing subjects, so that in their first few words readers see no consistent set of characters or concepts.

For example, in the sentences in this passage, notice how long it takes to get to the verb in the main clause (whole subjects are underlined; verbs are bold-faced):

> _Attempts_ at explanations for increases in voter participation in recent elections **came** from several candidates. A general _cynicism_ about honesty in government **was** a common claim of some conservative politicians. But the public's greater _interest_ in their private affairs than in national public affairs **is** also a possible reason for the drop in voting.

In the first sentence, the character _voter_ appears _in_ the subject, but not _as_ the subject, and the whole subjects are long and complex. It is a passage begging for revision.

Revise

1. Start by identifying important characters. In the above passage, they are _voters, candidates,_ and _conservative politicians._

2. Identify their actions. Voters _participate (less), are cynical,_ and _are not interested;_ candidates _attempt_ and _explain;_ conservative politicians _claim._

3. Revise so that most clauses (not necessarily all) begin with important characters as subjects and are followed by key actions in verbs.

   > Several candidates **tried to explain** why fewer people **voted** in recent elections. Some conservative politicians **claimed** that voters **were** generally cynical about honesty in government. But perhaps so few **voted** because they **were** more interested in their private affairs than in national public affairs.

4. Your diagnosis might find a long introductory phrase:

   > _Despite their role in creating a sense of loyalty among students and alumni and generating financial resources that support minor sports, on balance_ major intercollegiate sports damage the aims of higher education.

If so, revise in either of two ways:

- Make the phrase an independent clause:

  > Major intercollegiate sports **may create** a sense of loyalty among students and alumni and generate financial resources that support minor sports, but on balance they **damage** the aims of higher education.

- Make the phrase a subordinate clause. Move it after the main clause, if it communicates new information. If it is old information, try to shorten it.

On balance, <u>major intercollegiate sports</u> **damage** the aims of higher education, *even though* <u>they</u> create a sense of loyalty among students and alumni and generate financial resources that support minor sports.

Although <u>major intercollegiate sports</u> create loyalty and generate financial resources, on balance <u>they</u> **damage** the aims of higher education.

5. Your diagnosis might find a long whole subject whose simple subject is a flesh-and-blood character:

    <u>*Athletes* who receive special academic consideration because their time is taken up with training and competition</u> are not necessarily academically ill-prepared for the rigors of a high-quality education.

If so, revise in either of two ways:

- Turn the subject into an introductory subordinate clause. Make the simple subject its whole subject, if you can:

  Although <u>*athletes*</u> **might receive** special academic consideration because their time is taken up with training and competition, <u>*they*</u> **are** not necessarily academically ill-prepared for the rigors of a high-quality education.

- Or turn the subject into its own main clause:

  <u>Some athletes</u> **may receive** special academic consideration because their time is taken up with training and competition, but <u>they</u> **are** not necessarily academically ill-prepared for the rigors of a high-quality education.

6. Your diagnosis might turn up an interrupting element:

    <u>Major intercollegiate sports,</u> *because they undermine the intellectual integrity that higher education is supposed to support by lowering standards for athletes,* **should be abolished.** That kind of erosion will inevitably lead to . . .

If so, move that element to the beginning or end of its sentence, depending on whether it connects more closely to the preceding or following sentence.

> <u>Major intercollegiate sports</u> **should be abolished,** *because they undermine the intellectual integrity that higher education is supposed to support by lowering standards for athletes.* That kind of erosion will inevitably lead to . . .

A Note on Active and Passive Verbs

If you remember any advice about writing, it is probably to avoid writing in the passive voice. Generally, that's good advice, but often not. For example, after the first sentence in this next passage, imagine active and passive verb sentences:

> Some astonishing questions about the nature of the universe have been raised by scientists investigating black holes in space. <u>The collapse of a dead star into a point perhaps no larger than a marble</u> **creates** _{active verb} a black hole. So much matter compressed into so little space changes the fabric of space around it in surprising ways.

Some astonishing questions about the nature of the universe have been raised by scientists investigating black holes in space. <u>A black hole</u> **is created** _{passive verb} by the collapse of a dead star into a point perhaps no larger than a marble. So much matter compressed into so little space changes the fabric of space around it in surprising ways.

In that context, the passive verb would be the better choice:

- The subject of the active verb is long and abstract: *The collapse of a dead star into a point perhaps no larger than a marble.* But the subject of the passive verb is short, simple, and easily grasped: *A black hole.*

- The passive verb puts into the subject something we just read in the previous sentence:

  . . . exploring **black holes in space. A black hole** is created by . . .

We don't encourage the passive voice, but neither do we say always to avoid it. *Choose* active or passive, depending on what you want as a subject. That's what the passive is for.

IN A NUTSHELL

About Your Prose . . .

You cannot read your own prose as your readers will, because you know too well what you wanted it to mean when you wrote it, and so it will always be clear to you. To overcome that obstacle, you need a way to diagnose your prose objectively. Here are six principles of clear writing to take not as ironclad rules for every sentence, but as advice about how most of them should work:

1. Make your important characters the subjects of verbs. If they are abstractions, be sure that they are terms familiar to your readers.

2. Express the important actions not in abstract nouns but in verbs.

3. Get to the verb in the main clause quickly:

   Avoid long introductory elements.

   Keep whole subjects short.

   Don't interrupt subject + verb connections with long phrases or clauses.

4. Begin your sentences with information that seems familiar to your readers.

5. End sentences with information that seems new to them.

6. Keep your subjects consistent by using as subjects your most familiar characters. Avoid beginning successive sentences with unexpectedly different subjects.

In addition to writing sentences with distinct subjects and verbs, work to write prose that is more rather than less vivid. You do that in two ways:

- Avoid using words that add little or nothing to your ideas, such as *very, basically, really*, and so on.
- Avoid decomposing a meaning into several words if you can express it in a single word: *do not pay attention to* → *ignore.*
- Avoid stating what a word implies.

  Future events will unexpectedly surprise us.   →   The future will surprise us.

You are likely to write more vividly if you choose words that are common and down to earth: *belly button* vs. *navel*. Some writers, such as newspaper editorial writers, rarely use either slang or more formal words, sticking to a middle style. Other writers use a lot of slang and no formal words; still others—scientists, for example—use no slang and all formal words. And some good writers include an occasional formal or slang expressions to give their prose a little kick.

Another way to create a vivid style is to choose a word that conjures up an image in the mind of your readers. Just about every word is on a scale of words that range from more or less generality/specificity. But for many scales, there is a breakpoint where one word creates no particular image in our minds, but the next more specific one does: *object–weapon–gun–pistol–Glock 19*. We might have a vague image associated with *gun*, but *pistol* has a more distinct one.

Some arguments need words that are general and abstract enough to avoid evoking feelings or to assert general philosophical principles, to lay down warrants and assumptions that govern specific cases.

... and About Revising It

First, diagnose your prose: Underline the first seven or eight words in each major clause (ignore short introductory phrases and clauses, especially when they refer to previous sentences). Consider revising if you see these characteristics:

- Subjects are not a specific character named in a short phrase.
- By the seventh or eighth word, you don't see a verb.
- Those first seven or eight words express new information.
- Several sentences in a row keep changing subjects.

Revise like this:

1. Start by finding the important characters.
2. Identify the key actions they perform.
3. Revise so that most of your sentences begin with important characters as subjects and are immediately followed by key actions in verbs.

4. When you find a long introductory phrase, rewrite it into a sentence or clause of its own.

When you find a long subject, consider these revisions:

1. Revise it into an introductory subordinate clause.
2. Revise it into a sentence of its own.

When you find a long interrupting element between the subject and verb, move it to the beginning or end of its sentence, depending on whether it connects more closely to the preceding sentence or to the one that follows.

Chapter 13

The Overt and Covert Force of Language

In this chapter, we look at how words express values and evoke feelings, shaping belief in ways that are both obvious and subtle, sometimes even dishonest—not to help you be dishonest, but to make you aware of the power of language to lead and mislead. We discuss how the subjects of sentences influence who or what readers see as responsible for events and how metaphors enliven prose but may also mislead readers—and writers as well.

When we write clearly, concisely, and vividly, we help our readers read our argument quickly, understand it easily, and remember it accurately. But the force of language goes deeper than assisting understanding and memory. We can use words to evoke values and feelings that not only color our readers' reasoning, but shape it.

Invoking Values, Evoking Feeling

Value-Laden Words

We color how readers feel about our arguments when we use words that invoke their values. If we oppose a cut in the income tax, for example, we might claim that the cut will

> stuff the wallets of those fat cat rich who sit on most of our nation's wealth.

But if we support the cut, we might argue that it will

> restore to American workers some of our hard-earned wages that the IRS sucks out of our paychecks every month.

Both descriptions arguably refer to the same circumstance, but the words invoke different values: *stuff the wallets, fat cat rich,* and *sit on our nation's wealth* versus *restore to American workers, hard-earned wages,* and *IRS sucks out* (not to mention the more subtle ***those** fat cat rich* versus ***our** paychecks*).

We see such value-laden language most often in politics and advertising. Ads are covert arguments whose unexpressed main claim is obvious enough: *Buy this product.* But they usually support their claims more with feelings than with reasons. For example, look at the language of this ad for Lady Foot Locker, in a fashion magazine for older teens and young adults:

> Sure, working out's all fabulous the first month or so. And then somehow, the treadmill is about as appealing as that ex-boyfriend of yours with the color coordination issues. Luckily, new Nike Tuned Air (with the perfect combination of cushioning and stability) can help you fall in love with your workout all over again. Which is more than we can say for your ex.

This ad wants readers to imagine the tedium of working out when they read *the treadmill is about as appealing as that ex-boyfriend of yours with the color coordination issues.* But that language relies on values (as in *color coordination issues*) that are shared by only some women. How would readers of a woman's bodybuilding magazine respond?

Values in Academic Writing

In academic writing, you will rarely see words as value-laden as *swell the wallets of those fat cat rich who already hoard most of our nation's wealth.* That kind of language in a political science paper would damage your credibility. Academic readers expect you to project an ethos of cool, objective distance. That does not mean you eliminate all signs of value in your writing. (You couldn't if you tried.) You might, for example, write in a political science paper how the tax cut would *augment the personal wealth of those who already control most of the nation's resources.* That kind of language reflects values but does not seem crudely emotional.

You Can't Avoid Values

Some argue that we betray the spirit of fair, rational argument when we use value-laden language of any kind, because it "slants" or "biases" our argument. We should appeal, they claim, not to our readers' warmest feelings but to their coolest logic. Following that principle, both sides in the tax cut debate could describe it in terms emptied of emotion:

> The tax reduction will augment the financial resources of those with the highest incomes.

> The tax cut will raise net earned income for everyone.

But even when you drain language of emotion, as those two sentences almost do, you still project the value of dispassionate objectivity. Moreover, when you avoid words that express values, you risk betraying not only yourself, but your readers, because they have a right to know where you stand and how strongly you feel. How would you feel if after listening to an apparently disinterested argument about flawed statistics used to support gun control laws, you learned the speaker worked for the National Rifle Association?

You begin choosing values the moment you frame your problem. The Supreme Court, for example, will eventually decide an issue that contending parties frame in different ways, reflecting their different values:

The right to assisted suicide	vs.	The duty of the state to prevent physicians from killing patients
The right to a dignified end of life	vs.	The duty of the state to protect the helpless
The sanctity of bodily privacy	vs.	The sanctity of life

We gain a big advantage if we can get those who have to decide an issue to accept our way of framing the discussion, because that imposes on others the burden of denying our self-evident lofty values. Who can reject the value of human dignity or, alternatively, the sanctity of life? Those who can frame an issue in their own terms usually prevail.

Keep in mind, however, that those different ways of framing an issue need not set up polar oppositions. Real contraries oppose substantially different things out there in the world: the words *massive tax cut* cannot refer to the same one that others call *tiny*; those we call *fabulously rich* cannot also be called *dirt poor*. In contrast, those different ways of posing the issue of assisted suicide refer to the *same* thing out there in the world, choosing to die, but from a different framework of values.

That's why two people can look at exactly the same referent, but disagree over how to name it:

Lee is a reckless daydreamer!	No, he is a daring visionary!
Jones is a chauvinist reactionary!	No, he is a patriotic conservative!

We could probably agree that if Jones is anything like a left-wing, flag-burning radical, he cannot arguably be called a *chauvinist reactionary*. They are just different things. But if he waves the flag and boasts of being an American, he could arguably be called either a *chauvinist* or a *patriot*.

But how do we decide which he is? He waves the flag, speaks proudly of his country, is against gun control and for a constitutional amendment banning flag burning. Does that make him a chauvinist or a patriot? A conservative or a reactionary? Is it a matter of degree? Does he wave the flag too much? Talk too boastfully about his country? But what counts as "too much"?

In cases like this, we can't rely on common criteria of meaning or features of the referent to decide what someone or something *is* (review pp. 182–186). In fact, we ask the wrong question when we ask *What **is** he, a chauvinist or a patriot?* The real question is why we want *others* to *think* that he is one or the other. What problem occasions the need to decide what to call Jones in the first place? Why do we have to decide at all? What he "is" depends less on what he *objectively* is than on what we think is at stake in *calling* him by one term or the other. If we think we can solve a problem by getting people to think well of him, we call him *a conservative patriot;* if we can solve it by getting people to think badly of him, we call him *a chauvinist reactionary.* We cannot decide on the "right" term by checking its criteria against Jones' features. We *first* decide what problem we want to solve by naming Jones; *then* we pick the terms that support our solution. In matters like this, the debate over what to call Jones is almost certainly a surrogate argument for a larger issue (review pp. 179–182).

When Emotional Language Undermines Sound Thinking

It is fair to use value-laden words to elicit feelings in your readers, so long as your argument is otherwise sound. In fact, for some matters you would be wrong not to enlist your readers' emotional commitment. Given what's at stake in assisted suicide, those debating the issue are right to appeal to our deepest feelings, but not at the cost of our best thinking. The risk in emotional language is that it does just that.

Polarizing Language

If you call your views *sincere, normal,* and *reasoned,* you imply that those who hold different views must be *cynical, abnormal,* and *irrational,* thereby demonizing them. If your reader is not *pro-choice,* then she must be *anti-choice;* if not *pro-life,* then *anti-life.* That kind of language encourages us to reason in what are called *disjunctive syllogisms:*

> You are either a conservative or a liberal.
>
> You are not conservative?
>
> Therefore, you must be a liberal.

> The answer to the drug problem is either punishment or treatment.
>
> You think that more treatment programs are the answer?
>
> Therefore, you must be against tough drug laws.

In both examples, the reasoning is formally valid but substantively false, because it offers what seem to be mutually exclusive alternatives that in fact are not:

- Maybe both choices are right. Maybe we need both tougher laws and new drug treatment programs.
- Maybe we need *slightly* tougher laws and *some* new treatment programs.
- Maybe both are wrong and a third choice is right—more education.
- Maybe both are right along with the third choice.

Reality is almost always more complex than *either-or* language allows. You owe readers a duty to avoid not only making issues more complex than they have to be, but also, as Einstein once said, no simpler than they really are.

Respecting Differences of Degree

Here is how a prominent evolutionary biologist explains our need to find opposing features that definitively distinguish us from apes:

> We have generally tried to unite our intellectual duty to accept the established fact of evolutionary continuity with our continuing psychological need to see ourselves as separate and superior, by invoking one of our worst and oldest mental habits: dichotomization, or division into two opposite categories, usually with attributions of value expressed as good and bad or higher and lower. We therefore try to define a "golden barrier," a firm criterion to mark an unbridgeable gap between the mentality and behavior of humans and all other creatures. We may have evolved from them, but at some point in our advance, we crossed a Rubicon that brooks no passage by any other species ...The basic formulation of them vs. us, and the resulting search for a "golden barrier," represents a deep fallacy of human thought. We need not fear Darwin's correct conclusion that we differ from other animals only in degree. A sufficient difference in quantity translates into what we call a difference in quality *ipso facto*. A frozen pond is not the same object as a boiling pool—and New York City does not represent a mere extension of the tree nests [of chimpanzees in their native habitat] at Gombé.

Source: Stephen Jay Gould, "The Human Difference," *New York Times*, July 2, 1999.

Cynical Language

If intensely value-laden language can undermine sound thinking, it can also betray the ethical duty we owe our readers. In fact, we must condemn as ethically corrupt those who cynically use words to appeal to feelings alone. In the election of 1996, for example, a political consultant circulated a list of words that he urged his clients to use:

- To incite animosity toward their opponents, they were told to call them *liberals* and *liars*, to say they were *extreme, radical, wasteful, corrupt,* and *hypocritical* and to refer to themselves as *pioneers* with *vision*, as *fair* and *moral*, dedicated to principles of *truth* and *courage*.

- To exploit voters' decency, they were advised to talk about their own *pride in America*, their *families, common sense,* and *duty*, and to accuse others of *betraying* the *common good* by their *greed* and even *treason*.

Those words convey more than different shades of meaning, because we know that the difference between *courage* and *treason* is more than political "spin." When politicians use language cynically, they corrupt our civic life by undermining the foundations of democratic discourse, not just because they substitute feeling for thinking, but because they teach us to distrust all political discourse. As bad money drives out good, cynical language drives out thoughtful argument.

In addition to your ethical duty to avoid dishonest language, you also have a pragmatic reason: No matter how persuasive you think strong language is, it alienates thoughtful readers, because it discredits any way of looking at an issue other than your own, and that damages your ethos. To be sure, when you use moderate language, you risk being called wishy-washy by those taking a with-us-or-against-us attitude. And in some cases, nuanced language is wrong. Many people couldn't believe that Hitler was as unqualifiedly evil as he turned out to be. But except for such rare cases, you do well to err on the side of moderation, because nuanced language encourages nuanced thinking, in both you and your reader. Strong language might make you feel good, but it can also make you look very bad.

Emotional Language and Ethos

Here a reviewer complains that a writer of an otherwise good book loses credibility because of its extreme language:

[The author] makes his claims about Allied capabilities [to destroy German concentration camps during World War II] mostly persuasive, but does so in a style as dogmatic and vindictive as that of some of the "myth" purveyors he condemns ... Such invective detracts from his weighty evidence and illustrates a disturbing trend: some scholars shout as if engaged in "McLaughlin Group" combat or the exposé culture of the tabloids. Gray academic prose presents its own problems, and [the author] is not the first on this subject to shout. But his tone can cheapen his valuable scholarship.

Source: Ann Finkbeiner, *New York Times Book Review,* October 12, 1999.

Subjects and Point of View

In Chapter 12, we showed you that what readers take from sentences is not the words themselves, but a story—images, scenes, a mental scenario. That's why the most readable prose is storylike, with the key elements of sentences—subjects and verbs—matching key elements of a story—characters and actions. But storytelling offers an opportunity not only to be clear, but to shape how readers understand and judge by focusing them on particular characters.

Manipulating Subjects to Assign Responsibility

With every sentence you write, you have to decide who or what to make its subject and thereby its main character. But more than that, when you choose to make one character rather than another the subject of a sentence, you impose on your readers a point of view toward the story the sentence tells. For example, compare these pairs of sentences; both sentences in each pair arguably refer to the same state of affairs in the world.

    1a.   Smith obtained stolen goods from Jones.

    1b.   Jones provided stolen goods to Smith.

    2a.   We learn from history that we need free speech to strengthen democracy.

    2b.   History teaches us that a democracy grows strong from free speech.

    3a.   Susan McDougal defrauded the bank in the Whitewater affair by using a document prepared by Hillary Rodham Clinton.

    3b.   Hillary Rodham Clinton prepared a document that was used by Susan McDougal to defraud the bank in the Whitewater affair.

If the first sentence in each pair is true, then arguably so is the second. But we respond to them differently because each assigns responsibility to a different character, imposing on us different points of view about who's responsible.

Subjects and the Nature of Things

We might think that subjects are somehow in the nature of things "doers" of actions:

> The dog **chased** the cat for a while before <u>he</u> finally **caught** her.

In that world, the dog did something to a cat; so it seems natural to make it the subject of *chase* and *caught*. But events do not determine subjects of sentences. We can *choose* to make the cat the center of attention:

> The cat **ran away** from the dog until <u>it</u> finally **got caught.**

By reshaping that sentence around the cat, we change which character seems to claim the center of our attention.

That story, of course, is a trivial one. Here is one more consequential:

> Reporters grilled the mayor until they finally got the information they wanted: Companies owned by friends who got contracts with the city contributed more than $100,000 to his campaign.

> The mayor went through a grilling from reporters until he finally admitted what he had tried not to reveal: He had taken more than $100,000 in campaign contributions from friends whose companies got contracts with the city.

The first sentence focuses on the press and the companies; the second on the mayor. Which is "truer"? Wrong question: if one is true, so arguably is the other. The right question is which better serves the aims of an argument. Who does the writer want us to focus on as the responsible character, the mayor or the press?

We tend to remember best the character that appears most often in subjects, and we tend to make that character most responsible for what happened in a story. So by managing the subjects of sentences, deft writers can get us to make judgments without consciously knowing that we have, much less why.

Managing Subjects by Managing Verbs

To manage subjects, however, you have to manage verbs. The easiest way to change subjects is to shift between active and passive verbs:

<u>My friend</u> **taught** me Spanish.

<u>I</u> **was taught** Spanish by my friend.

<u>We</u> **recorded** the fluid velocity at thirty-second intervals.

<u>The fluid velocity</u> **was recorded** at thirty-second intervals.

(Those of you in technical fields will write many sentences like that last one, because technical writers usually tell stories about things like velocity or fluids rather than about those who measure them.)

A more subtle technique is to find verbs that tell roughly the same story, but from different points of view:

<u>My friend</u> **taught** me Spanish.

<u>I</u> **learned** Spanish from my friend.

<u>George</u> **bought** a handgun from Fred.

<u>Fred</u> **sold** a handgun to George.

Sometimes, we have to think hard to find alternatives:

<u>The New York Yankees</u> **are losing** fans to the Mets.

<u>The New York Mets</u> **are attracting** fans from the Yankees.

<u>Fans</u> **are moving** from the Yankees to the Mets.

All three sentences arguably refer to the same action "out there," but lead us to assign the responsibility for that action to different characters. When you make an argument that depends on making one character responsible for an action, make that character the subject of as many verbs as you can. When you want to downplay the role of a character, make that character anything but the subject of an action.

Making Qualities Characters

In Chapter 12 we saw how we displace judgments about style from our impressions to the sentence that causes them:

I had to work hard to understand this book.   →   This book is unclear.

We displace judgments about many other qualities as well:

I don't feel close to you.   →   You are aloof.

When I look at that light, my eyes hurt.   →   That light is too bright.

Words that seem to describe the world often describe how we feel about it.

As simple as this point seems, behind it are some vexing philosophical issues that have been debated for centuries. In some cases, it is clear where to locate qualities we call *round, metallic,* or *combustible*—they are in the object. But qualities we call *hot, tasty, loud,* or *red* seem to be in the perceiver.

More complicated yet, some qualities seem to be shared by all perceivers, but others not. Contrast these five pairs of sentences: the (a) sentences focus on an object, the (b) sentences on the person judging it:

1a. The sun is hot today.
1b. I felt hot in the sun today.

2a. Vinegar tastes sharp.
2b. When I taste vinegar, I feel a sharp sensation on my tongue.

3a. Killing children is bad.
3b. I strongly condemn the killing of children.

4a. Expensive wine is a waste of money.
4b. When I buy expensive wine, I waste my money.

5a. Homosexuality is immoral.
5b. I condemn homosexuality for moral reasons.

If someone makes those (b) statements sincerely, then for that person each is "true." But would they be true for everyone? To determine that, we have to substitute *we all* for *I.* For most of us, the first three might be true.

1c. If we were all in the sun today, we all would have felt hot.

2c. When we all sip vinegar, we all get a sharp taste on our tongue.

3c. We all strongly condemn the killing of children.

But the next two are more problematic:

4c. When we all buy expensive wine, we all waste our money.

5c. We all condemn homosexuality for moral reasons.

Though (4b) and (5b) might be true for the writer, (4c) and (5c) are by no means true for every reader.

This issue of where a quality resides—in the referent or in our judgment of it—has been debated for millennia, so we will not try even to scratch its surface. But however philosophers decide that question, you can *choose* to write a sentence that seems to locate the quality in the thing (*Homosexuality is immoral*) or in a person's experience of it (*I morally condemn homosexuality*). It's worth a minute to think through such sentences, because when you attribute qualities to a thing, you may be referring to everyone's experience of it, or only to your own.

Treating Means as Agents

Another way to shift responsibility from flesh-and-blood actors to an object is just this side of metaphor:

I can't buy love with money.   →   Money can't buy me love.

You can conquer all with love.   →   Love conquers all.

The English language lets us make that kind of transformation systematically:

A does B to C by means of D		D does B to C
I cut my finger with the knife.	→	The knife cut my finger.
I can't buy love with money.	→	Money can't buy me love.
You can conquer all with love.	→	Love conquers all.

As common and as innocuous as this stylistic device seems, people argue over it. We've all seen or heard the slogan on this bumper sticker:

Guns don't kill, people do.

Those who oppose gun control focus on the agents of shootings—people; those who support it focus on the means—guns. Thus we have a battle over two forms of the "same" concept, one a transformation of the other:

A does B to C by means of D		D does B to C
People kill people with guns.	→	Guns kill people.

This pattern also lets you attribute a claim to an objective-seeming source:

<u>We</u> **have proved** with these data that we need a raise.

→ <u>These data</u> **prove** that we need a raise.

In their recent study, <u>Smith and Yang</u> **found** evidence from which <u>they</u> **conclude** that <u>those who smoke</u> **become** prematurely senile.

→ <u>A recent study (Smith and Yang, 1997)</u> **found** <u>evidence</u> **pointing** to the conclusion that <u>smoking</u> **causes** premature senility.

→ <u>Evidence from a recent study (Smith and Yang, 1997)</u> **points** to the conclusion that <u>premature senility</u> **results** from smoking.

Those sentences refer to the same "facts," but each slants who or what is responsible for actions and outcomes in a different way. So, think twice when you read a sentence suggesting that a "study" or "evidence" "proves" something, because such a sentence conceals an important variable: the human judgment behind the evidence.

Language and Responsibility

Shortly after 15-year-old Andrew Williams killed two classmates at Santana High School in March 2001, Daniel R. Weinberger of the National Institute of Health explained how the prefrontal cortex controls impulsive behavior but does not fully mature until a person is close to 20 years old. He wrote this in conclusion:

> This brief lesson in brain development is not meant to absolve criminal behavior or make the horrors any less unconscionable. But the shooter at Santana High, like other adolescents, needed people or institutions to prevent him from being in a potentially deadly situation where his immature brain was left to its own devices. No matter what the town or the school, if a gun is put in the control of the prefrontal cortex of a hurt and vengeful 15-year-old, and it is pointed at a human target, it will very likely go off.
>
> *Source:* "A Brain Too Young for Good Judgment," *New York Times*, March 10, 2001, p. A27.

Notice in the last sentence how Weinberger de-emphasizes Williams's responsibility by making *a gun* the main character: *a gun is put . . . it is pointed . . . it will very likely go off.*

Abstractions as Characters

Another way to shift responsibility takes us into the realm of metaphor:

> <u>Life</u> **will find** a way.

> <u>Nature</u> always **tells** us when <u>she</u> **thinks** we have violated her laws.

> <u>Duty</u> **requires** us to sacrifice.

We turn *Nature* into a person by making it the subject of verbs implying human action, such as *tell* and *think*. The technical term for doing that is *reification;* we also call it *personifying* or *anthropomorphizing,* which means to treat something not human as if it were. It's a kind of metaphor.

Sometimes we reify abstractions to deflect readers from a human cause:

> <u>Science</u> **has** the power to reveal nature's laws, but <u>it</u> **cannot define** our values; only <u>religious faith</u> **can guide** us down the moral path.

When we think about science and religion, we typically prefer not to focus on the fact that both are constructed through human action. So few writers would revise that sentence into this:

> <u>Scientists</u> **have** the power to **reveal** the patterns in the natural world, but <u>they</u> **cannot define** our values; only <u>religious leaders</u> **can guide** us down the moral path.

More commonly, however, we reify abstractions not to hide human agency but to express matters too complex for readers to picture easily. If we say,

> <u>Your ethical responsibility</u> **demands** that you resign.

we are not deflecting attention from some obvious agent:

> <u>People</u> **will think** you are unethical if you do not resign.

Instead, by reifying abstractions, we describe a situation in which there are no specific agents as if there were. Similarly, when the scientist in the movie *Jurassic Park* warns that the cloned dinosaurs will reproduce despite the efforts to prevent it, he says,

> <u>Life</u> **will find** a way.

He is not hiding a human agent, but using the reified abstraction to describe a situation without one.

By no means is reification always dishonest or unethical. Indeed, in our most revered political document, the drafters of the Declaration of Independence did just that. Here are just two examples, with our translations:

> **Original**: . . . <u>a decent respect</u> to the opinions of mankind **requires** that they should declare the causes which impel them to the separation.
>
> **Revised**: If <u>we</u> decently **respect** the opinions of mankind, <u>we</u> **should** declare why we do so.

> **Original**: . . . such is now <u>the necessity</u> which **constrains** them to alter their former systems of government.
>
> **Revised**: As a result, <u>we</u> **decided** that <u>we</u> **must** alter our former system of government.

In that first sentence, the drafters were reaching beyond specifics to generality. In the second, they used a metaphor that made themselves not agents free to act, but an oppressed people forced to act by circumstances and duty: *necessity constrains them to alter*. These reifications are not just clever wordplay, because the rest of the Declaration is a model of sound reasoning. The drafters used reifications not to mislead, but to support a larger and more complex argument.

Metaphorical Scenarios

The most dramatic way we use language to shape belief is by spinning out metaphorical scenarios. Metaphors can do more than reify a single abstraction. They can create a virtual world in which we play out many implications, some illuminating, some misleading. The problem is that when we create a metaphor, we may imply things we do not mean.

We earlier discussed two metaphors and some of their consequences: argument as war and communication as shipping a package of meaning. The two metaphors are easy to combine:

> I will *advance* my claims as *forcefully* as I can until you *yield* to the weight of my evidence. But if you can just *see into* my thinking about this, you'll *get the picture*.

In that sentence, we imagine two ways of coming to agreement: We force a claim on a reader, or the reader can look inside the argument to find its meaning.

We can imagine a different model for communication: guiding readers along a path that gets them from here to there:

> I will *lead* you *through* a line of reasoning that together we can *follow* to *reach* agreement.

So what if these metaphors differ? They invite us to see an event in different ways, and those differences may have consequences. For example, what if your reader fails to agree with your argument?

- If argument is war, then you lose the battle because you are too weak or your reader too strong.
- If communication is a bundle of meaning sent and received, you can blame yourself for packaging it badly or the reader for unwrapping it incorrectly.
- If communication is a path down which you lead readers, you can blame yourself for being a bad guide or your reader for being a bad follower.

A metaphor can also be so vivid that it creates networks of implications that are simply wrong. Consider these metaphors:

- A school official explains why a student was suspended from school for expounding unpopular ideas:

> That kind of hate speech is a *virulence* we had to *stamp out*. We *isolated* the student because his *sick* views could have *infected* and *spread through* our community.

Beliefs are not communicable diseases, but the metaphor encourages us to think that it is in the public interest to quarantine those who might spread unpopular ideas.

- An environmentalist defends those who vandalize logging equipment:

> A living thing has the *right* to protect itself from predators. And if it cannot *defend* itself, then those who love it have a duty to do so. The redwoods cannot *defend* themselves, so we who *love* them must *defend* them and *punish* their *attackers*. That's *nature's law*.

Trees do not have rights; only people do. But if we think in terms of "nature's law," then the metaphors of prosecution, defense, and punishment follow.

- A police officer might say this about the accidental shooting of an innocent person in a drug raid on the wrong apartment:

  The *war* on drugs is no picnic. *Wars* have *casualties,* but that can't stop us from *fighting* an *enemy* that *attacks* innocent children. We cannot *surrender* to the *tyranny* of heroin and cocaine.

In the heat of battle, armed forces kill innocents, but should we judge police as we do soldiers? In short, metaphors can infiltrate our thinking and shape it in ways that are seriously misleading.

We do not say that you should never use value words, manipulate subjects, reify abstractions, or create metaphors. We cannot think without metaphors. Just be aware of the language you choose, because it can mislead not only your readers, but yourself.

The Use and Abuse of Natural Selection

Scientists have long personified nature. When Darwin called evolution *natural selection,* he helped his readers understand a complex matter through a memorable metaphor: Nature selects those species most fit to survive. He combined an agent his readers knew well, *Mother Nature,* with a process they also knew well, *selective breeding:*

> We have seen that man by selection can produce great results, and can adapt organic beings to his own uses, through the accumulation of slight but useful variations, given to him by the hand of Nature. But Natural Selection . . . is immeasurably superior to man's feeble efforts as the works of Nature are to those of Art. (*Origin of Species,* ch. 2)

When Darwin defended natural selection against the charge that he spoke of it "as an active power of Deity," he pointed out that scientists had done the same for centuries: magnets **attract** or **repel** one another, gravity **holds** the planets in their orbits, water **finds** its own level. He claimed this was a harmless way of talking because "Every one knows what is meant and is implied by such metaphorical expressions" (*Origin,* ch. 4).

Perhaps, but Darwin could not predict how others would use his metaphor. At the end of the nineteenth century, John D. Rockefeller used *natural selection* and its rugged cousin, *the survival of the fittest,* to defend his brutal business practices:

> The growth of a large business is merely the survival of the fittest . . . The American Beauty rose can be produced . . . only by sacrificing the early buds which grow up around it. This is not an evil tendency in business. It is merely the working-out of a law of nature and a law of God.

It's a view still current today: "Darwin was right. Only the fittest survive—especially when the creatures involved are graying commodities companies battling in the pits of a downcycle."

Source: Robert Matthews, Susan Warren, and Bernard Wysocki, Jr., "Fitness Test: Alcoa-Reynolds Union Bears Stamp of Deals Rocking Commodities," *Wall Street Journal,* August 20, 1999.

WRITING PROCESS
The Overt and Covert Force of Language

REVISING

Subjects and Point of View

After you are sure your prose is clear and direct, check whether you have used the subjects of your sentences to focus readers on those characters that you want them to see as most responsible for the events in your story. Here is a simple test:

1. Pick out the characters that your sentences focus on:

   • Circle or boldface the subject of each main clause and subordinate clause.

   • If an important character appears in a phrase before the subject, circle or boldface it. For example,

   Thinking about **politicians,** Americans cannot help but be cynical about the future of argument as a tool of democracy.

   Then if you can, revise so that the first character is the subject of the sentence:

   <u>Politicians</u> make most Americans cynical about the future of argument as a tool of democracy.

2. Have you repeated a few characters or used many different ones?

   • If you find a few, do you want readers to see them as your main characters? If not, revise so that they appear elsewhere in their sentences.

   • If you find many characters, would you improve your story by focusing on fewer?

3. Are your subject-characters people or abstractions?

   • If abstractions, are they so familiar to readers that they can build a story around them? If not, revise to focus on people or familiar abstractions.

IN A NUTSHELL

About Your Prose . . .

All words imply values, so you cannot write in a completely value-free way. Your problem is to figure out what values you want to invoke, because values evoke feelings, and feelings are often as powerful an element in an argument as is "pure" logic.

The most difficult issues in framing a question arise not from polar opposi-tions—tall versus short or rich versus poor—but when you and your readers disagree about a point of view: *filthy rich* versus *wealthy, poor* versus *impover-ished.* In such debates, you waste your time if you try to match criteria to features. Instead, you have to think clearly about the problem you are trying to solve. If one term solves the problem better than the other, then that is the term you argue for.

You use value-laden words unethically when you knowingly use them to replace the rational force of an argument, rather than to augment it. When you use polarizing words, you polarize choices. You force your reader to be with you or against you, rather than somewhere in between, which is where most thoughtful people find themselves. Polarizing language squeezes out nuance, moderation, and complexity.

Every story has more than one character, so you can tell your story from different points of view. You make a character dominate a passage when you make it the subject of all or most of its sentences. Readers then focus on that character as responsible for most of the events in that part of your story.

. . . and About Writing It

- If you are a slow drafter, watch your words as you draft. Decide on an emotional tone before you begin drafting.

- If you are a fast drafter, pay attention to your words later in the revision stage.

You lead readers to focus on a character by working that character into the subjects of sentences. You do that in six ways:

- You can switch between active and passive verbs, which is the simplest way: *I recorded the observations* versus *The observations were recorded.*

- You can find verbs that let you move into the subject the character you want readers to focus on: *I bought a car from you* versus *You sold a car to me.*

- You can displace a feeling onto what makes you feel that way: *I had a hard time solving that problem* versus *That problem is difficult.*

- You can move the means or instrumentality of an action into a subject: *You can't buy happiness with money* versus *Money can't buy happiness.*

- You can reify abstractions by making them subjects of verbs you usually use with flesh-and-blood characters: *Love conquers all.*

- You can create metaphoric scenarios: *Racism contaminates the thinking of many people.*

Checklists for Planning and Revising

We have recommended that when you make an argument you ask yourself and your readers many questions. But if you are new to writing arguments, their number may overwhelm you. (You'll find more than ninety in the complete list below.) Not even the most experienced writers can hold them all in mind, much less systematically answer them. As you gain experience, however, you'll find that you won't need to think about them all, because you'll answer most of them without asking. But since even the most experienced writers need help to see their work objectively, we include here four checklists for looking at aspects of your paper. The first three you can run through quickly. The last is a complete list for when you have time to revise more carefully. At the end, you'll find a step-by-step procedure for storyboarding a long paper.

A Checklist for Evaluating Discussion/Paper Questions

This short checklist will help you find good questions that you can raise in class or use to formulate a conceptual problem for a paper. If you answer "No" to the first five questions, you may have to find a new topic for your argument.

1. Do you care about answering the question you have posed?
2. Will anyone else care about hearing your answer?
3. Can you imagine finding an answer?
4. Can you imagine evidence that would support your answer?
5. Can you imagine finding that evidence?

If you answer "Yes" to these next questions, you may also have to find a new topic.

6. Can you answer the question in just a few words?
7. Does the question call for a simple yes-no answer?
8. Is it a question of fact that a reader could answer just by looking something up?
9. Will your readers accept your answer without asking for reasons and evidence?
10. If they disagree, will they think the answer is just a matter of opinion?

A Checklist for Argument

This checklist will help you analyze the structure of your argument as you plan and as you revise. If you are checking a draft, you don't have to copy from it word-for-word: a brief paraphrase will do. But do write complete sentences, not just topics or phrases.

1. Do your reasons/subclaims "add up" to a strong case for the main claim?

2. Can you think of any other reasons that support the main claim? If so, add them.

3. Are the reasons/subclaims in the best order? If not, reorder them.

4. Will readers recognize the principle of order for your reasons/subclaims? If not, add a transitional word or phrase to signal that order.

5. Does the evidence under each reason/subclaim in fact support it?

6. Is there enough evidence for each reason/subclaim?

7. Is there other evidence that would support a reason/subclaim?

Once you answer those questions and fill in missing information, use the diagram on the following page to guide further drafting and revising.

Ten Steps to a Coherent Paper

This checklist will help you predict whether your readers will judge your argument to be coherent. Use it for drafts that are close to finished. A "No" answer to any of the questions suggests that you have to do some revising.

1. Draw a line between the introduction and the body and between the body and conclusion.
   • Does the body begin with a new paragraph?
   • Does the conclusion begin with a new paragraph?

2. In your introduction, underline the sentences that state the problem or question.
   • Have you told your readers why it should matter to them?
   • If not, will they think it matters for the same reason you do?

3. Box the sentence that states the main claim of the paper.
   • Does it respond directly to the problem or question?
   • Does it make an arguable claim?
   • Is it at or near the end of the introduction? If not, is it in the conclusion?

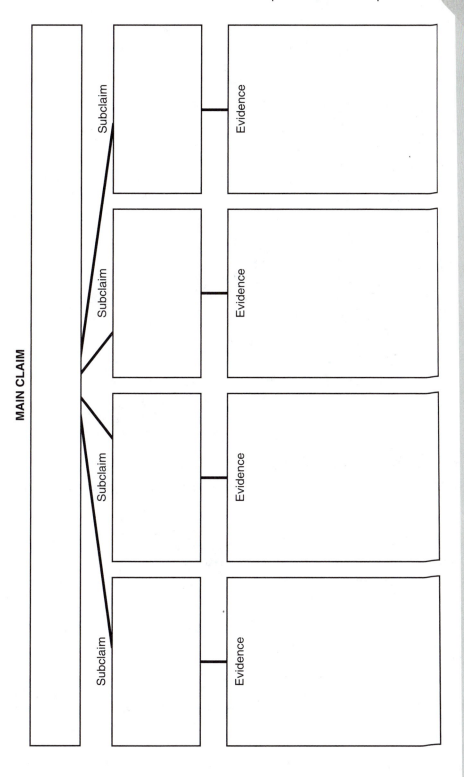

- If the claim is in the conclusion, do the last sentences of the introduction announce the key terms that appear in the main claim?
- If your main claim is stated in both your introduction and conclusion, are the two statements similar?
- If they are similar, is the one in the conclusion more specific, more informative?

4. Circle the key words in the last two sentences of the introduction and the most important sentence in your conclusion. Then circle those same words throughout the paper. Bracket words that refer to roughly the same concepts as the circled words or to concepts that are clearly related to them.
   - Are there three or more circled or bracketed words per paragraph?

5. Circle key words in the title.
   - Are the words that you circled the same ones that you circled in the introduction and conclusion?
   - Are they words that did not appear in your written assignment?

6. Draw a line between each major section of your paper. Box the sentence that states its main point.
   - Does it make an arguable claim?
   - Is it a reason supporting the main point/claim?
   - Do most of the main points appear at the beginning of their sections?
   - Now if you can, do the same thing for each paragraph.

7. Look at the beginning words of each section.
   - Do they begin with words that signal why the paragraphs come in the order they do, words such as *first, second; on the other hand, however; therefore, in conclusion,* and so on?

8. For each paragraph, underline every sentence that reports evidence supporting the point/claim of the paragraph.
   - Have you underlined at least half of the paragraph?

9. Underline the first half of the first sentence in each paragraph.
   - Do the words you have underlined refer back to something already mentioned earlier in the essay?

10. Underline the first six words in each sentence.
    - Do they refer to information that would be familiar to readers, or at least would not surprise them? Are they words that are mentioned earlier in the essay, obviously connected to a concept mentioned earlier, or related to concepts that readers are likely to have in mind?

A Complete List of Questions

This checklist will help you keep track of all the questions you might ask about your argument. The questions are in categories organized top down, from the most general questions about your readers and problem to the details of sentences. We have marked the most important questions with a star (★), the more important ones with an arrow (➷). If you can't cover every question, review the marked ones, and if you're *really* pressed for time, focus on the starred ones.

1. Preliminary Questions About Your Audience

★ 1. What are the general values of your readers? Liberal? Conservative? Middle of the road? Religious? Secular? Do their values reflect their race? Ethnicity? Marital status? Economic level? Profession? Expertise?

➷ 2. What kinds of arguments do your readers prefer? From lots of individual bits of evidence to a generalization? From settled principles and warrants to deductions from them? Will they expect to see the kind of argument that is common in their field of expertise?

➷ 3. What kind of evidence do they prefer? Hard statistical evidence? Field observation? Personal experience? Quotes from authorities? Primary reports of evidence? Anecdotes?

4. How much time do they have for your argument? Will they want a summary of it up front, or will they patiently read through it all?

2. Questions About Your Particular Problem

★ 1. What kind of problem are you addressing, pragmatic or conceptual? Do you want your readers simply to believe something? Or do you want them to act, or at least support an action?

➷ 2. What costs or benefits are at stake *for your readers* in your problem? Would they agree?

3. Have your readers tried to solve this problem? Do they think they have already solved it? How committed are they to a different solution? If so, what is at stake for them in giving up their solution in favor of yours?

4. What level of agreement are you seeking: Understanding? Respect? Approval? Endorsement? Wholehearted assent?

3. Questions About Your Solution/Claim

★ 1. Is your claim significant enough to make an argument about? Is it contestable? Is it capable of being proved wrong?

↩ 2. If your claim solves a pragmatic problem, will the solution cost less than the problem does? Will it create a bigger problem than the one it solves? Can it be implemented? Why is it better than alternative solutions?

↩ 3. Is your claim sufficiently rich in concepts to anticipate the key concepts in your argument?

4. Is it appropriately complex? Does it open with clauses introduced with *although, if,* or *when*? Does it close with clauses introduced with *because*? Would a shorter, simpler claim be more effective?

5. Is it appropriately hedged? Are there limiting conditions? Exceptions?

6. Is your solution feasible? Ethical? Prudent?

7. If your claim solves a conceptual problem, could other facts, concepts, theories, etc., contradict it?

4. Questions About Your Title

★ 1. Does your title include key words from your main claim? Are there words that someone who knew the assignment would not predict?

2. Have you taken advantage of using a two-line title?

5. Questions About Your Introduction

★ 1. If your problem is pragmatic, have you stated the destabilizing condition clearly? Have you clearly stated the costs and/or benefits from the point of view of your readers?

↩ 2. If your problem is conceptual, have you stated clearly what is not known or not well enough understood? Have you stated the consequences in a way that shows they are more significant than the destabilizing condition?

↩ 3. Where have you located your main claim/solution? If it is in both the introduction and conclusion, do both statements harmonize? If you state it for the first time in the conclusion, did you end the introduction with language that introduces the key concepts you develop in the rest of the argument and repeat in the claim at the end?

↩ 4. Can your reader plainly see where you have ended your introduction and where you begin the body of your argument?

5. Can you find common ground to establish a context for your problem? Does it introduce key concepts about the problem?

6. Would you improve your introduction by adding a prelude, a pithy quotation, an interesting fact, or a brief anecdote that encapsulates the problem? Would a prelude suit the kind of argument you make?

6. Questions About Your Conclusion

★ 1. Have you stated your claim/solution in your conclusion?

2. Have you suggested why it is significant? Have you suggested what is still unknown, uncertain, left to be done?

3. Would you improve your conclusion by adding a coda? Would a coda suit the kind of argument you make?

7. Questions About the Body of Your Argument

★ 1. Why have you ordered the parts of your argument as you have?

☞ 2. If you have divided your argument into two or more parallel parts, can you explain their order? Is it clear to your reader? Have you introduced each part with words that signal the order?

☞ 3. If you have divided your argument into two or more sequential parts, have you ordered them from the beginning of the process to its end or from the end back to the beginning? Is that order clear to your reader?

☞ 4. Can you pick out in the body of your argument key words that you use in your title, at the end of your introduction, and in your conclusion?

5. Have you avoided laying out your argument as a history of your thinking or as a summary of your sources? Have you avoided dividing it into blocks organized around the things given to you by your topic rather than around ideas or qualities *you* discovered and choose to discuss?

6. Have you avoided opening the body of your argument with a long summary of background?

8. Questions About the Body of Your Sections and Paragraphs

★ 1. Have you organized sections as you organize a whole essay? Does each section open with its own introduction? Do you state the point of the section at the end of its introduction?

☞ 2. Do you state in the introduction to each section the key words you develop in the rest of that section?

3. If a section is longer than a couple of pages, have you concluded each section by restating the claim of the section?

4. Have you organized your longest paragraphs like your sections?

9. Questions About Your Evidence

★ 1. Have you based your reasons on reliable reports of evidence? Are your sources authoritative? Have you cited them?

★ 2. Are you sure your readers will accept what you offer as a report of evidence or will they think it is only another reason?

★ 3. Do you have sufficient evidence? Is your evidence accurate? Precise? Representative? Authoritative?

4. Have you been careful not to paraphrase your sources so closely that you have risked a charge of plagiarism?

5. Have you distinguished between quoting an authority just to paraphrase your claims and reasons and quoting an authority as evidence?

6. Have you introduced complex quantitative evidence and long quotations with a reason that interprets the evidence for the reader?

7. Are you depending too much on your memory for evidence? Are you depending too much on a vivid anecdote?

10. Questions About Your Warrants

★ 1. Have you made explicit what your readers must believe in general before they will consider your particular claims and reasons? Have you taken important definitions, values, assumptions for granted?

↩ 2. Should you treat your warrant as a subordinate claim that you must support in a subordinate argument?

3. Do your warrants actually cover your reasons and claims?

4. Are your warrants appropriately limited and qualified?

5. Are your warrants appropriate to your community of readers?

11. Questions About Acknowledgment and Response

★ 1. Can you imagine your readers' objections and reservations? Can you respond to them? Can you support your response as if it were a subordinate claim in a subordinate argument?

2. Can you imagine a reader offering counterreasons, counterevidence, counteranalogies to your own? Can you imagine responding to them?

12. Questions About Your Reasoning

★ 1. Have you avoided becoming fixated on your first hypothesis? Have you kept your mind open to alternative ones? Can you imagine at least one hypothesis as an alternative to your own?

2. If you reasoned deductively, from a warrant and reason to a claim, are you certain of the truth of the warrant? Or have your taken it for granted?

3. If you reasoned inductively, from specifics to a generalization, are you certain that you have observed enough instances to draw a generalization?

13. Questions About Meaning and Definitions

★ 1. If your argument turns on a definition, do you want your readers simply to understand a concept in a new way, or once they understand it, do you want them to do something?

☞ 2. Are you obliged to work within the four corners of a technical definition or can you work with a common one? Are you relying on a technical definition when your readers expect a common one (and vice versa)?

☞ 3. If you rely on a common definition, can you state the criteria of meaning that best serve your purposes and then match features of the referent to those criteria?

☞ 4. If you rely on a common definition, can you describe a model member of a category that your readers will accept and then describe your referent to match that model?

5. Can you shape the criteria of meaning and the features of the referent to match each other?

6. If your problem seems to be a conceptual one, is it possible you are addressing a surrogate problem in place of a pragmatic one?

7. Have you become a prisoner of an authoritative definition, either from a standard dictionary or a specialized source?

14. Questions About Causation

★ 1. If your problem is a pragmatic one, have you focused on those causes that you think you can fix?

★ 2. If your problem is conceptual, have you focused on those causes that are highlighted by the special interests you and your readers bring to the question?

☞ 3. Have you avoided the "One True Cause" mentality? Have you considered causes that do not immediately precede the effect? Causes that are absent? Causes that are routine rather than unusual? Causes whose magnitude is less significant than the effect? Causes that do not confirm your assumptions?

☞ 4. If your problem is a pragmatic one, have you considered offering all five narratives that explain the causes of an effect? Have you explained the problem? How the solution will work? Why the solution will cost less than the problem? Why it won't create a bigger problem? How you can implement it? Why it is better than alternatives?

5. Have you analyzed your theory of causation using an ANOVA table?

6. Have you considered the possibility of multiple causes? Of mutual feed-back of causes?

7. Have you begun your analysis of causes far enough back in the chain of causes and effects? Or too far back?

8. Have you analyzed causes at a level of detail that suits the solution to your problem?

15. Questions About Language

★ 1. Do most of the subjects of your sentences name the main characters in your story? Do your verbs name the specific actions those characters are involved with?

★ 2. Do you begin all of your sentences with information that is familiar to your readers?

★ 3. Are your subjects relatively consistent? Are they the characters most significant to your story?

➾ 4. Do your sentences get to main verbs quickly? Do they have relatively short introductory elements? Relatively short subjects? Few interruptions between subjects and verbs?

➾ 5. Have you eliminated empty words, redundant implications of words? Have you compressed several words into one, when you can?

6. Have you tried to choose words that are specific enough to create an image in the mind's eye of your readers? Have you chosen general words for your warrants and definitions?

7. When you use words that invoke values and evoke feelings, do you do so in the context of an otherwise sound argument? Are you clear why you are using them? What problem do you think you are solving?

8. Have you avoided inappropriately trying to deflect your readers' attention away from flesh and blood characters by reifying abstractions and relying on metaphors?

Storyboarding a Long Paper

We've offered advice about organization in several Writing Process sections, and that advice should get you through most short papers. But for a longer, more complicated one, you may need help planning and managing all its parts. We recommend that you try a storyboard.

When you create a storyboard, you group related parts of your paper on separate pages, in rough outline form at first, but in greater detail as you develop your argument. A storyboard has all the advantages of an outline, but without the fussiness of indentations, having a "b" for every "a", and getting the numbering right. And unlike an outline, a storyboard reduces the complexity that you have to deal with at one time.

- You isolate the units of your paper so that you can work on each one separately without worrying about how it fits into the whole.
- You see at a glance where you have lots of information and where you have gaps.

A storyboard also helps you *see* a complex argument in its entirety, especially when you lay it out on a table or tape it to a wall.

- You take in the organization at a glance, like a physical structure with layers and sublayers all laid out before you.
- You can easily move pages around to try out different arrangements, seeing the structure of each new arrangement at a glance.
- You can easily add or delete sections.

Some people feel that they think better when they physically move around their storyboard, actually looking at it from different angles to get new perspectives on it. If you are a verbal person, better with words than shapes, think of a storyboard as a flexible, expanded outline. If you are a visual person, think of it as a picture of the structure of your paper. In either case, you'll manage a complex argument better if you use one.

1. Create templates.

To start the process, create template pages for your introduction and conclusion, with a heading for each possible element. Use whole pages.

Introduction/Problem	Conclusion
Prelude:	Main claim:
Common ground:	
Destabilizing condition:	Significance of claim:
Costs/consequences:	Work still to be done:
Solution:	Coda:

Next, create two kinds of reason templates: one for those reasons that you think you can support only with evidence (you should have few of these) and another for reasons that you have to support with a complete nuclear argument. So depending on how complex the support for your reason will be, create one or the other of the two templates below for each reason.

Reason #_____
Main reason:
Reports of evidence to support main reason:

Conclusion
Main reason claim:
Reasons in support of main reason/claim:
Reports of evidence to support reasons:
Acknowledgment and response:

Finally, create templates for warrants and their supporting arguments and for acknowledgments and responses and their supporting arguments:

Warrant for Reason #_____
Warrant/claim:
Reasons in support of warrants:
Reports of evidence to support reasons:
Acknowledgment and response:

Acknowledgment and Response for Reason #_____
Objection/reservation/alternative:
Response/claim:
Reasons:
Reports of evidence:
Warrant/acknowledgment and response:

For the reason, warrant, and acknowledgment/response templates, make as many copies as your argument has major reasons. Save the blank template pages on your computer, but you'll start out working with them in hard copy.

2. Fill out the templates.

Fill in as many blanks as you can with what you know right now. At first, you may not have much to add, and some of it may be guesses that you have to confirm later. If you have to do some research to find something to add, do it quickly. Don't wait until the pages are full to go on to the next step.

3. Arrange the templates as they will appear in your paper.

As soon as you have enough to go on, tape the sheets to a wall or lay them out on a table, your bed, or the floor as shown below.

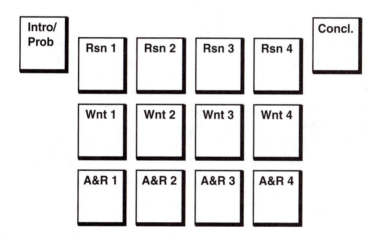

Move the pages around until you feel that you have a workable order. Add ideas as they occur to you.

If the pages get messy with notes, enter them in your computer template and print clean copies on which you can add even more notes. You can also use sticky notes that you can easily add to or delete.

4. Draft, but then revisit your storyboard.

Once you have a workable plan, build your argument piece by piece. As you draft, try different arrangements. From time to time, check the skeleton of your argument by reading straight through the whole *Introduction/Problem* page, the main reasons at the top of the *Reason* pages, and the whole *Conclusion* page. If some sheets remain empty, so be it. They will remind you of opportunities. The point is to decompose your task into parts so that you are not paralyzed by the kind of complexity that even the most experienced writers cannot deal with all at once.

Appendix 1

∞

Fallacies

Throughout this book we've discussed both how the quality of your thinking contributes to the quality of your argument and, no less important, how the quality of your argument can improve the quality of your thinking. We've shown you how to use the elements of a written argument to guard against common mistakes in reasoning, even to avoid those deep-seated biases that can lead us all astray. When you look for and evaluate reasons, evidence, warrants, and especially acknowledgments and responses in your arguments, you think more systematically and more carefully about the soundness of your claims.

There is, however, another common way to encourage sound thinking, one that is almost 2,500 years old. In this approach, logicians study systematic errors in reasoning that they call fallacies. A fallacy is not a false belief, like thinking that the earth is flat. Rather, fallacies are missteps in the process of reasoning your way to a logically sound conclusion. By this definition, you can reason validly and conclude that the earth is flat or fallaciously and conclude that it is round.

Over the centuries, logicians have identified scores of these fallacies and given them formidable Latin names such as *post hoc ergo propter hoc, ad verecundiam, non sequitur.* Some of them will always undermine your reasoning, while others do so only in certain circumstances. So we group them into two categories to help you distinguish blunders in reasoning: those that you should always avoid and those that you should question carefully.

Errors in Reasoning

These fallacies are outright errors in getting from a reason to a claim. They can all be explained in terms of "technical" problems in one or more elements of the argument. We'll introduce each of these fallacies as if we're being charged with it, and then add the technical explanation.

1. "But what you said doesn't follow!" (Your reason is irrelevant to your claim.)

Cyberspace will make government irrelevant _{main claim} by making all data instantly available. _{reason 1} Once we can be in instant contact with everyone else, _{reason 2} artificial national borders will wither away _{claim/reason 3} and government will have nothing to do. _{claim/reason 4}

You might be right, but I can't follow the steps in your chain of reasoning. First, I don't see why making information available faster makes government irrelevant. Second, I don't see how being in contact with everyone will make national borders disappear. And third, I don't see why the lack of borders leaves government nothing to do. Maybe I can see some connection between governments having nothing to do and their being irrelevant, but the steps between are too much of a stretch.

When a claim follows a reason with no good warrant to connect them, we call the claim a *non sequitur,* pronounced "nahn SE-kwi-toor," which means literally *It doesn't follow.* If your readers might think you've committed a *non sequitur,* you have to think about warrants: Do readers share your underlying assumptions, and have you failed to state warrants you should have?

2. "You're arguing in a circle and begging the question!" (Your reasons just restate your claim.)

To ensure our safety, we should be free to carry concealed guns _{claim 1} because we should have the right to carry a weapon to protect ourselves. _{reason 1} When criminals worry that we might have a gun and would use it, _{reason 2} that knowledge will make them realize that we are ready to defend ourselves. _{claim 2} Only when criminals worry about their own safety _{reason 3} will we be able to stop worrying about our own. _{claim 3}

You are reasoning in a circle. You keep saying the same thing—we should be free to do something because we have the right to do it. That makes no sense. Then you say that when criminals know something they know something. That may be true, but it doesn't make sense either.

You argue in a circle when your claim and reason mean the same thing. You can test for circular arguments by switching claims and reasons. If the sentence means the same after the switch, you're arguing in a circle:

To ensure our safety, we should be free to carry concealed guns _{claim} because we need the right to carry one to protect ourselves. _{reason}

We need the right to carry a weapon to protect ourselves _{claim} because we should be free to carry concealed guns to ensure our safety. _{reason}

If you cannot reverse the reason and claim and make sense, your argument is not circular. Compare the last sentence in the example, which does not reason in a circle:

Only when criminals worry about their own safety _{reason} will we be able to stop worrying about our own. _{claim}

Only when we are able to stop worrying about our own safety _{reason} will criminals worry about theirs. _{claim}

If your readers might think you are arguing in a circle, you have to think about your claims and reasons. If they are too similar, then you must find better reasons to support your claim.

3. "You're assuming things that we haven't settled!" (Your reason is not supported with evidence or an argument.)

We should reject the mere opinion _{implied claim} of a known liar like Smith. _{reason}

Who says that what Smith says is "mere opinion," and who says he is a "known liar"?

This is cousin to begging the question. It's a little like that nasty question, *When did you stop beating your dog?* It occurs when someone tries to support a claim with statements that assume a judgment or fact that readers do not accept because it has not been proven.

4. "But you can't use the lack of evidence to prove an affirmative claim!" (You rely on a false warrant: When something has not been disproved, we should believe it.)

People who say they have been kidnapped by UFOs should be taken seriously, _{claim} because no one has proved that their stories are false. _{reason}

Hold on! No one has proved that I don't have an oilfield under my back yard, but that doesn't mean that I'm going to start drilling. I don't know something is true because I don't know for sure that it's not.

The technical term for this fallacy is *ad ignorantiam,* pronounced "add ignore-AHN-tee-em." If you make a claim, you bear the burden of offering affirmative reasons for believing it. It is not up to the other person to disprove it. Those who make these arguments often say, *Well, if you can't think of a good alternative to my claim, then I must be right.* But a claim is not true simply because no one can think of a good alternative.

A somewhat weaker strategy is to say, *Well, it could be true.* In a sense, anything could be true, even alien abductions. We can leave room for the chance that a claim could be true, but we should file such claims in a corner of our minds reserved for possibilities waiting on evidence.

5. "You can't prove something by claiming that the consequences of not accepting it are intolerable!" (You rely on a false warrant: When it would hurt us not to believe something, we should believe it.)

The Constitution protects our right to privacy, _{claim} because if it did not, then states could regulate our most intimate behavior, including our sexual lives. _{reason} That would be intolerable. _{reason}

You're right; it's intolerable that states should be able to interfere in our private lives. But that's irrelevant to what the Constitution does or does not say. As bad as it may seem, the Constitution gives states the power to snoop in our bedrooms.

This fallacy is called *ad baculum,* pronounced "add BAck-yu-lum." It means "with force." Those who argue like this imply that if we do not agree, something bad will happen to us.

Inappropriate Rhetorical Appeals

Unlike fallacies we just discussed, these may or may not be errors, depending on the circumstances of the case. The problem is not that the writer misuses an element of argument but that he relies on a warrant that applies in some cases, but not all. The trick is to know when your readers will accept these appeals and when they will not.

Inappropriate Appeals to Intellectual Consistency

6. "But what you said last month contradicts what you say now!"

You claim that students should evaluate teachers every quarter, because only then will they know whether they are helping you achieve your goals._{acknowl-edgment} But last month, you argued that teachers should not evaluate students because their tests do not fairly represent your strengths and abilities._{response} How can you say that you should evaluate us when you reject our evaluations of you? _{appeal to consistency}

What I say now may not be perfectly consistent with what I said a month ago. But that was a different situation, and the world is too complex for us to be perfectly consistent. That was then; this is now.

This fallacy is called *tu quoque* (pronounced "too kwo-kway"), literally "You too." It is a charge of inconsistency, at worst of dishonesty. But this charge is tricky: It feels legitimate to point out inconsistency—we distrust those who are. But that may have nothing to do with the merits of the case at hand: So what if someone contradicts herself? Regardless of what the writer said before, we have to judge the issue before us on its own merits: Should students evaluate teachers? Yet so strongly do we dislike those who contradict themselves that we reject even a good argument when made by hypocrites. If readers might think that you contradict yourself, you should consider acknowledging the objection and responding with an argument showing why the inconsistency is not fatal.

7. "If you take this one step you will go all the way!"

We can't legalize marijuana for medical purposes _{claim} because if physicians prescribe pot for dying patients, they'll soon prescribe it for people only in pain, then for people who just claim to be in pain. _{reason}

You insult the intelligence of physicians, implying that they don't know the difference between taking this one step and going all the way. It is like claiming that if you drive one mile over the speed limit, you will end up driving 100 miles an hour.

This fallacy is called the *slippery slope* argument. It is a claim that one step must inevitably lead to the next, and the next, and the next. But we know that this is not always true. On the other hand, as every parent knows, there are occasions where a first step does lead to the next:

Daughter: Oh, can't I have one little cookie?

Father: Well, OK, but just one, and just this once!

A particular kind of slippery slope is called *reductio ad absurdum*—reduction to absurdity, pronounced "ruh-DUK-tee-o add ab-ZERD-um." Instead of claiming that an argument begins a slippery slope, it asserts that it has hit bottom.

> You want students to evaluate their teachers? I suppose you also want the criminally insane to evaluate their psychologists or criminals to evaluate their judges or children to evaluate their parents.

When a critic reduces an argument to an absurd version and then attacks it, we say the critic has built a straw man. It is never fair to do that.

Appeals to Inappropriate Perspectives

8. "You offer a false choice between only two alternatives. There are more!"

> It is time to end the debate between "whole word" reading and phonics. The failure of "whole word" pedagogy $_{reason,}$ demands that we return to the time-tested phonics method. $_{claim}$

> *But most good teachers use some of both and a few other ways of teaching as well.*

It is misleading to insist on either-or choices when the facts of the matter allow both more-or-less or some-of-both. In some cases, however, the choice really is between two and only two mutually exclusive alternatives:

> We must decide whether we are going to administer capital punishment or not. It is not fair to sentence people to death and then let them live out their lives as the delays drag on. $_{reason}$ It is not fair to the criminals, who must wait in limbo as their death is postponed; and it is not fair to the families of their victims, who must wait for closure on their grief. $_{reason}$ If we sentence people to death, they should be executed; if they are going to live out their lives in prison, that is the sentence they should receive. $_{claim}$

As you plan your argument and find yourself arguing for a choice between two exclusive alternatives, stop and think: Could you choose both, or at least some combination? Are there third, fourth, or even fifth choices?

9. "That's just a metaphor! You can't act as though it's literally true."

> Sick ideas such as X can infect those too weak to resist them $_{reason}$ so we must keep people from spreading their ideas by isolating them. $_{claim}$

> *You may be right that the idea may spread, but ideas are not diseases. You can't stop ideas from spreading the way you stop TB.*

Metaphors may mislead us, but the fact is, we can't communicate without them: The problem is not the metaphoric language itself; it's how it's used. So think hard about whether you are pushing the metaphors too far.

Inappropriate Appeals to Social Solidarity

10. **"You're just appealing to the crowd! Why should we go along with everyone else?"**

When parents pay for the education of their children, they have the right to decide what should be taught. _{warrant} Most people think creationism should be taught alongside evolution, _{reason} so that's what school systems should teach. _{claim}

That caters to popular ignorance. We don't vote on scientific truth. The only relevant issue is what the facts are. Suppose most parents thought that the earth was flat? Should that be taught?

This fallacy is called *ad populum*, pronounced "add PAH-poo-lum." It means the arguer puts more weight on majority beliefs than on the truth. The basis of an ad populum argument is probably our inherited human bias to conform with the thinking of the tribe. But an appeal to popular will is not always a fallacy:

The city council must reject the plan to build a new stadium, _{claim} because the people don't want to pay for it. _{reason} This is a democracy. _{warrant}

If readers might think your appeal to popular opinion is inappropriate, acknowledge and respond to the objection:

The city council must reject the plan to build a new stadium, _{claim} because the people don't want to pay for it. _{reason} We know that the team might move _{acknowledgment} and that some businesses might suffer. _{acknowledgment} But in matters of public spending, the people and not the Chamber of Commerce decides. _{response} This is a democracy. _{warrant}

Your argument will legitimately appeal to the popular will when you can legitimately use this warrant:

When most people believe/decide X, we should accept X.

11. **"We don't have to accept your claim just because X says so!"**

According to Senator Wise, the predicted rise in atmospheric carbon dioxide will help plant growth, _{reason} because plants take in carbon dioxide and give off oxygen. _{report of evidence} He was born on a farm, _{reason} and he knows plants. _{claimed authority} So we ought not fear green house gases. _{claim}

Senator Wise may be an admirable person, but being born on a farm doesn't make him an expert on atmospheric chemistry.

This fallacy is called *ad verecundiam*, pronounced "add vare-uh-COON-dee-ahm." It literally means the "modesty" we should exhibit before authority. The psychological basis for this appeal is probably the deference we feel to power and prestige. An appeal to authority goes wrong when the authority has no reason to deserve our trust. The fact that Wise was born on a farm is irrelevant to his standing to make predictions about greenhouse gases.

But the problem is some people are real authorities whose expertise we should respect. So when you want to use an authority, you have to weigh three questions: Is this a case where expertise matters? Is your authority truly an expert in this field? Will your readers be willing to defer ("be modest") in this case?

If readers might question an authority, anticipate their questions. You address the first two by telling them why they should accept your authority as an expert in this case and the third by reporting not just what the authority claims but the reason for claiming it.

> According to Dr. Studious, we would be prudent to stockpile medication in anticipation of a new outbreak of Asian flu. _{claim} As Director of Epidemiology at the National Institute of Health, he was responsible for our being ready for the epidemic of 1987. _{basis of authority} In his research on that and twenty other epidemics, _{basis of authority} he found that the lag between the first cases and an epidemic is about two months. _{reason} Now that the first cases have begun to appear, we know that we have about two months to prepare. _{reason}

12. "You are just engaging in mud-slinging! Unfair personal attacks have nothing to do with the issues."

> Senator Boomer avoided the draft during the Vietnam War, _{reason} so he is disqualified from judging the use of military power. _{claim} No one who shirks his duty can say anything about the service he scorned. _{warrant}

Stick to the issue instead of making a personal attack! His actions as a 20-year old are irrelevant to his current analysis of the facts of the matter.

This fallacy is called *ad hominem,* pronounced "add HA-mi-nim." It literally means "against the person." It is the corollary of a fallacious appeal to authority: Just as we err when we accept an argument because we admire the person making it, so can we err when we reject an argument because it is made by someone we dislike. At times, however, we should question an argument on the basis of who makes it, if that person is regularly dishonest, unreliable, or careless.

A version of this appeal is "guilt by association," which is sometimes fair and sometimes not.

> Professor Hack claims that crime drops when citizens carry concealed weapons. But his research is funded by gun manufacturers, _{reason} and he serves on a committee for the National Rifle Association. _{reason 2} We should look at his research skeptically. _{claim}

If readers might think you are unfairly attacking the person who makes an argument, then you have to acknowledge and respond to their objection:

> . . . We should look at his research skeptically. _{claim} That does not mean his research is necessarily unreliable, _{acknowledgment} but the source of his support gives us reason to look at his methodology carefully. _{response} Even a cautious researcher can be influenced by the interests of those who support his or her work. _{warrant}

13. "Don't give me that sob story. You're just appealing to my pity!"

Teachers here at State U. are so anxious over rumors about eliminating departments _{reason} that adding a new teaching evaluation form will make them insecure and fearful. _{claim}

Our job is to improve teaching. If that makes teachers unhappy, that's too bad. It's irrelevant to creating a sound undergraduate education.

This technical term for this fallacy is *ad misericordiam*, pronounced "add miz-ÁIR-uh-CORE-dee-um." It asks us to put our sympathies ahead of relevant reasons and evidence. The foundation of such an appeal is our sound intuition that we should respond sympathetically to the suffering of others and act to mitigate it when we can.

Although we can be wrong to put sympathies ahead of our reasons, we can also be right to do so:

States have released people from institutions for the mentally ill, pushing them onto the streets, where they are homeless and helpless. It is inhuman _{claim} to abandon those who cannot care for themselves to a life of suffering they did not cause and from which they cannot escape. _{reason}

If readers might reject an argument based on sympathy, you have to give them reasons that go beyond it:

. . . cause and cannot escape. _{reason} We must never put politics and economics above basic human dignity. _{warrant} That's not being a bleeding-heart. _{acknowledgment} If we knowingly refuse to help the helpless, _{reason} we become a morally callous people who will lose all sensitivity to injustice. _{claim}

There are dozens of other so-called "fallacies," but these are the ones readers complain of most often. Be alert to these fallacies in what you read, but their real value is that they help you reflect on your own thinking.

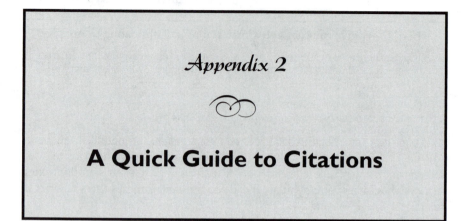

Appendix 2

A Quick Guide to Citations

Readers expect you to cite your sources accurately. Since no one can see the "evidence itself," they have to be satisfied with your reports of it. But that means you have to draw your evidence from reliable sources and describe them precisely enough that readers can, if they want, find the source and check the evidence themselves. Some students wonder why their teachers demand that citations precisely follow a set form. When you follow a form that readers can anticipate, they can find your sources most easily.

There are two parts to a complete citation:

- The citation of a source in the body of the paper.

- The list of references at the end of the paper.

There are many forms of citations, but two are most common:

- Modern Language Association (MLA) citations, common in the humanities.

- American Psychological Association (APA) citations, common in the social sciences.

So you should first find out which style your reader expects, MLA or APA. We cannot cover every form of citation or every kind of source, so you should buy a short guide to citation style. You will get plenty of use out of it. Here we will explain the most common kinds of sources in the two most common forms, MLA style and APA style.

MLA Citations

We'll first discuss listing your references. Then we'll discuss how to cite them in the body of your paper.

Books (Including Collections of Articles)
General Format
The general format is as follows:

> Author. Title. Publication information.

> Last name, First name, Middle initial. <u>Title: Subtitle.</u> City: Publisher, year.

> Meargham, Paul R. <u>The History of Wit and Practical Jokes: How Humor Coexists with Cruelty.</u> Boston: Smith, 1988.

Note that (1) titles must be either underlined or italicized, (2) there is a period after each unit of information, and (3) the second line of the entry is indented.

Special Formats
Multiple Books by the Same Author

- List each book in chronological order, but instead of repeating the author's name, type three dashes and a period:

  > Meargham, Paul. <u>The History of Wit and Practical Jokes: How Humor Coexits with Cruelty.</u> Boston: Smith, 1988.

  > ———. <u>Wit: Its Meaning.</u> Boston: Smith, 1988.

Multiple Authors

- For the first author, put the last name first; for remaining authors, start with their first names. Put a comma after each author but the last.

  > Meargham, Paul, Harry Winston, and John Holt. <u>Wit: Its Meaning.</u> Boston: Smith, 1984.

- For four or more authors, you can give just the first author's name followed by et al.

  > Meargham, Paul, et al. <u>Wit: Its Tragic Meaning.</u> Boston: Smith, 1989.

Multiple Volumes

- When referring to a multivolume work as a whole, indicate the number of volumes after the title (abbreviate the word *volumes*).

  Meargham, Paul. <u>Wit: Its Meaning.</u> 2 vols. Boston: Smith, 1984.

- When referring to a particular volume, indicate which one you are using.

  Meargham, Paul. <u>Wit: Its Meaning.</u> Vol. 1. Boston: Smith, 1984.

- When referring to a particular volume in a series, indicate which one you are using and give the title of the series.

Meargham, Paul. <u>Wit: Its Meaning.</u> Boston: Smith, 1984. Vol 1. of <u>Wit and History.</u> 2 vols.

Multiple Editions

- When referring to any edition other than the first, indicate which one after the title but before the volumes (abbreviate the word *edition*).

Meargham, Paul. <u>Wit: Its Meaning.</u> 3rd ed. 2 vols. Boston: Smith, 1984.

Translation

Meargham, Paul. <u>Wit: Its Meaning.</u> Trans. George Playe. Boston: Smith, 1984.

Edited Book

Meargham, Paul, ed. <u>Wit: Its Meaning.</u> Boston: Smith, 1984.

Individual Item in an Edited Collection

Meargham, Paul. "The History of Jokes." <u>Wit: Its Meaning.</u> Ed. George Playe. Boston: Smith, 1984. 123–46. Note: that the page numbers have been elided—123–46 rather than 123–146.

Individual Item in Reference Work

Meargham, Paul. "The History of Jokes." <u>Encyclopedia of Humor.</u> Boston: Smith, 1984.

Articles

General Format

The general format for journal articles has the same general categories as books:

Author. Article Title. Publication information.

Last name, First name Middle initial. "Article Title." <u>Journal Title</u> vol. number (year): page numbers.

O'Connell, James. "Wit and War." <u>Theory of Humor</u> 21 (1983): 55–60.

Note that article titles are not underlined and that the publication information includes the title of the journal (underlined or italicized), data on the specific issue, and page numbers for the article.

General Circulation Magazine

O'Connell, James. "Wit and War." <u>Humor Today</u> May 1996: 45–66.

If there is no author, start with the article title.

Newspapers

O'Connell, James. "Wit and War." <u>Tulsa Clarion</u> 13 June 1983: 1B.

If there is no author, start with the title.

Scholarly Journal

O'Connell, James. "Wit and War." <u>Theory of Humor</u> 14 (1997): 335–60.

Special Formats

Journals that Do Not Number Pages Continuously

Most scholarly journals number pages continuously through the year. If you are citing one that starts the pages numbers over with each issue, add the issue number to the volume number.

O'Connell, James. "Wit and War." <u>Theory of Humor</u> 14.2 (1997): 33–60.

Reviews

If the article is a review of another work, put the name of the reviewer and the title of the review (if any) first, then the name and title of the work reviewed.

Abbot, Andrew. "I'm Not Laughing." Rev. of <u>Wit and War</u> by James O'Connell. <u>Theory of Humor</u> 14 (1997): 401–19.

Films

Start with the title (italicized or underlined), then name the director, the distributor, and the year of release. You can add other information (such as the screenwriter) between the title and the distributor.

<u>It's a Funny War.</u> <u>Dir.</u> Nate Ruddle. Wri. Francis Kinahan. RKO. 1958.

Television

Include the title of the episode, the series title, the network and local station that broadcast it, and the broadcast dates. You can include other information (such as the name of the director or screenwriter) after the series title.

"The Last Laugh's on Bart." The Simpsons. FOX. May 22, 1996.

On-line Print Sources

If you cite a book or article that was originally printed but you obtained on-line, add the date of access and the URL to the end of the citation. (Never cite a work that has been posted without the permission of the copyright holder.)

O'Connell, James. "Wit and War." <u>Theory of Humor</u> 14.2 (1997): 33–60. 15 Nov. 2001 <http://www.funnystuff.hope.edu/theory/wit.html.>

If you cite a book or article that you obtained from an on-line database, add to the end of the citation the name of the database, your on-line connection, the date of access, and the URL.

O'Connell, James. "Wit and War." <u>Theory of Humor</u> 14.2 (1997): 33–60. WilsonWeb. Bulwinkle College, Lake Forest, IL. 23 Oct. 2001 <http://wilsonweb2.hwwilson.com>.

Web Pages

Start with the author/owner of the page, if you can find one; otherwise, use the best identifying information you can find. Include the date of the last update, if you can find it, and the URL.

<u>Center for Wartime Humor Home Page.</u> 23 May 1999. 15 Nov.2001 http://warjokes.org.

Citing Sources in the Body of Your Paper

The principle is to let your reader know exactly where to look in your source to find what you refer to. There are three variables you have to consider.

- If you mention your source in your text and your reader unambiguously knows to whom you are referring, you can simply insert a page number in parentheses before the final period:

  In arguing that wit is closely allied to tragedy as a way to deflect the experience of pain and death, O'Connell points to the gravedigger scene in Hamlet as an example of how wit and humor can relieve the oppressive weight of the unendurable (34).

- If, however, the reader cannot unambiguously find the source, you have to be more explicit. For example, if you include more than one book or article by O'Connell, you have to make clear which work you are drawing from. You do that by inserting a word from the title before the page number:

  In arguing that wit is closely allied to tragedy as a way to deflect the experience of pain and death, O'Connell points to the gravedigger scene in Hamlet as an example of how wit and humor can relieve the oppressive weight of the unendurable (<u>Wit</u>, 34).

- If you refer to more than one writer in a passage, insert the source's name before the page number (and if necessary, a title):

  In arguing that wit is closely allied to tragedy as a way to deflect the experience of pain and death, O'Connell disagrees with Halliday, who points to the gravedigger scene in Hamlet as an example of how wit and humor can relieve the oppressive weight of the unendurable, (O'Connell, <u>Wit</u>, 34).

APA Citations

Books (Including Collections of Articles)

General Format

The general format is as follows:

Author (Date). Title. Publication information.

Last name, Initials (date). *Title: subtitle.* City: Publisher.

Meargham, P. (1988). *The history of wit and practical jokes: how humor coexists with cruelty.* Boston: Smith, 1988.

Note that (1) the year of publication is included in parentheses after the author, (2) titles are underlined or italicized, (3) only the first word of a title is capitalized, (4) there is a period after each unit of information, and (5) the second line of the entry is indented.

Special Formats

Multiple Books by the Same Author

- List each book in chronological order. If there is more than one entry for a single year, order them alphabetically and add a letter after the year.
  Meargham, P. (1984). *Wit: its meaning.* Boston: Smith.
  Meargham, P. (1988a). *The history of wit and practical jokes.* Boston: Smith.
  Meargham, P. (1988b). *War jokes.* Boston: Smith.

Multiple Authors

- List all authors last name first followed by initials. Use an ampersand (&) in place of the word *and*:
  Meargham, P., Winston, H. & Holt, J. (1984). *Wit: its meaning.* Boston: Smith.

- For six or more authors, you can use just the first author followed by et al.
  Meargham, P., et al. (1984). *Wit: its meaning.* Boston: Smith.

Multiple Volumes

- When referring to a multivolume work as a whole, indicate how many volumes in parentheses after the title (abbreviate volumes).
  Meargham, P. (1984). *Wit: its meaning.* (Vols. 1–2). Boston: Smith

- When referring to a particular volume, indicate which one you are using.
  Meargham, P. (1984). *Wit: its meaning.* (Vol. 1). Boston: Smith.

- When referring to a particular volume in a series, indicate the title of the series, the volume number, and then the title of the volume.
  Meargham, P. (1984). *Wit and history.* (Vol. 1). *Wit: its meaning.* Boston: Smith.

Multiple Editions

- When referring to any edition other than the first, indicate which one in parentheses after the title (abbreviate the word *edition*).
  Meargham, P. (1984). *Wit: its meaning.* (3rd ed.). Boston: Smith.

Translation

Meargham, P. (1984). *Wit: its meaning.* (G. Playe, Trans.). Boston: Smith.

Edited Book

Meargham, P. (Ed.) (1984). *Wit: its meaning.* Boston: Smith.

Individual Item in an Edited Collection

Meargham, P. (1984). *The history of jokes.* In G. Playe (Ed.), *Wit: its meaning* (pp. 125–142). Boston: Smith.

Note that page numbers are listed in full, 125–142 rather than 125–42.

Individual Item in Reference Work

Meargham, P. (1984). *The history of jokes.* In *Encyclopedia of humor* (pp. 173–200). Boston: Smith.

Articles

General Format

The general format has the same categories as books:

Author. (Date). Article title. Publication information.

Last name, Initial. (Date). Article title. *Journal title,* vol. number, pages.

O'Connell, J. (1983). Wit and war. *Theory of humor* 21, 155–160.

Note that article titles are not underlined and that the publication information includes the title of the journal (italicized), data on the specific issue, and page numbers for the article.

General Circulation Magazine

O'Connell, J. (1996, May). Wit and war. *Humor today,* pp. 45–66.
If there is no author, start with the title.

Newspapers

O'Connell, J. (1983, June 13). Wit and war. *Tulsa Clarion,* p. 1B.
If there is no author, start with the title.

Scholarly Journal

O'Connell, J. (1983). Wit and war. *Theory of humor* 21, 55–60.

Special Formats

Journals that Do Not Number Pages Continuously

Most scholarly journals number pages continuously through the year. If you are citing one that starts the pages numbers over with each issue, add the issue number to the volume number.

O'Connell, J. (1983). Wit and war. *Theory of humor* 14.2, 33–60.

Reviews
If the article is a review of another work, put the name of the reviewer and the title of the review (if any) first, then the name and title of the work reviewed inside square brackets.

Abbot, A. (1977). I'm not laughing. [Rev. of the book *Wit and War*]. *Theory of humor* 14, 401–19.

Films
Start with the director and anyone else responsible for the film (such as a producer), then the year in parentheses, the title underlined, and the distributor.

Ruddle, N. (Director). (1958) *It's a funny war* [Motion picture]. United States: RKO.

Television
Start with the name(s) of the producer, director, or other significant contributors, then the date in parentheses, the title (italicized), identify the work as a television broadcast or series in brackets, and identify the city and the network or local station that broadcast it.

Kinahan, F. (Writer). (1996, May 22). *The last laugh's on Bart.* [Television series episode]. In J. Doe (Producer), *The Simpsons.* Reno, NV: Fox.

On-line Print Sources
If you cite a book or article that was originally printed but you obtained on-line, add the date you retrieved it and the URL to the end of the citation. (Never cite a work that has been posted without the permission of the copyright holder.)

O'Connell, James. (1997). Wit and war [Electronic version]. *Theory of humor* 14(2), 33–60. <http://www.funnystuff.hope.edu/ theory/wit.html.>

If you cite a book or article that you obtained from an on-line database, add to the end of the citation the name of the database, your on-line connection, the date of access, and the URL.

O'Connell, James. "Wit and War." <u>Theory of humor</u> 14.2 (1997): 33–60. WilsonWeb. Bulwinkle College, Lake Forest, IL. 23 Oct. 2001 <http://wilsonweb2.hwwilson.com>.

Internet and Web Pages
Start with the author/owner of the page, if you can find one; otherwise, use the best identifying information you can find. Include the date of the last update, if you can find it, and the URL:

Center for Wartime Humor Home Page. (1999, May 23). Retrieved Nov. 15, 2001 from http://warjokes.org.

Citing Sources in the Body of Your Paper

The principle is to let your reader know exactly where to look in your source to find what you refer to. There are three variables you have to consider.

- If you mention your source in your text and your reader unambiguously knows to whom you are referring, you can simply insert the year.

  In arguing that wit is closely allied to tragedy as a way to deflect the experience of pain and death, O'Connell points to the gravedigger scene in Hamlet as an example of how wit and humor can relieve the oppressive weight of the unendurable.

- If there is more than one publication from the same year, distinguish them with a lowercase letter:

  In arguing that wit is closely allied to tragedy as a way to deflect the experience of pain and death, O'Connell points to the gravedigger scene in Hamlet as an example of how wit and humor can relieve the oppressive weight of the unendurable (1992a).

- If there is any chance of ambiguity, insert the source's name before the year:

  In arguing that wit is closely allied to tragedy as a way to deflect the experience of pain and death, O'Connell disagrees with Halliday, who points to the gravedigger scene in Hamlet as an example of how wit and humor can relieve the oppressive weight of the unendurable (O'Connell, 1992a).

Index